www.itsallimagined.com
ISBN—9798397721110
First Edition, July 2023

IT'S ALL IMAGINED

REFRAME YOUR REALITY TO EVOLVE YOUR EXISTENCE

Lars Vegas

CONTENT

Happiness.................................... 265

Frame 274

Reframe 290

DISCLAIMER

This book is intended for informational and educational purposes only and is not intended to replace the advice or guidance of a qualified healthcare professional, financial advisor, or mental health specialist. The author and publisher have made every effort to ensure the accuracy and completeness of the information provided; however, they cannot guarantee that the strategies and recommendations presented will work for every individual or in every situation.

The information in this book should not be considered medical, psychological, or financial advice, and readers should always consult with the appropriate professionals before making decisions that affect their health, mental wellbeing, or finances. The author and publisher disclaim any liability or responsibility for any loss, damage, or adverse consequences that may arise directly or indirectly from the application or use of the information and strategies in this book. Any action taken by the reader is solely at their own risk and discretion.

BE MORE HUMAN

*Life is long if you know how to use it. But
one man is gripped by insatiable greed, another by a laborious dedication to useless
tasks. One man is soaked in wine, another
sluggish with idleness. One man is worn out
by political ambition, which is always at the
mercy of the judgment of others. Another
through hope of profit is driven headlong
over all lands and seas by the greed of
trading. Many are occupied by pursuing
other people's money or complaining about
their own. Some have no aims at all for
their life's course, but death takes them
unawares as they yawn languidly.*

— Seneca, On the Shortness of Life

I am 47, married, and a father to two shelter dogs. I grew up in Germany in a moderately wealthy household provided for by my hard-working German father and culturally dominated by my Ukrainian American mother.

We were not the most harmonious family, but I enjoyed a stimulating childhood. I credit this to my parents, who created an environment in which I could thrive. Their focus was on how to learn and improve. In their view, achieving mastery was more important than the specific domain. Whatever my sister and I showed interest in — sports, music, culture, or science — my parents would provide the resources for us to excel in that field. Provided we put in the work.

We had access to cutting-edge technology of the time, including a large TV with a versatile VCR that supported both European PAL and American NTSC video cassette tapes, a digital video camera, and a personal computer, the Commodore C-64, which I became obsessed with when I was 11 years old. Although my parents were not always proficient in using these tools, they still recognized their value and encouraged me to explore them.

As a result, I enjoyed a diverse upbringing filled with unique experiences and opportunities. We traveled extensively. I got to visit America annually, graduated from high school in Seattle, traveled most of Europe, and studied in Australia for a year. I also had the chance to explore less frequented countries such as Ukraine, Russia, China, and Vietnam.

At times it was challenging to reconcile the different perspectives I encountered. Our conservative middle-class neighborhood in West Germany embraced humility and social equality, trying to erase the legacy of fascism and genocide. Our American family and friends from the suburbs of Detroit, however, celebrated status and material wealth with grand houses, speed boats, and oversized cars as markers of success. Adding to the complexity, our marginalized Ukrainian community struggled to articulate their experiences of Russian oppression to a world that often failed to recognize their unique identity.

Growing up amidst these partially conflicting cultures ironically helped me maintain a level of detachment from any particular group. It created some distance to observe events and people from. As a result, I rarely favored one ideology or tribe over another. This gave me the freedom to explore all options. Free university education in Germany with access to American jeans, films, and gadgets, combined with a Slavic backstory reaching back to the Cossack riders.

It also had drawbacks. I missed out on the sense of community that comes with identifying with a group. I never felt strongly about sports teams or rivalries between cities, countries, or regions. These create bonds that people usually connect over. My German wife is sometimes amazed at the things I don't seem to know about fundamental elements of German culture, music, or folklore.

My parents knew to enjoy life — but on a budget. We went to the movies and theaters, dined at restaurants, spent time at the beach, and celebrated special moments with our loved ones at home. But there was an element of thriftiness in everything. We did not splurge. At restaurants, we only ordered one drink since my parents believed beverages offered the least value for money. At buffets, we became skilled at stacking our plates to maximize the amount of food we could carry away. As children, we were taught to be self-sufficient and earn our pocket money by completing chores. At the age of six, I knew how to operate the washing machine and do my laundry independently, something my friends only figured out when they moved out of their parents' homes.

This lifestyle perfectly complemented my inherent curiosity. I am naturally drawn to new experiences and enjoy combining them with my existing knowledge to create something new. I thrive on broadening my horizons and tend to lose interest if I have to focus on a single topic for too long. While I may not always come up with the best solution when problem-solving, I am rarely at a loss and can usually see a way forward, even in complex situations.

My world is full of possibilities. I have always been optimistic about my prospects and the ability to shape my life. A German proverb perfectly captures my sentiment — "everyone cooks with water." It means that what you admire about others is also accessible to you. With time, I trust I can figure out most things.

This book is not about me or my life but rather about you and your potential. My upbringing serves only to explain why I have a natural inclination to step back and observe how seriously people take everything. My father instilled reason and humanism in me, while my mother taught me entrepreneurship and agility. Combined with my inherent self-confidence, I became relatively immune to the tribalism that defines many individuals. I noticed how fatalistic some can become because they experience the world as a series of events happening to them. Some even get to the point of suicide, such as traders losing their money or samurais who brought shame to their families. I often wondered why people would jump out of a window because of an external event like a stock market crash. What narratives did they believe in so strongly they would end their life over them? Why would they not recognize that everything we think, believe, and experience is made up by our brains? Brains that have no direct access to reality or are particularly accurate in processing our sensory inputs.

Consider Plato's Cave, an allegory attributed to Socrates but presented by the Greek philosopher Plato. In it, we perceive the world as chained prisoners who can only see shadows on the wall. These shadows are cast by a fire illuminating objects behind us, out of sight. All we know are the shadows, so they are what we consider reality. If this is all we have ever known, it is hard to imagine that there is anything else or that the actual objects are separate from the shadows. It is plausible to mistake the representations of the objects for the objects themselves.

I am in Plato's Cave, just like everyone else. I don't claim to know anything about the true nature of the objects behind us. However, due in part to my upbringing, I've had the opportunity to sit in a few different caves and observe similar shadows from different perspectives. This has led me to conclude that what we see, tell each other, and believe might be something we made up to represent the objects we cannot see.

This also applies to science, the pinnacle of objective truth. Nobody has ever directly observed fundamental particles, black holes, or other galaxies with their own eyes. We created models and representations to describe them and validated these using the scientific method. In describing a photon or gravity, we look at their shadows on the wall. The models do not claim to represent the truth. They merely serve as a means to an end.

For instance, Albert Einstein proved in 1915 that Newton's law of gravity was wrong. As early as 1687, Newton published his Law of Universal Gravitation and claimed that gravity originated directly from the mass of objects. Einstein, however, proposed that gravity derives from a curvature in a four-dimensional space-time fabric. So, 228 years after its publication, did Newton's theory suddenly become obsolete? Of course not. Newton's law of gravity works well for most practical purposes on Earth, including rocket launches. To explain how gravity behaves at the edge of a black hole, however, you need Einstein's theory of general relativity. And though Einstein's theory has been confirmed through experimentation, it still has limitations. At some point deep into the black hole, the curvature of space-time becomes so extreme that Einstein's formula no longer applies, and a new theory is required. Same object, different shadows. Ultimately, we choose to use whatever serves our purpose.

Growing up in the cultural mashup of my family, I realized that many of the ideologies and social conventions we hold dearly have a profound element of randomness to them. My core beliefs would likely have differed if I had grown up elsewhere, in another era, or in another socio-economic reality. I might defend other norms and values than I do today. We are a product of the caves we get to sit in.

I find it curious how passionate football fans can become over the fate of "their" team. They usually have no direct connection to any of the players, the club itself, and certainly no influence over the outcome of a particular match. Nevertheless, the events of a game can drastically alter their state of mind, make them happy or sad, impact their physiological state like heartbeat and respiratory rate, and influence how they spend their time and resources. Had they grown up in another country or another city in the same region, this particular sports team and its trajectory of achievements would have been irrelevant to them. The random place of upbringing is sufficient for many football fans to become firmly attached to a string of events ultimately outside their control.

In my case, diverse inputs have not led to stronger convictions on any particular narrative. The underlying premise I developed instead is that there is value in keeping a healthy distance from all dogma, ideology, and even your own beliefs. Ben and Rosamund Zander capture the idea in their mantra: "Remember Rule Number 6". What is Rule Number 6? In their book "The Art of Possibility," there are no other rules except for this one: "Don't take yourself so g—damn seriously."

No one can claim to know absolute truth. Everything we say and do derives from representations of concepts and objects overlayed by specific contexts and perspectives. That does not make them fictitious. These representations can be very real in how they impact behavior or the physical world. They can be true or false in general or contingent on a set of variables. They can be within or outside of the ethical boundaries set by a particular group. But they are all more or less granular shadows on the wall. You probably know and recognize this at the macro level of religions, state doctrines, advertisements, or political ideologies. But in my experience, we don't expect this kind of perception distortion at the micro level of social conventions, dress codes, conventional wisdom, and what your peer groups tell you daily.

Being aware of these distortions can be helpful. If several mutually exclusive representations of reality exist, this introduces an element of choice to shape better outcomes for your life. If all is imagined, why not choose the most functional narrative to achieve your goals? I stress the criterion of functionality. Narratives are less useful if they violate fundamental laws of nature (angels and demons) or do not have a proven impact on the outcome you are trying to shape (homeopathic medicine in veterinarian use).

To deconstruct our view of reality and start identifying our perception distortions, let's take a giant step back and look at the cosmos and our role in it. The more we understand the natural sciences, the more sobering it is for our sense of self. It seems like down to the smallest particles that make up the world, everything is built from inert matter and energy that behave in predictable ways but have no discernible purpose. Everything you are or find remarkable about this life is explained by mechanical, physical, and chemical processes against an incomprehensible amount of trial and error over time, which we call evolution. Life is a chance concert of lifeless components without a director or musical score governed only by the laws of nature. It is aimless and circumstantial. Given trillions of random actions and reactions, the emergence of a DNA code that can copy itself and hence perpetuate and scale the process is just that — a random occurrence in an otherwise inert universe. No divine intervention, no mystery of life, just chemical and physical processes that formed stars and planets, also happened to create a self-replicating molecule strand that became more complex over time as random mutations added to the sequence.

The notion of a unique, immortal soul has no place in this contemporary view. Thoughts, emotions, and decisions are ultimately made or guided by subconscious processes following evolutionarily optimized programming. In the end, the replication of DNA is all that matters, and our bodies are just vessels to create more copies. Our role in the cosmos is to be the Xerox machines for DNA, and we share this with all other species on the planet — and perhaps other planets.

If this doesn't remind us of Rule Number 6, then nothing will. But there is a silver lining. If our lives are ultimately governed by mechanistic forces, then stepping back and reframing our reality should come easily. What better way to reclaim free will than by selecting your personal narrative? How you perceive and process a setback or a victory, how you deal with a social norm or the hierarchy in your company, does not change the underlying events. But it can profoundly affect your mental and even your physical state. It can widen or narrow the set of options at your disposal. We will see how powerful this can be in the following chapters, as alternative narratives can easily impact the physical world. Not in a mystical sense but in a very explainable, scientific way. Borrowing from Iain McGilchrist, you can take control over your life and make it more enjoyable when you intersect three areas:

- Metaphysics — The nature of what we find in the physical world surrounding us.
- Epistemology — How we come to know anything at all.
- Neuropsychology — How our brains shape reality.

Based on research in these fields and the feedback loops of my existence, I propose reframing your reality to more functional narratives (the *How*). This method is universally applicable, but I will not attempt to apply it to every conceivable situation. Instead, I will focus on three areas I consider fundamental to the human condition: health, happiness, and wealth (the *What*). Improving the value of any or all of these dimensions will significantly impact your quality of life.

But *Why*?

My motivation for writing this book is to promote humanism. The potential of our species lies in providing the intentionality the cosmos apparently lacks. Humanism recognizes the value and agency of all human beings. It is based on critical thinking and evidence and rejects religious or societal dogma. The goal of life is human flourishing, enhancing the capabilities of humans to enjoy life and contribute to the welfare of society and our biosphere. To unlock this potential, we need to work through our constraints, such as the limits of our cognition, the limits of our biology, and our base instincts of greed, fear, envy, and instant gratification. Unlike any other life form on Earth, we are born as animals but undergo a massive intellectual transformation as we grow up and mature. Only after a process of intense learning that builds skills and knowledge can we confidently call ourselves human.

I encourage you to become even more human. To continue on the path of learning and improvement. To become physically strong and able, mentally resilient and calm, and blessed with the resources to be a force for good. Once you embrace some of the principles and virtues in this book, you will become and act better. By improving yourself, you will contribute to improving humankind. But wherein lies this uniquely human power? Where does human agency come from? What does it even mean to be human? What, if anything, sets us apart from other species?

Genetically, the differences are subtle. All living organisms on Earth have DNA, and 50 percent of our DNA code is shared with all plants and animals. Believe it or not, 60 percent of your DNA code is the same as in bananas.

Life on Earth started over 4.3 billion years ago with protocells containing early genetic material, most likely RNA, that was already capable of self-replication. More stable DNA developed 300 million years later in single-cell organisms called prokaryotes, which began producing the atmospheric oxygen we breathe today.

DNA's main aim is to self-replicate, but there is no delete function. Over millions of years of evolution, we have accumulated a lot of irrelevant code that may have been useful to some common ancestor species but no longer contains any relevant information to build a human. A significant portion of our DNA is "silent," which is why we often find surprising overlaps with other organisms, such as bananas.

We share 98.7 percent of our genome with chimpanzees and bonobos, our closest relatives. Genetically, we are closer to bonobos than African elephants are to Indian elephants. With other members of the homo sapiens species, you share 99.9 percent of DNA. What makes you unique in terms of appearance, character traits, and propensity to certain diseases is the remaining 0.1 percent.

As a species, we share a significant amount of our genetic makeup with other creatures. However, in just two million years, we've come a long way from being one of several homo species. In relation to Earth's age of 4.54 billion years, this period is like one second out of 75 minutes. As homo sapiens, we have climbed the food chain, grown in population from a few thousand to eight billion individuals, impacted every other species, and even caused global climate change. What drove this unprecedented development? Compared to other animals, we are not particularly strong, fast, or adaptable. Without the aid of tools, clothing, or shelter, we would struggle to survive in nature for long. Additionally, traits we commonly associate with being human are not necessarily exclusive to us. For instance, various mammals experience emotions and have a sense of self. Dogs can manipulate and deceive other dogs (and their human companions). Rats exhibit empathy and altruism. Many primates possess self-awareness and a sense of fairness. Capuchin monkeys have established a form of currency exchange, while chimps display goal-directed actions and in-group politics, as well as the ability to kiss, laugh, and lie.

What is uniquely human, however, is what you are doing right now — reading a book and engaging in symbolic, abstract thinking, transferring knowledge through stories and memes using speech and language, and being able to self-reflect. We can ponder our existence and even our inevitable death. We can imagine things that do not exist in the physical world, like a company or a country, and use them to collaborate with others. These core characteristics that make us human are ultimately linked to our brains. We can think about anything. What the cosmos is made of, infinity, or how the brain we are using right now works. We can think about thinking.

Other physiological features have contributed to our evolutionary success, such as bipedalism or our optimization for endurance running. Without fur and with many sweat glands, we effectively disperse heat. Therefore, we can run at a moderate pace for a long time. This allowed us to hunt faster prey to exhaustion by chasing them until they would overheat and collapse. Another anatomical specialty of humans is the structure of our shoulders. We have very flexible shoulder joints, which enable us to throw spears overhead and with high accuracy. But neither our ability to exhaust hunt nor our propensity for spear throwing helped us much in building New York City, inventing the airplane, or traveling to the moon. Those are all due to our larger brains.

Our ancestors' brains gradually increased in size between 800,000 and 200,000 years ago. Multiple theories attempt to explain this phenomenon. The extinction of larger African megafauna left humans with smaller prey and plants to feed on, requiring greater intelligence to navigate the faster game and uncertain toxicity of plants. Extreme climate variability after the Mid-Pleistocene

Transition intensified the situation and resulted in frequent migrations for early humans. The ability to control fire allowed them to cook food and consume more calories, providing resources for the energy-hungry brain. Additionally, selection for effective collaboration through communication and social skills to share resources and divide labor increased the likelihood of survival and reproduction for Homo.

However, brain size alone didn't tip the scale in our favor. Human brains weigh 1.5 kilograms on average, which is small compared to the brain of a sperm whale, typically weighing in at eight kilograms. The relative size, then? While a sperm whale's brain-to-body-mass ratio would be 1:5,000, humans have a more favorable ratio of 1:40. Rodents, incidentally, have the same ratio. Brachymyrmex, a tiny type of ant, has an average body mass of 0.049 milligrams and an average brain mass of 0.006 milligrams. This ant has the largest relative brain size at a ratio of 1:8 and should therefore be the most intelligent species on Earth (which it is not).

If not absolute or relative size, maybe brain composition, then? The human brain is composed of three areas: the hindbrain, which controls basic body functions and movement; the midbrain, which is responsible for our seeing and hearing, emotions, and instinctive reactions; and the forebrain, which controls our thinking, reasoning, and problem-solving abilities.

Our distinct human abilities reside in the forebrain. It is folded into different lobes specializing in various functions associated with thought and action. The occipital lobe, at the back of your head, processes vision and allows you to navigate through space and interpret other people's body language. The temporal lobe near your ears enables you to process auditory signals. It filters out one voice and helps understand language. The parietal lobe, mid-top of your head, controls complex behavior that integrates your senses from various body parts. Finally, the frontal lobe directly beneath your forehead is the powerhouse. It allows you to reason, organize, plan, speak, move, make facial expressions, serial task, problem solve, control inhibition, initiate and self-regulate behaviors, pay attention, remember, and control emotions.

The size of the forebrain is remarkable relative to the rest of the brain, but again not unique. Recent studies of the neuron count of various brain parts relative to their size have been similar to other primates. A study at the Institute of Biomedical Science in Rio de Janeiro concluded that the human brain is just a linearly scaled-up primate brain.

A crucial difference to primates, however, is our neuroplasticity. This refers to our ability to form new connections, to rewire ourselves through growth and reorganization, and to function in some way that differs from before. Studies at George Washington University showed that the organization of the cerebral cortex in humans, i.e., the forebrain, is less inherited, that is, determined by genes, than in primate brains. Since our brains are much less developed at birth than our primate relatives, these areas responsible for higher-order thinking have more time to be shaped by our surroundings after birth.

Being human comes down to neuroplasticity — the ability to rewire our brain on the go rather than rely on evolution and hereditary formation. Herein lies the key to human agency. We don't just passively develop new traits through the trial and error of random mutation over eons. We can come up with ideas and insights anytime and transfer these to our fellow humans through speech and writing. We call these bits of knowledge and behaviors "memes."

In "The Selfish Gene," Richard Dawkins likens memes to genes as their success is equally determined by their replication rate, which either makes them stick or die out. When people "knock on wood," a superstition that is still widespread in Western cultures, this behavior is not caused by a random mutation in our genetic code that has led to increased wood knocking in affected individuals. This would require wood knockers to somehow be better adapted to their environment and better able to produce offspring. There is no wood-knocking gene. Instead, knocking on wood is a behavioral meme rooted in superstition for good luck. Its origins are buried in history and folklore, but the behavioral pattern continues to replicate through observation and imitation.

Memes need not wait for generations to be selected or go extinct. Some have been around for a long time ("eye for an eye"), and others have deeply penetrated cultures within a matter of days or weeks ("Make America great again"). Our capacity for neuroplasticity allows us to integrate memes into our canon of knowledge that we develop and pass on at lightning speed. Through memes, we have supercharged the slow genetic evolutionary process. This explains the exponential development of humankind since the invention of language 50,000 to 150,000 years ago, further accelerated by the creation of the Sumerian script around 3400 BCE.

Most animal behavior is guided by instinct based on some hereditary background. Primates can pass on knowledge through memes, like how to crack open a nut with a tool. But most animal behavior is coded in their genes. A foal can stand on its legs one hour after being born. After two hours, it can run. Spiders know how to spin a web, and birds can build a nest without consulting internet tutorials.

By contrast, human babies can do next to nothing after birth. Each of the roughly 100 billion neurons of the newborn's brain starts off connected by 2,500 synapses on average. But in the first decade of its life, the number of connections per neuron grows to 15,000. That's where most of the learning is acquired around motion, speech, and interacting with the physical world. Information is incorporated almost indiscriminately during that early phase of life. Only later do we start pruning less valuable connections based on the experiences we made and re-enforce those that matter. But the system of the brain remains flexible throughout. We can create new connections at any point in our lives.

Our unique cognitive features, therefore, are superior reasoning abilities matched with an endlessly adaptable brain. To be human — from the perspective of neuropsychology, epistemology, and metaphysics — is challenging your forebrain with new stimuli and using the frontal lobe's ability to rationalize, exercise restraint, and plan for the long term. Without these, you would merely be another ape particularly good at spear-throwing and exhaust hunting, but not reading this book curious about how you can further improve your existence.

Using this particular part of the brain is energy intensive and therefore feels hard. As evidenced by the research of Daniel Kahneman and Amos Tversky ("Thinking Fast and Slow"), our brain tries to employ heuristics (rules of thumb), biases, and pattern recognition methods to economize. If we try to solve a complex problem while walking, we sometimes stop mid-stride. That's how energy intensive the process is. Your brain subconsciously puts motion and associated visual processing on hold to give your forebrain more bandwidth to solve the problem. When on the phone while driving, you often arrive at your destination without remembering anything about the journey. The driving got delegated to your subconscious while you focused on the conversation.

What it looks like to be without your prefrontal cortex is something you experience while dreaming or drunk. During rapid eye movement (REM) sleep, the prefrontal cortex shuts off, and your limbic system takes over. This is an area involved in emotionally processing your sensory input. What you remember from these "limbic episodes" are typically non-sequential and vivid storylines that seem random and strange.

Many people voluntarily shut down their frontal lobe by drinking alcohol and taking other drugs. Alcohol successively sedates different parts of your central nervous system. Before targeting the parietal lobe (slowing down your reaction time), the cerebellum (impacting balance and coordination), and the hippocampus (memory loss and blackout), it first hits your prefrontal cortex. With the first glass of wine, you are targeting the most valuable part of your body, the pinnacle of evolution.

If "Being Human" is so energy intensive that our natural inclination is to avoid or even shut it down with drugs, why would we want to "Be *more* Human?" In a universe and existence devoid of purpose, what are we solving for?

Abraham Maslow visualizes our basic human needs as a pyramid. At the base is the need for food, shelter, and safety, something we are achieving for an ever-growing number of people. Above that are our social needs that are also generally met in our societies, albeit in an increasingly anonymous way. We used to live in bands of 20 to 100 individuals. Today, many of us live in huge cities surrounded by thousands of people, yet we hardly know our neighbors. Technology allows us to connect and collaborate remotely, but the lockdowns of the Covid-19 pandemic revealed that it wasn't a complete substitute for in-person social interaction.

After socializing, we need to self-actualize and be our unique, authentic selves. Again, from tattoos to consumerism, there is ample opportunity to stand out from the crowd, albeit in a shallow way. On a deeper level, the current emphasis on diversity and inclusion in Western cultures takes a meaningful step toward addressing this need.

At the top of the pyramid, we need self-transcendence, our quest for meaning and spirituality, the sense that we are somehow in unity with the cosmos, that there is something greater beyond ourselves.

Self-transcendence is becoming harder to achieve nowadays. Traditionally, religious belief systems were able to resolve the cognitive dissonance we experience when contemplating death and the perceived infinity of time and space. Religions provided hope and the promise of transcendence in an eternal soul, a rebirth on Earth, or some afterlife in paradise. These thoughts have increasingly become difficult to reconcile with science.

In business, colleagues invoke the idea of "legacy." They hope to be remembered for their inspirational leadership, the great deals they made, or the visionary innovation that changed our lives. Like kings and dukes conquering territory in former times, today's business tycoons try to amass wealth and immortalize their names with philanthropic or other heroic endeavors. In private equity and investment banking, people showcase intricately designed plastic paperweights to commemorate a deal. Some have dozens of these transparent plastic blocks in their office, which are aptly called "tombstones." When leaving their important roles, people struggle with how quickly they are forgotten. To remind the new Pope of the transitory nature of life and earthly honors, a monk would burn flax during the coronation ceremony, producing a momentary flame. The monk would proclaim, "Sic transit gloria mundi," which means, "Thus passes the glory of the world."

Others, more realistic about their chances of making it into the history books, think they will live on through the memory of their children. Their genes indeed passed on and might continue the lineage if successive generations continue to have offspring. The sad truth, however, is they will also most likely not be remembered. Everyone you know and who is alive today will be dead in less than 150 years. Chances are you will be forgotten in no more than three generations. What do you still know about your great-grandparents? By definition, you have eight great-grandparents. Do you know their names?

For the vast majority of people, there is no legacy. Even though we crave it, self-transcendence is a delusion, just like the meaning of life. From a strictly scientific perspective, our existence has no higher purpose. We are the byproduct of a blind evolutionary process perpetuated and self-regulated by random variation and replication over billions of years. As far as we can tell, there is no divine plan. If our planet were destroyed today, the universe would carry on.

Any meaning you ascribe to your life is a delusion. This is not a judgment but a fact. There is nothing wrong with deluding yourself about your role on the planet. This is precisely what this book is about! But you should be aware of it as a starting point.

Whether you die for your country, invent nuclear fusion, or build a new company, whatever you tell yourself to feel good about your existence, it's all imagined. If you think it means anything to the cosmos, remember Rule Number 6.

How, then, should we find the motivation to "Be more Human?" Why not choose hedonism or nihilism over humanism? Let me try to make the case. When you think about your existence, for a moment, contemplate the opposite, the absence of life. Non-life is abundant. Outside of the thin layer of about four kilometers thickness around the crust of this planet, there is no other place we know of currently that could sustain our lives.

There probably is life elsewhere in the universe. But given the necessary conditions are so rare, we still haven't found evidence of it. You need a planet at a habitable distance from a star, the so-called Goldilocks zone, not too cold or hot so that water can be liquid. After an unfathomable number of chance encounters, a bunch of chemical elements needs to form some molecule chain that can replicate itself by biological and physical processes alone. Minor imperfections in the replication process (random mutation) cause a virtuous feedback loop that automatically reinforces those variations that increase replication success. Replication success is driven by intrinsic but also extrinsic factors of a constantly changing environment. The process never reaches the end. Adaptation is the necessary factor leading to more complex life forms. If some chance biochemical process had created early DNA that perfectly replicated itself without errors, evolution couldn't have happened. Change and adaptation are the keys to life and existence. If mutations, for example, from radiation, would be repaired with 100 percent precision, the molecule would stay the same forever and would never develop.

You can get to simple life forms with all the right ingredients in a few hundred million years. With a couple of billion years at your disposal, you might also form more complex life forms and maybe even higher forms of intelligence as ours. Like with the black swan, even improbable events will likely happen at some point.

There is nothing special about humans in the cosmic sense. But as far as our evidence suggests today, we got the furthest in the evolution of consciousness, at least anywhere near our solar system. We think the universe has been around for 13.7 billion years, and the oldest planet we have detected has been dated 12.8 billion years. Our solar system formed 4.6 billion years ago, so intelligent life could have happened in other galaxies already and even to a much higher degree. But the probability of life in general and the emergence of intelligence that leads to the kind of technological species we are today is very low. According to the Drake equation, the odds of a habitable zone planet hosting a technological species are less than 1 in 60 billion. You are 250 times more likely to win the jackpot of the Euromillions lottery.

While probably not unique to Earth, life seems precious and rare. It is extremely unlikely to evolve in the first place and vulnerable where it does, able to exist only under a narrow set of conditions. My purpose is not to give all that away. I admit it's delusional because life on Earth has no meaning to the cosmos. But being alive — in the here and now — is like winning the biggest jackpot in the Universe. We are incredibly fortunate. It is so inexplicably rare that you are alive at all, but also in a time and age that allows you to explore the full potential of it. You don't have to spend most of your energy just staying alive like most ancestors. You can shape this journey any way you want.

But after millions of years of development, we also have the power to destroy it all. To eradicate our existence and throw evolution back into a primal state. Of all species that have evolved on Earth, probably 99.9 percent have gone extinct — through catastrophic events like the famous meteor that wiped out the dinosaurs or their failure to adapt to environmental changes. Tony Barnosky, a Stanford biologist who works with fossil records to map changes in ecosystems over time, suggests that current extinction rates in species are 100 times the rate typically seen in Earth's known history. He and his colleagues at Stanford predict that the next few decades will be the end of the kind of civilization we're used to. The reason they point to this is apparent: "too many people, too much consumption, and growth mania."

Humans have progressed in the evolutionary process due to their ability to invent things. Good things like philosophy and bad things like nuclear weapons. And things that are good and bad simultaneously, like combustion engines. We have grown to a population size that completely dislocated our ecosystems' balance, leading to the mass extinction rates mentioned. The next two decades will decide if we can re-establish the balance or if we inevitably ruin this journey that started so long ago. If we made the planet uninhabitable for humans, life as such would carry on. Cockroaches and other more resilient forms of life like bacteria would even survive a massive nuclear winter. But it would potentially take hundreds of thousands of years to re-establish habitable conditions for higher life forms. The chance of again forming higher-order intelligence in the evolutionary process is less than certain.

The simplest solution to the most prevailing problems of our unsustainable lifestyle would be population control, something we routinely do with other species overpopulating their habitat. Given the value we attribute to each individual of the human race, the rights to life, freedom, and the pursuit of happiness we have struggled to achieve over time, it is not a path we want to contemplate. Certainly not for humans alive today, nor for restricting people's right to procreate and have their own offspring.

At least indirectly, economic progress and prosperity seem to slow down population growth which is currently at an annual rate of 1.1 percent globally. In the revised World Population Prospects report of the UN of 2022, the world will peak at 10.4 billion people in 2080. This means, on top of dealing with all the problems we face today with 8 billion individuals, we will need to find solutions to accommodate a good life for at least 2 billion additional earthlings.

As a species, we must innovate and discover new solutions that can restore balance to our environment. As individuals, we need to become better in order to provide the intellectual and financial resources to fuel this systemic change. Health, wealth, and happiness are the vectors that make us better and unlock the ingenuity of human progress.

We will find new ways to generate power, feed ourselves, build things, and move around without exhausting the planet's natural resources. We must avoid the ecological imbalances that lead to global warming, degradation of soil and forests, destruction of marine life, and the massive reduction in biodiversity we have caused so far. The alternative is catastrophic, with mass extinction events that could impact humans and lead to a horrific existence for many.

We have to be at our best to achieve this. We need to think long-term and potentially trade off short-term comforts we have gotten used to. We must stop spending fortunes on treating people for preventable conditions like obesity and heart disease linked to a poor lifestyle and dementia from a lifetime of drinking alcohol and poor sleep. About 10 percent of the global GDP is spent on healthcare. We could free up an unbelievable amount of resources, creativity, and innovation if more people were happier with their lives, physically able and financially independent, to pursue endeavors that benefit the species and the planet. And we should wake millions from their lives on autopilot, lulled into promises of quick fixes, simple truths, and instant gratification.

So far, progress has been slow, if we can even call it that. Our impact on the habitat has only gotten worse — year after year. We understand the challenges and their root causes well by now and have elevated environmental concerns to the top of most agendas. But people's inertia is high, while the pace of real change is low. Published in 2021, Bill Gates formulated a clear plan on "how to prevent a climate disaster" in his book with this exact title. Yet people around me keep telling me why they prefer combustion engine cars or heating with oil. Even when faced with shocks like the atrocious Russian war waged on Ukraine, we don't grasp the opportunity presented by the crisis. In Europe, we manage the short-term challenge of redistributing energy sources to make up for a loss of the Russian supply. But we do not seem to articulate the mid-term plan that could make us fully independent of fossil fuels. We are too caught up in the trap of satisfying short-term needs at the expense of long-term gains and adaptation.

With the abundance of resources available today and the tools at our disposal, we should, as a species, be able to solve all our current and future challenges. Our human brains are trained on adaptation. We are born with an unfinished brain that keeps rewiring itself until we die. We are able to reframe, rethink, and reshape. As we live and age, the requirements constantly change to keep our minds and bodies at their best. So, let's selfishly use our uniquely human qualities to live longer and stronger, but also for the good of our collective existence.

As we don't have any effective collective governance, it is down to the individual to make a difference. The challenges of today are not likely to be solved top-down. We need to make a difference bottom-up. We need to *Be more Human* to enjoy life fully and advance human consciousness into the next chapter.

About this book

This is not a self-help book or a collection of tactics to fix something about your life. My framework is based on humanistic principles that branch out into strategies and mindsets that will allow you to determine the right tactics for your situation. I have organized my thoughts in four layers:

1. **The motivation** — We all benefit if more people, including you, become better versions of themselves. The cosmos is inert, mechanistic, and likely indifferent to us. Even life and evolution seem aimless and circumstantial at best. Against this backdrop, humans stand out. We are unique in the sense that

we decoupled and accelerated our intellectual development from the slow-moving adaptation of our biological evolution. The neuroplasticity of our brains enables us to learn, invent, and evaluate, which gives us agency, at least in how we process the world. So, if we learn to overcome our worst instincts, we can evolve as individuals and as a species. This is the main idea conveyed in this chapter.

2. **The reframe concept** — In the upcoming chapters, I aim to demonstrate that your reality is merely a matter of perspective and choice. It's all imagined. Acknowledging this fact is a significant step towards personal growth. However, proactively seeking out alternative viewpoints and selecting the most beneficial ones is a rare and valuable skill. Sadly, we often operate on autopilot and fall prey to cognitive biases that reinforce our existing beliefs. We know that diversity of thought leads to better outcomes, yet we still struggle with confirmation bias, selection bias, hindsight bias, overconfidence effect, and many more. Reframing is a trainable skill that can help us make sound decisions in any area of our lives.

3. **The application in life** — I believe health, wealth, and happiness are fundamental sources of power. There is no limit to how much we can have of them; the more, the better. And we know instantly when

any of them are missing or below a critical threshold. Health is your ability to act in this world. Wealth is the supply of resources you can tap into to generate options. And happiness enables you to *Be more Human*. You can take the reframe concept and apply it anywhere you like. But increasing health, wealth, and happiness is universally beneficial and will enable individuals to do the right thing.

4. **My choices** — In the last chapter, I offer a view of my concrete life choices and tactics regarding health. These are not instructional, best practices, or claim any universal application or truth. I included them as an example and inspiration to start thinking about the choices you want to make yourself.

The underlying assumption you will encounter throughout the following chapters is that our thinking should be based on reason and evidence, not dogma or convention. Therefore, we have the freedom to question everything, regardless of how widely accepted it may be. If there is no proven outcome to a particular life choice, it has no value to me. I understand that some people believe in pseudo-sciences like astrology, but since their predictions cannot be verified or falsified through the scientific method, I don't consider them relevant. Of course, I don't want to discount the power of the placebo effect, as it can indeed lead to positive outcomes. The problem is that it is solely based on belief. To be replicable, everyone would need to hold that same conviction. It's a steep requirement, and not everyone will be convinced. That's why I prefer to offer choices that have proven outcomes, so they can work regardless of whether you believe in them or not.

There would be no need for this book if everyone accepted scientifically established facts and behaved accordingly. People love doing things that ultimately harm them and sabotage their goals. They will devise brilliant justifications and counter-narratives to keep behaving in self-destructive ways. Smokers, for instance, know very well how bad smoking is for them. There is no need for warnings on cigarette packs. According to recent data in the EU, 70 percent of smokers would like to quit. But instead of quitting, they find ways to justify their behavior. They say smoking tastes good, calms them down, makes them skinny, or is more social. Their friends reinforce these beliefs because they also smoke. Smoking together, asking for a light, and sharing cigarettes becomes the very ritual that expresses their bond. It is not about scientific evidence. It becomes an imagined order that makes it hard for the individual to break out of. And the same is true for alcohol consumption, diet, exercise, sleep, status symbols, recreational activities, career expectations, parenting, and so on. Reframing the situation and devising a more functional narrative helps you step back from these imagined orders.

I would like to acknowledge that I also live in imagined orders. My cultural heritage, social conditioning, and personal biases impact everything I write here. Many of my points reflect the values and socio-economic realities of "Western civilization" and might be irrelevant, not applicable, or even offensive to people from other backgrounds. For this, I apologize. Again, none of my judgments or concrete choices are relevant here. I am trying to disseminate a methodological approach rooted in science: neuropsychology, epistemology, and metaphysics.

To make my arguments, I have shamelessly copied from others where it made sense, directly and indirectly, without listing the sources. If you want proof or to understand the science, I invite you to conduct your own research. I did and adopted views that have credible evidence against them, but I am not trying to build a scientific argument here. I try to provide mental models that help you elect and feel good about decisions to expand your optionality, value, and enjoyability of life.

I believe in the discipline of mastering the best of what other people have figured out.

—*Charlie Munger*

IT'S ALL
IMAGINED

You take the blue pill, the story ends, you wake up in your bed and believe whatever you want to believe. You take the red pill, you stay in Wonderland, and I show you how deep the rabbit hole goes.

— *Morpheus in The Matrix*

Creativity and Criticism

Imagine living 1,000 years ago as a member of a Viking tribe in present-day Norway. Your days would have been spent on a longship, engaging in raiding, pirating, trading, and settling across Europe. Occasionally, you would have participated in battles, wielding your sword or axe to defend or attack a village. Your chances of survival were influenced by both your skill as a warrior and the quality and strength of your weapon. Battles were often decided by the superiority of equipment, and you faced opposition from Romans, Christian settlers, neighboring warlords, and other clans. However, during the early Iron Age, Viking swords were lacking in quality. They sourced their iron from bogs and swamps in Scandinavia, where bacteria had oxidized trace amounts of iron and thereby concentrated it. This so-called bog iron was impure and soft, leading to inferior weapons. In contrast, Romans had been mining for iron ore deep in the ground for centuries, providing access to much purer grades.

How did Vikings then prevail as warriors and conquer so much territory around the turn of the first millennium? The answer is that they found an unusual way to strengthen their bog iron harnessing the power of their ancestors. They discovered that they could extract the spirit of a mighty warrior and insert it into the iron during smelting. This "spirit insertion" seemed to make the resulting weapon much more effective in battle. Archeological excavations showed that burial mounds were indeed opened a few years after the initial burial of a deceased warrior to collect their bones. Viking smiths would then burn them in the same fire they used to forge the weapons. During this ritual, the ancestral powers somehow transferred to the material, strengthening it. This was not a myth. The material of the inspirited weapon was actually harder than without the spirit.

Naturally, people believed that magic was involved. By using the spirits of former warriors, the smiths gave birth to a new being. In the Scandinavian poetry collection called the "Poetic Edda," many swords had names and personalities. Some could speak or sing, provide guidance, or even cause misfortunate to the wielder. What the Viking smiths did not realize at the time was that they were making an early form of steel. Steel is an alloy consisting of iron with added carbon to improve its strength and fracture resistance. Carbon is present in all organic matter, including bones, and burning bones in a furnace alongside iron would have released carbon into the iron. Researchers have recreated the forging process using these traditional methods and found that the carbon from the bones can penetrate up to three millimeters deep into bog iron, enough to strengthen the sword significantly.

We know of many myths that try to explain natural phenomena, such as the shape of the Earth (round or flat), its place in the solar system (center, orbit around the sun, or sitting on a stack of turtles), and its creation (God, Rainbow Serpent, or other Deities). As far back as we can trace human storytelling, we have evidence of how people tried to explain the natural world around us and our role in it.

Earthquakes particularly aroused our ancestors' imagination, with each culture providing its own unique explanation. For instance, in Assam, India, people believed that inside the Earth, there lived a race of humans that, from time to time, would shake the ground to find out if anyone was still living up on the surface. When they felt a quake, they would shout, "Alive, alive!" to let the people beneath the ground know they were okay and stop the shaking. Meanwhile, other tribes in India believed that the Earth was supported by four elephants standing on a turtle's back, which was balanced on a cobra. Whenever these animals moved, the Earth shook, leaving one to wonder when it would ever be still. In Scandinavia, people believed that the god Loki was being punished for killing his brother, Baldur. He was tied to a rock in an underground cave, and a serpent dripping poison was placed above his face. Loki's sister would catch the poison in a bowl, but sometimes she had to leave to empty it, causing the poison to fall on Loki's face, which made him wriggle and twist, resulting in the ground shaking above him.

Across various cultures, Earth has been regarded as a living entity that can fall ill occasionally. Mozambicans believed that when our planet experiences fever and chills, it shakes just like any other person. In Greek mythology, Poseidon, the god with a notorious temper, was believed to be responsible for earthquakes. He would strike the ground with his trident, resulting in violent tremors.

However, in Ancient Greece, people started looking for better explanations than the ones provided by mythology. Philosophers of the era sought to establish knowledge by utilizing mathematics and reasoning. They created physics as a new discipline to understand and explain the natural world, predominantly by thought experiments rather than scientific observation and experimentation.

In the 5th Century BCE, Leucippus of Miletus introduced the theory that all matter consists of fundamental particles. His student, Democritus of Abdera, named them "atomos," meaning indivisible, as they believed that these atoms were uniform, solid, rigid, incompressible, and indestructible. They were wrong, but nevertheless, a remarkable idea for a period that only relied on thinking and had no tools to observe, measure, test, or experiment, especially at the atomic level. Leucippus, Democritus, Epicurus, and other supporters of the

Atomic Theory never saw an atom. They arrived at this idea solely through reasoning.

The logic behind their theory is that all things have to be made of something "that is" versus "that is not." Everything "that is" can be divided and further subdivided, but the process must end somewhere. If it were possible to infinitely divide matter, it would eventually become nothing or something "that is not," which goes against the principle that everything must be made of something that does exist. Therefore, there must be a fundamental particle that cannot be divided any further. All matter is composed of these particles, and just as letters form words, atoms combine to create all matter. Why atoms must be uniform and cannot vary like letters in an alphabet was one of the points of contention among philosophers.

Unlike in mythology, philosophers had to ensure their ideas were logically sound. The answer to a question had to be rational and linked to proven concepts. The Atomic Theory is a logical argument. If matter could be infinitely divided, it would ultimately result in nothingness, which contradicts the idea of matter.

Today, we still adhere to this principle of rational proof. All mathematical laws, for instance, are logically linked to a few axioms, or fundamental assumptions, that are thought to be true. From these, they are derived by direct or contrapositive proof, contradiction, or mathematical induction.

In the natural sciences, logic is a necessary but not a sufficient condition. Even the predictions of mathematically proven models must align with our observations of nature. So, by experimentation, we need to validate that the model indeed describes what is happening in the real world. Today, we understand that mass and energy are equivalent, as stated by Einstein's Theory of Relativity and his formula $E=mc^2$. So, mass particles are not indivisible and can transform into radiation. But we discovered fundamental particles that cannot be divided further, as far as we know. These include electrons, fermions (quarks, leptons, antiquarks, and antileptons), which make up matter and antimatter, and bosons (gauge boson and Higgs boson), which make up the different forces like the electromagnetic interaction through a photon. We built gigantic particle accelerators, like the Large Hadron Collider at CERN, which lies 100 meters underground and has a circumference of 27 kilometers, just to find them. Some of these particles, like the "graviton," remain hypothetical and are yet undiscovered.

The physics of Ancient Greece did not have the same rigor. You could agree with the Atomic Theory or not. There was no method like science today to settle the dispute or at least generate evidence to validate or falsify the theory.

For example, the famous Greek philosopher and mathematician Aristotle fiercely opposed the Atomic

Theory. He believed that all materials on Earth were made of the four elements earth, water, fire, and air.

He also had his own theory on earthquakes. Aristotle believed that powerful winds were trapped in underground caverns and struggled to escape, resulting in earthquakes. While this theory holds little scientific value, it can at least be scrutinized and tested, unlike the mythological theory involving Poseidon's trident. The idea can be verified by digging deep into the ground to find the caverns, although people of his era lacked the necessary equipment to do so. With advancements in mining equipment, we can now drill deep into the Earth's crust and search for these caverns. The Kola Superdeep Borehole SG-3, which is the deepest hole ever dug, reaches 12,262 meters, but no caverns have been found there. This does not disprove Aristotle's theory since the Earth's crust is 30-70 kilometers thick where there is land, and the Earth's radius is 6,371 kilometers to its midpoint. The caverns could exist deeper down or in a different location than the Kola borehole.

But we do not need to rely on further excavations. We discovered that sound travels at varying speeds depending on the material it passes through. By sending sonar waves into the ground and recording the echoes, we can deduce the composition of the earth's surface and detect any large air pockets. Even without knowledge of tectonic plates, which actually cause earthquakes, we can use sonic measurements to conclude that there are no caverns containing trapped wind. Aristotle's theory on earthquakes was wrong.

Wrong or right, we are the only creature on Earth to develop these theories, stories, inventions, and other conjectures. In "Sapiens," Yuval Harari credits human imagination and its ability to unlock effective collaboration as one of the most decisive success factors in the advancement of humanity: "How did Homo sapiens manage to cross this critical threshold, eventually founding cities comprising tens of thousands of inhabitants and empires ruling hundreds of millions? The secret was probably the appearance of fiction. Large numbers of strangers can cooperate successfully by believing in common myths."

Other organisms can collaborate with members of their species, but only in evolved ways imprinted in the genetic code. Some animals can hunt in groups, and ant or bee colonies have intricate ways of collaborating almost as complex organisms.

But bees do not choose to behave this way, nor can they change it. Ants cannot one day decide to follow a God and build cathedrals rather than nests to worship their ant deity. Bees cannot choose to stop serving their queen and establish a republic.

Humans, however, can come up with hundreds of different ways to distribute power, determine roles for individuals, and define collective goals to achieve. It all comes down to narratives, stories, myths, and other explanations we tell each other.

Harari calls the imagined order we live in an "inter-subjective reality." Subjective is what one person believes, but inter-subjective is what everyone in a community takes for granted. It remains subjective and fictional but is broadly accepted and agreed on by many members of a particular group. This creates a culture within which individuals can maneuver and collaborate effectively with total strangers: "Two Serbs who have never met might risk their lives to save one another because both believe in the existence of the Serbian nation, the Serbian homeland, and the Serbian flag. Judicial systems are rooted in common legal myths. Two lawyers who have never met can nevertheless combine efforts to defend a stranger because they both believe in the existence of laws, justice, human rights – and the money paid out in fees."

But inter-subjective realities do more than just enable collaboration. They also set aspirational incentives, such as freedom, prosperity, or the afterlife, to motivate or justify everyone following the established order. They evolve or sometimes fall apart abruptly in revolutions to be replaced by a new consensus. This allows our collaboration to adapt to the environment, to our state of knowledge, or to a shift in power. Adaptation, the signature skill for survival in nature, is what makes inter-subjective realities so effective.

One factor that drives these adaptations is our capacity for critical thinking. Crafting a compelling story is not easy, as you may have experienced yourself. Without resorting to violence or coercion, persuading others requires a convincing narrative. Individuals retain their independence to think critically. This is exemplified in Monty Python's "Life of Brian" when the protagonist is compelled to relate a parable.

BRIAN: *Look. There was this man, and he had two servants.*

ARTHUR: *What were they called?*

BRIAN: *What?*

ARTHUR: *What were their names?*

BRIAN: *I don't know. And he gave them some talents.*

EDDIE: *You don't know?!*

BRIAN: *Well, it doesn't matter!*

ARTHUR: *He doesn't know what they were called!*

BRIAN: *Oh, they were called 'Simon' and 'Adrian.' Now-*

ARTHUR: *Oh! You said you didn't know!*

BRIAN: *It really doesn't matter. The point is there were these two servants-*

ARTHUR: *He's making it up as he goes along.*

As humans, we love the illusion of a magic trick but also want to know how it worked. We can develop hypotheses explaining what we observed and then think through the consequences of each theory, all in our heads. We can assign probabilities to each version based on our prior knowledge and experience and then narrow in on the likely solution. The ability to combine imagination with rational thought is a unique strength of the human brain. Before even taking action, we can theorize multiple solutions to a problem and analyze the potential outcomes. We have the power to question information presented to us and form our own conclusions. When we disagree, we can construct a counterargument and potentially establish a new shared reality if enough people agree.

Throughout history, societal norms and cultural beliefs have been established by those in power. These beliefs, in turn, served as a justification for the existing societal structures. The Pharaohs used the construction of pyramids to solidify the idea that they were indeed gods on Earth. Why else would such immense resources be devoted to constructing these objectively useless buildings? As a peasant during that time, you likely believed this myth as there was no evidence to the contrary. Everything around you supported the idea that Pharaohs were superhuman and, therefore, rightfully in charge. There was no reason to question the existing order. During the Pharaonic period, there were several uprisings due to social unrest, but none challenged the Pharaoh as a divine ruler.

It took 2,000 years before the Ancient Greeks started using logic and deduction as tools to create knowledge.

Narratives and theories had to adhere to the higher standard of reason and make sense in and of themselves. However, an Egyptian peasant, even if blessed with higher reasoning skills, would have still come to the conclusion that the Pharaoh is a king-god. The inter-subjective reality they had created made sense in and of itself. In fact, the Greek philosophers didn't conclude that their Gods didn't exist, even though they were certain that the Gods must be subject to the laws of nature. The Atomists insisted that the Gods must be made of atoms like everything else.

It wasn't until the Age of Enlightenment, another 2,000 years later, that the scientific method we use today was established. In the 16th and 17th centuries, the ideas of empiricism and rational thought emerged, which sparked an unprecedented scientific revolution. Scientific societies and academies formed outside of universities, and knowledge was further democratized through encyclopedias and translations of Latin texts. The revolutionary idea of the time was that being wrong had value, as it helped to advance thinking and narrow down viable solutions. The culture at the time was open to change, tolerating dissent and relying on evidence and data instead of trusting dogma or authority. This led to a proliferation of innovations and discoveries in various fields of science, such as astronomy, physics, chemistry, and engineering. Rene Descartes wrote, "To seek truth, it is necessary once in the course of our life to doubt, as far as possible, all things."

It is remarkable that it took so long for the scientific method of creativity and criticism to become available. Nothing had to be invented or discovered for it to exist. It is simply a mindset that is open to new questions and ideas. But those in power, including religious leaders, had used dogma and myths to successfully silence critical thinking for centuries. The recent coronation ceremony of the British King Charles III. would have made perfect sense to most people a hundred years ago, but today it seems anachronistic and comical.

With the mindset of creativity and criticism, millions could have altered and improved their fates long ago. The Egyptian peasants could have verified whether the Pharaoh was a god or just a mortal human without any special powers. The Viking smiths could have detected that it wasn't the spirit that made the steel but the combination of iron and bone. With further testing, they would have concluded that any bone worked, be it from warriors, non-warriors, or animals. This insight would have greatly increased the available raw material for producing better-grade weapons. While upscaling their steel production, they could have started using it for their ships, shields, tools, and fortifications. So much progress could have resulted from the curiosity of asking the simple question, "Why?" Instead of blindly accepting some tale about spiritual intervention, the critical mind could have unlocked tremendous value for the tribe. They had the technology, the resources, and the tools. What they lacked was the curiosity to identify what was really driving the outcome they observed.

Human progress is based on imagining solutions and applying criticism to validate their functionality. Like evolution, this process has no endpoint. We will never have achieved complete knowledge. Sensory limitations and cognitive distortions aside, knowledge itself has limitations. For instance, in Heisenberg's Principle of Uncertainty, one cannot know the exact position of a mobile particle in space and its momentum simultaneously. Increasing your knowledge on one of them comes at the expense of accuracy on the other. The more you know about the exact position of a mobile particle, the less you can understand its current velocity. So, you need to make a choice and prioritize one over the other depending on the question you are trying to answer.

Progress is not linearly refining the knowledge of a deterministic world until we can accurately predict every next step with precision. Progress occurs when we refine our mental models and narratives to produce more functional outcomes.

The Imagined Order

Critical assessment requires detachment. Being too invested in a particular narrative clouds your judgment and prevents you from accepting opposing viewpoints or admitting when you're wrong. The Age of Enlightenment marks a turning point in human development precisely because it dared to question existing beliefs and paradigms. Scientific discoveries disproved the foundations of religion, and revolutions upended dynasties of rulers. The starting point for this explosion in knowledge was to step back from everything people took for granted and reassess.

To advance your life, you must, therefore, first step back from your own deeply held beliefs about yourself. The smoker, drinker, workaholic, sugar addict, sleep-deprived, or sedentary person will find themselves rationalizing and justifying their habits instead of taking an honest look at where they stand and where they want to be. To attempt to change, we need to challenge the stories we tell ourselves. The gods we pray to, the nations we die for, the money we chase, the human rights we invoke, the laws we abide by, and the justice and fairness we demand are all constructs of the human mind. And the imagined order penetrates much deeper into our lives than we realize. Your social groups, the sports you play or follow, how you are expected to behave in a church, a restaurant, or a club, what you consider luxury, which clothes you put on in the morning, what you do for leisure, your holiday destinations, everything follows a set of local, regional, national, social, or global rules that you never think about and accept at face value.

Every so often, we are forced to notice the underlying social norms we unconsciously adhere to when they are violated or conflict with other standards. Fictional characters like Mr. Bean or, at the extreme, Borat are considered funny because they so blatantly disregard the social order: "My wife she is dead. She die in a field. She die from work, an accident. But is not important. I have new wife."

Walking through Central London, I often observe a minor yet bothersome clash of customs. In the United Kingdom, people drive and walk on the left side of the road, while the rest of Europe and North America drives and walks on the right. Although driving on a specific side is legally mandated for obvious safety reasons, where one walks is usually left up to personal preference. However, as a matter of convention, people tend to walk on the same side as they drive. If they did not adhere to this, they would constantly have to maneuver around others in their path.

In Central London, however, the established order is disrupted, particularly around tourist hotspots. Left-walking locals find themselves walking alongside tourists and foreign workers who are used to walking on the other side. Suddenly, the efficient rule is no longer universally shared among all pedestrians, resulting in chaos. Everyone follows the rule of "walking on the same side you would drive on," but differing backgrounds lead to divergent individual outcomes. People walk everywhere, causing congestion, the need for frequent evasive maneuvers, and the occasional collision with others. If most people consistently walked on one side, the rest would understand and adapt. However, collaboration becomes less effective when neither group, locals nor foreigners, has the critical mass to enforce their view of the right side to walk on. Try walking down Piccadilly at 6 PM, and you will see what I mean.

Ordinarily, we are on autopilot, driven by our habits. It makes us function in society and helps us navigate a complex world alongside millions of others. But when you step back and observe everything with fresh eyes, sometimes you wonder where all this is coming from. Coca-Cola for Christmas? Gendered body wash, soaps, and shampoos? Carrying takeaway coffee with you anywhere you go in the city? These behaviors can, at least in part, be attributed to advertisement. Companies introduce new desires that no one knew they had before and then offer the products and services to fulfill them. Every commercial is a short story about what is missing in your life and how to fill that gap. These stories set the standards and norms for you to compare your life against.

Are you celebrating something with your friends? Then everyone must have a glass of champagne and make an awkward toasting gesture. A sparkling drink is the gold standard for celebrating something. But why? This goes back a couple of hundred years. Wine from the Champagne region used to be considered inferior to the products from other areas. The Champagne is a bit too high in altitude, and the bottles kept fermenting and sometimes exploding. Dom Perignon, a monk-wine-maker of the 17th Century and now brand-name of exclusive champagne, ironically spent most of his life trying to rid the local wine of its fizz.

This second-rate Champagne wine got mainly exported to England. They would cork the bottles in winter, and in Spring, the yeast would activate in the warmer temperatures and make the wine sparkle. The British aristocrats loved it and developed a taste for champagne. Wineries in Champagne cleverly exploited this development and deployed the complete marketing playbook on turning the sparkling characteristic of their wine — formally a weakness — into a strength. From removing the cork with a saber, christening ships with champagne, or endorsements by artists like Paul Cézanne, they positioned their drink as the must-have ingredient for any celebration.

Why do engagement rings have to feature diamonds these days? Because "Diamonds are forever," and what better way to express eternal love than through one of the hardest and most durable carbon compounds on the planet that also sparkles beautifully? Interestingly, just a hundred years ago, hardly anybody was getting engaged with a diamond ring. It wasn't until a diamond mining company launched a marketing campaign in 1947 that the idea really took off. De Beers invested heavily in advertising, increasing their budget from US$ 200,000 to 10 million per year between 1939 and 1979. The move paid off, with annual sales skyrocketing from US$ 23 million to 2.1 billion in the United States alone during the same period. De Beers even suggested that couples should spend two months' salary on a ring — a notion that would have seemed absurd a century ago. Today, however, it has become the norm, and many brides-to-be expect nothing less.

Luxury is largely a matter of imagination. People love a shrimp cocktail but are revolted by maggots. Shrimp don't seem very different if you take a close look. Similarly, delicacies like oysters or caviar look quite unappetizing, yet they are highly sought after and considered a symbol of social status. The appeal of luxury food and beverages lies not only in their taste but also in the exclusivity they offer. So, once such foods become widely available, their exclusivity diminishes, and the luxury category shifts to even rarer or more inaccessible foods or preparation methods. For instance, smoked salmon no longer holds the same status as a luxury item since it became widely available through salmon farming. It would have to be scarce, hand-caught, or prepared in a time-consuming manner to be considered a luxury again.

The product that is overwhelmingly defined by imagination is wine. In blind tastings, research has repeatedly shown that a higher-priced bottle of wine does not necessarily correspond to higher enjoyment. A study published in 2008 in the Journal of Wine Economics analyzed a large sample of 6,000 blind tastings and found a slightly negative correlation between price and enjoyment. On average, individuals enjoy more expensive wines slightly less if they are unaware of the price or its appreciation by experts.

However, if people are aware of the price, their enjoyment and demand are suddenly positively correlated with it. These types of products are called Veblen goods, which are primarily desirable as status symbols and become more desirable the more expensive they are. Veblen goods are consistent with The Law of Demand, despite their inverse relation of price and demand. In fact, the higher price point combined with the scarcity of the product gives it a higher social value, thus elevating the product to a different category in society's imagination.

The Hermès Birkin bag, for instance, is more than just a simple accessory for carrying items. It serves as a symbol of wealth and power due to its exclusivity. It is made of French bovine leather and takes about 18 hours to manufacture end-to-end. According to Luca Solca, an equity analyst at Exane BNP Paribas, the production cost of a standard Birkin bag is estimated to be around US$ 800. Compare this to an entry list price of about US$ 11,000 in 2020, with an average waiting time for a new purse of about six years. You can shorten the wait by settling for a color assigned to you by the Hermès staff or paying up to US$ 40,000 in unofficial channels. But the absurdity of the price and the artificial supply restrictions seem to have no impact on consumer demand. The purse continues to be one of the most sought-after luxury items.

Similarly, a US$ 30,000 mechanical watch isn't necessarily a superior timekeeper. It can only tell the time accurately if you wind it, move your wrist frequently, or store it in a special apparatus that keeps the mechanism running. On the other hand, an Apple Watch can connect to satellites in space to determine your geo-location, communicates with cell towers to exchange data, measures your heart rate and blood oxygen saturation, records an EEG of your heartbeat, plays music, makes phone calls, records your steps or a run, and even functions 100 meters underwater. It can remind you to take your medicine or warn you of severe weather conditions. And above all, it tells the time accurately wherever you are.

When it comes to functionality, the smartwatch outshines the exclusive mechanical timepiece by offering endless features. In fact, you can purchase more than 70

Apple Watches for the price of a single Patek Philippe "Ellipse d'Or" which features two rosé gold watch hands. Despite the lower functionality and reliability of luxury products like ink fountain pens, manual-geared cars, and corked wine bottles, they still sell well. This is because their owners are more concerned with the perceived status and the resulting experience.

The experience of enjoying fine wine is particularly well-defined. There are nudges and incentives everywhere that you don't realize until you take a step back. To start with, your experience of the wine is influenced by someone else before you even take the first sip. A wine menu, the bottle itself, or a sommelier will provide a quality metric like Parker points to give you an idea of how people more sophisticated than you rate this particular wine. They often describe the taste and aroma, mentioning notes of cocoa, hints of elderberries, and nutmeg. These descriptions are vague enough for you to interpret and confirm your opinion that the wine is indeed excellent, like a horoscope.

Expectations are particularly high when it comes to expensive wine. If you bring a bottle of Tignanello, Sassacaia, Solaia, or a similar brand to the table, the consensus is that it will be outstanding. If it's not, people will blame the temperature of the drink. You could argue that the cork was bad, but it's wise not to challenge the predetermined view that the product is excellent. After all, you paid €500 for the bottle, so it must be good. This helps to resolve the cognitive dissonance of spending such a large sum of money on fermented grape juice.

Restaurants take advantage of people's insecurities about wine. Upon arriving at a decent restaurant, you will find wine glasses already waiting for you at the table. This signals that everyone is expected to have some with their meal. If you indicate that you will pass, the waiter will quickly remove your glass as if it's an insult. The glass has been on the table all day, but it cannot bear to sit in front of a non-drinker for another moment!

The wine menu is a separate, leather-bound volume that is treated with great care. It is carefully handed to one person at the table as if it's the only copy of the Mona Lisa. There are numerous food menus available, and each person gets their own, but the wine list is so exclusive that only one person can handle it. It's given to the host or the highest-ranking member of the group. This ensures that the table will order whole bottles of wine rather than each person selecting their preferred beverage.

After the wine is chosen, the amusing ceremony of tasting a sample follows. Again, one person is tasked with determining whether the wine is of acceptable quality. People often misunderstand this and say, "Yes, it tastes great." However, it's not about whether you like the wine or not. It's about identifying any quality flaws, such as issues with the cork or incorrect temperature.

I find the whole spectacle entertaining. The key to winning this game, it seems, is making bold statements.

You can say practically anything like, "Could you please decant this wine? It needs oxygen," and as long as you remain confident with a serious expression, no one will challenge you. It's all a show.

The restaurant will always play along. They have just sold you an overpriced product you selected based on a brand name, label, region, or grape, or realistically based on the price point you are willing to pay. They successfully made the entire decision your accountability. You picked the wine, tasted it, and verified that it was acceptable to drink. If someone does not enjoy it, what does that say about you?

Rarely do we reflect on the absurdity of many customs and conventions because it can be uncomfortable. Staying within the social order is beneficial and even recommended. Stepping out too boldly will impact your ability to collaborate with others and can make you a pariah. You can go shopping in pajamas or paint your house purple with maroon stripes. Objectively there is nothing wrong with that. You can eat cereal for dinner and pizza for breakfast. But the social cost of these deviations can be high if you leave the narrow band of conventions we have collectively established.

Luckily, conventions change all the time, albeit at a slow pace. Social norms on acceptable business attire and facial hair are one of the most visible (and welcome) changes I have experienced in the past 20 years of working. What also seems to be reaching a tipping point is, indeed, tipping. It started with the courtesy tipping jar you would leave some change in. Then it became customary to add ten percent to the restaurant bill to support a server with a low wage. But things have gone crazy lately. Digital payment terminals at coffee shops now sometimes automatically suggest a 20 percent tip for a brief transaction at the counter, and the stigma of ignoring the request is considerable. I believe amount and scope of tipping have increased so much since the Covid-19 pandemic that it will trigger a backlash. The Wall Street Journal is calling it "tip creep" now that customers are even prompted to leave tips in self-checkout lines at airports, grocery stores, and cafes — leaving you unsure whom exactly your generosity would benefit.

Similarly, I expect the social norms and conventions defined by the current generation of 40–60-year-olds in power to fade out. Noisy combustion engine sports cars, golf, making a big deal about red wine, or exclusive holiday destinations will move on to be replaced by other signs of tribal identification.

Ultimately, it is about signaling who is part of the in-group and, more importantly, who belongs in the out-group. We have a deep neurological desire to be part of a social in-group whose members we treat preferentially versus members of the out-group. This is why true diversity of thought is so hard to achieve, as the in-group preference and out-group skepticism is deeply rooted in how our brain subconsciously processes inputs from other people.

In experiments by Michael Billig and Henri Tajfel in 1973, people were randomly assigned to groups of which the subjects were aware. They were tasked to award real money to others only identified by a code number. The number revealed which group people belonged to, and group members consistently awarded more to members of their own group. Subsequent experiments based on this minimal group paradigm confirmed that belonging to a particular group led to favoritism to that group, even if the basis for group formation was transparently arbitrary and meaningless. Worse, studies showed that in-group bias often led to hostility toward other groups. In the case of the Robbers Cave study (dubbed "a real-life Lord of the Flies"), randomly assigned groups of boys escalated their rivalry to the point of violence and had to be separated to prevent serious injuries.

Based on nothing.

Reality isn't real

In my early teens, I discovered I was color blind. As a passionate sailor, I was eager to obtain my sailing license and diligently prepared for the exams, which included several medical tests. Everything went as expected until I was confronted with the Ishihara test.

Many colored dots in a circle were arranged so a number would be visible in one specific hue. In some cases, the number was evident to me. In others, all I saw were colorful dots but no numbers.

To determine the extent of my red-green color blindness, which is known as deuteranopia, I visited a specialized clinic where I had to align colors in a scope. By adjusting various dials, I had to match two halves of a circle perfectly in color. Upon completing the task, my mother would examine the scope and point out how different the colors appeared to her. She even began to suspect that I was intentionally sabotaging my physical exam to avoid taking the test for the permit.

The reality is I am what is called a strong protan. Because of a genetic disorder, the cones in my eyes responsible for detecting long-wavelength light (L-opsins) have a neutral point at 492 nanometers. Color blindness is inherited and affects eight percent of men. It is passed on through the recessive X chromosome of the … mother.

In my case, the signal strength and, therefore, the brightness of red is much reduced. It sometimes seems like black or dark grey to me, especially if the objects are small. But in most situations, I do perceive red. Or at least I can identify what everyone calls red, which is distinct from other colors. When I mention my disorder, people instinctively point at something red in the vicinity and ask me, "What color is this?" Red is always the correct answer, even without looking at where they are pointing.

I find it remarkable that my brain can identify red objects even without the corresponding data. It is the reason I never realized I was color blind until I had to take special tests for a sailing permit. From early on, my brain seemed to realize that it was missing information and tried to fill in the blanks independently. It does a phenomenal job taking all environmental cues into account. Like everyone else, I know strawberries are red, as well as the backlights of cars, warning signs, or tomatoes. So, in these cases, I perceive them clearly as red. It might not be the same red a person with full-color vision sees. For others, red stands out, for me, it doesn't. It is a color like any other. The key difference is that I don't actually see it, as none of my senses can detect any information about an object reflecting light at that frequency. I physically cannot see red. But somehow, I do.

You don't have to be color-blind for your brain to alter or supplement your senses. A famous optical illusion pictures a pie with strawberries on top. People nearly always say that the strawberries in the photo are red. But the picture is monochrome and does not contain a single red pixel. Even the brains of people with working color perception will mistrust and override the actual sensory information they receive.

How do we know what is real, then? We don't have any direct access to the world outside our skulls. Our senses translate inputs into electromagnetic impulses that get transferred to and interpreted by the brain. From this overwhelming mass of information arriving every second, the brain selects a few highly edited points for our consciousness to focus on.

To start with, our senses are not much to write home about. We don't see ultraviolet light like bees or can sense the Earth's magnetic field like turtles, worms, or wolves. Our hearing and sense of smell are underdeveloped compared to most other mammals.

What we call color does not exist in reality. In nature, there are different wavelengths of radiation. Our eyes cover only about one ten-trillionth of that spectrum. Within that small bandwidth of visible light, we have assigned colors to different wavelengths, and even those are imagined. Russians, for example, are raised to see two different types of blue and therefore see an eight-striped rainbow rather than our seven stripes. They see "goluboy" (lighter blue) and "siniy" (darker blue) as two distinct colors.

Reality is probably more like the flowing code from The Matrix. Our perception evolved to allow us to function in it. We see colors as it helps us identify ripe fruit or avoid dangers like fire. Colors trigger emotions and memories that re-enforce or discourage behaviors. But they are interpretations of the story-telling brain. Of course, our perception is not entirely decoupled from reality. That would not allow us to survive in the physical world. But perception is a director's cut of what the brain thinks is essential.

Cognitive psychologist Donald Kauffman likens our perception of the world to a computer interface. If you look at a file icon on your desktop, you know this isn't actually your file. It is just a representation that hides the reality of transistors, memory storage, binary code, layers of software, and so on, so you can easily access and manipulate it. Plato's Cave all over again. Similarly, our perception does not try to detect reality but hides everything that is not functional to our survival and procreation. Our perception has evolved to be a filter rather than a sensor.

If you took the raw data from both of your eyes and put it together, you would be disappointed. Much of the action in the video stream would be covered by an enormous object — your nose. From the perspective of your eyes, the nose is a big blind spot in your field of vision. However, we don't see it. It gets edited out.

Have you ever attached a GoPro camera to a helmet or backpack and recorded some footage while walking? Unwatchable. The video looks like it was taken from a roller coaster ride violently swinging up and down, left and right. Again, your brain edits out all that vertical and lateral movement.

Remember the last time you walked through a forest near dusk and started seeing people and shadows everywhere? At close inspection, they turned out to be tree stumps or branches. When you thought you saw a crazy guy with an axe in the bushes, your brain actually put that image there. While scanning your sensory information for danger, a pattern recognition algorithm in your subconscious thought it detected a threat. So, your brain places that image in your mind along with the emotion of fear to heighten your alertness. You did see a crazy guy with an axe. Only when you inspected the area more closely did the hallucination get updated by an image of harmless branches of a tree.

Because of the signal delay from the eye to the brain and the processing involved, our vision runs roughly 100 milliseconds behind real-time. So, everything we see happened 0.1 seconds ago. That does not sound like much. But a car driving 120 kilometers per hour will move 3.3 meters in that time. The average fastball in the MLB baseball league comes flying at the batter with an average speed of 91 miles per hour, or 147 kilometers per hour. In 0.1 seconds, the ball travels 4 meters, so your perception of the ball should be off by the same distance. How can anyone accurately hit the ball?

The brain knows its deficits and makes selective adjustments to your perception. For objects on a motion path, the brain will predict their position in space and adapt your vision to reflect the calculation. Objects in motion could be prey or predator, so accurately locating these is an evolutionary benefit. Stationary objects don't have the same criticality.

There is an optical illusion that demonstrates how this works. It features a green dot scrolling across the screen from left to right. At one point on the journey, a red dot flashes right next to the position of the green dot. However, you don't see them at the same location. As the green dot is in motion, the brain adjusts its position to account for the 0.1-second time lag. It cannot do that for the one-time flash of the red dot because it is stationary. It, therefore, seems that the red dot flashes up at a position that the green dot has already passed. Our brain photoshops the scene to make sure you know where the green dot should likely be.

The same kind of editing happens with our memories. People sometimes tell me that life is all about our experiences and memories. They travel, go to concerts, climb mountains, and go through a lot of effort to capture and collect mental images of their lives. These diverse inputs and emotions will undoubtedly benefit you over a lifetime. However, if you expect your brain to accurately and faithfully record these events as they happened, then think again.

Modern psychology divides your self-awareness into the experiencing and the remembering self. Your experiencing self records how you feel in the present moment. It asks, "How does it feel right now?" Your remembering self records how the entire event unfolded after the fact and asks the question, "How was it on the whole?"

Looking back, your remembering self has more screen editing rights and will compress and alter your memory according to the heuristics it has developed. What we don't remember particularly well is the duration of an event, an effect called duration neglect. Entire episodes get condensed into one scene. Another heuristic called the peak-end rule, will make your memories overemphasize what happened at the end of an event. In a study involving colonoscopies, patients had to record the pain they experienced real-time in fixed intervals throughout the procedure. With some delay, they were later asked to rank how painful the colonoscopy was in hindsight. Even if their process was much shorter than others, patients remembered the event as more painful if they experienced pain toward the end.

Even the memory of so-called flashbulb events, significant events that trigger strong emotions and therefore are remembered especially vividly, gets distorted over time. Researchers asked more than 3,000 individuals from seven US cities to report their recollections of how they learned about the September 11 terrorist attacks one week, 11 months, and 35 months after the event. They found that people changed the details of what they remembered and sometimes presented new facts later that were inconsistent with earlier reports.

In the famous "Bugs Bunny in Disneyland" experiment, researcher Elizabeth Loftus even planted false memories in test subjects. While being interviewed, a cut-out of the Bugs Bunny character was present in the room for some subjects but not mentioned. Others saw a fake advertisement for Disneyland that featured Bugs. With these cues present, more than 30 percent of test subjects recalled meeting and shaking hands with Bugs Bunny during their visits to Disneyland. The problem is that Bugs Bunny is a Warner Brothers character and does not appear in Disneyland.

It might seem unnerving to think about how little control you have over the window you experience the world through and your memory of it. From how you perceive reality to the stories and norms of the imagined order we take so seriously, it's all imagined.

Focus on the part that is in your control. Use it to your advantage. The story you tell yourself becomes your reality. Mind over matter. If that sounds like magic, that's right. The origin of the word "Abrakadabra" is not fully known, but one explanation is that it stems from the Aramaic כדברא אברא, avrah k'davra, which means "I create as I speak."

It's all invented anyway, so we might as well invent a story or a framework of meaning that enhances our quality of life and the life of those around us.

— Ben and Rosamund Zander

REFRAME YOUR REALITY

Life is long enough, and a sufficiently generous amount has been given to us for the highest achievements if it were all well invested. But when it is wasted in heedless luxury and spent on no good activity, we are forced at last by death's final constraint to realize that it has passed away before we knew it was passing. So it is: we are not given a short life, but we make it short, and we are not ill-supplied but wasteful of it. Just as when ample and princely wealth falls to a bad owner, it is squandered in a moment, but wealth, however modest, if entrusted to a good custodian, increases with use, so our lifetime extends amply if you manage it properly.

— Seneca, Letter to Paulinus

In 2015, Reckitt Benckiser, a pharmaceutical company based in the UK, faced a hefty fine of AU$ 6 million and was compelled to remove its successful range of painkillers, the "Nurofen Specific Pain Range," from the Australian market. The Federal Court agreed with the Australian Competition and Consumer Commission (ACCC) that these products were misleading consumers, and consequently, an order was placed to ban them. The decision was drastic, but why was it necessary?

Reckitt is known for one of the most popular pain relief brands globally, Nurofen, which contains ibuprofen, similar to Advil or Motrin. Ibuprofen is a nonsteroidal anti-inflammatory drug that was first developed in 1961 and is useful in treating pain, fever, and inflammation. It is available over the counter in the form of branded or generic products in most countries. In the UK, Reckitt had already launched tailored versions of their medication for specific pain symptoms, and they brought these products to Australia. These included Nurofen for Migraine Pain (violet box), Nurofen for Tension Headache (burgundy box), Nurofen for Period Pain (magenta box), and Nurofen for Back Pain (green box).

The ACCC took offense at the fact that all of these differently marketed Nurofens contained the same active ingredient. Regardless of whether it was for migraines or back pain, all variants contained precisely 342 milligrams of ibuprofen lysine, which is a faster-acting version of ibuprofen. The court concluded that selling consumers the same product under different brand names and for specific indications was misleading.

An unfortunate decision. Research shows that a more specific positioning of a drug can increase its therapeutic response. Due to the placebo effect, a medication will subjectively work faster and more effectively if the patient believes strongly in its potency. This is the driver behind homeopathic "medicine," but it also works with ordinary chemical compounds. A study in 2019 showed that branded medication triggers a more significant placebo effect, resulting in a higher therapeutic response. In contrast, generics are associated with greater side effect reporting, even though they are biochemically identical. As seen in the wine example above, people will generally associate pricier branded products with higher quality. The difference is that in the case of medication, this perception of quality and effectiveness can translate into a physiological response that alleviates pain.

Other research has shown a higher contribution from the placebo effect for medication marketed specifically for the patient's condition. Artificial restrictions on dosage, such as "no more than six capsules in 24 hours," also signal greater potency to consumers. Special preparation requirements, such as combining two ingredients, can further enhance the patient's belief in the effectiveness of the drug.

The same psychology is behind the fact that you must add an egg to the Betty Crocker cake mix. When the General Mills food company launched its first cake mix in the 1950s, all ingredients were already contained in the dry powder, including eggs and milk. All you had to do was add water, mix, and bake. However, the product didn't take off. Consumers at the time were skeptical and felt like they were cheating. The process was just too simple and reflected poorly on the user. When General Mills realized the problem, they responded brilliantly and made the product slightly harder to use. By having to add an egg, the cake mix suddenly became acceptable to consumers, and sales shot through the roof.

So, why shouldn't you be able to buy a Nurofen specifically for your tension headache if that will make you feel better than taking an (identical) all-purpose ibuprofen pill? After all, the branded version of Nurofen already suggests it is better than the generic or white-label ibuprofen lysine, even though these are identical as well. A strict application of the Australian court's reasoning would mean that all branded medication is misleading where cheaper, generic versions exist.

In my view, Reckitt Benckiser successfully reframed the act of taking a standard, nonsteroidal anti-inflammatory drug and provided the consumer with a narrative that leads to better outcomes. This ibuprofen will solve your menstrual pain, and this one will work specifically on your back. If it helps people, why not? I am sure they could create even more tailored versions like Nurofen for paper cuts or people talking loudly in restaurants.

Reframing is a time-tested approach to problem-solving that involves altering the question being asked. Take for instance the issue of pedestrians becoming impatient at red traffic lights, which can lead to them crossing the road dangerously. Rather than asking, "How can we shorten the waiting time at red lights?" — hard to solve as it takes time for cars to pass and shortening wait times for some can impede traffic flow overall — a better question to ask would be, "How can we prevent people from becoming frustrated while waiting?" Taiwan tackled this issue by developing animated traffic lights that display the remaining waiting time in seconds, similar to how ride-share apps inform you of your driver's location and estimated arrival time. Although it does nothing to reduce waiting time, it makes the experience less unpredictable and thus more manageable. Imagine being put on hold during a phone call without any music or sound — that would certainly be worse than listening to the tedious waiting music many companies play. The music signals that your call is still active.

We can't just make up stories and expect everything to change. There are limits to what mental models and cognitive reframing can provide. We cannot change the laws of nature, including space and time, the forces of physics and chemistry, and the resources available to us in the biosphere. While we can influence how we perceive these things and how they make us feel, ultimately, the cosmic order and the relentless march of time govern everything we do. Science may uncover new insights and capabilities for energy generation, motion, food production, and extending our lifespan. We may even find ways to leave the biosphere of our planet and thrive elsewhere. However, all of these advancements represent a better understanding and more efficient use of the physical world as it is, rather than a way of changing it.

Consequently, it is hard or even impossible to shield yourself from externalities. There is a constant low-level risk of your demise that is a direct consequence of living in the physical world. Freak accidents, fatal genetic dispositions or mutations, unlucky exposure to substances or pathogens, and the uncontrollable acts of others resulting in wars, mass shootings, or drunk-driving accidents are all possible. They happen to someone somewhere all the time. No matter how strong you are mentally and physically or how much money you have, there is always the risk of meeting an untimely end. Nowadays, the base rate probability of this is low. Being fit and financially independent with a positive outlook certainly lowers the likelihood of a spontaneous fatal outcome. But no matter how small the risk, if it happens to you, the effect is binary.

Externalities don't have to be fatal to limit your ability to reframe your life. Your socio-economic starting

93

point, the laws and social norms governing your community, the opportunities and support you got early in life, the experiences you make in your social circles and family — every interaction with the people and things around us can either improve or reduce our chances of being more human and improving ourselves. But unlike the laws of nature, we can often mitigate or shape the externalities affecting us to our advantage. They form the environment we live in. Across environments, people have very different starting points, day-to-day influences, and varying prospects and rates of reaching a specific level of health, wealth, and happiness.

If you live in Ukraine and a Russian missile tears up your apartment building killing your family and upending your hopes and plans, the improvement path is much harder to see. You can always better adapt to and partially shape your environment to your benefit — at least relative to doing nothing. However, experiencing the horrors of war or genocide is an indescribable tragedy that can leave one struggling for survival at the base of Maslow's hierarchy of needs. In these dire circumstances, being able to step back and reframe one's narrative can be an incredibly valuable skill. The movie "Life is Beautiful" by Roberto Benigni, which depicts life in a Nazi concentration camp, highlights the importance of maintaining hope and finding joy even in the most atrocious of settings.

In contrast, I have enjoyed a life full of opportunities with minimal setbacks or hardships. It is easy for me to say that you can improve your existence no matter the circumstances. I would, of course, argue that my intrinsic motivation and ability to reframe social conventions have contributed. A favorable environment on its own does not automatically lead to good outcomes. Think of people you know who had it reasonably easy in life. Are they consistently able to be the best version of themselves? Are they happy, capable, and fit?

Ironically, the brain itself forms another barrier to creating better narratives and habits. Despite being the organ that enables self-reflection and imagination, our grey matter can hold us back because of the way it developed. Homo sapiens had to reconcile the comparatively high energetic cost of operating such a big brain with an environment of scarcity. Hence, we developed metabolic strategies to preserve and store every calorie we could spare. This makes us fat now that we live in a world of abundance. But it also enabled us to survive over the millennia by maximizing storage and economizing usage of energy.

Particularly the brain, which accounts for circa 20 percent of total energy requirements, has several power-saving strategies. Our conscious mind, one of the largest energy sinks when fully engaged, can only focus on a few things at a time. While our senses send circa 11 million bits of information to the brain every second, the conscious mind can only process 50-120 bits of them. Researcher Mihaly Csikszentmihalyi and, independently, Bell Labs engineer Robert Lucky estimated that we could only process 5-7 bits at any one time, called an apperception. Processing each apperception takes the brain about 1/15 of a second. So, you will only consciously notice and process 1 bit of information for every 100,000 to 200,000 bits of input you receive. For comparison: the 16-core Neural Engine of the Apple M1 processor in the iPad I am writing this book on is capable of 11 trillion operations per second.

The brain uses several data compression and prioritization techniques to make the most of our limited bandwidth. Instead of being aware of everything all the time, we only see changes in a very narrow focal area. In our emotions, we rarely appreciate the full breadth of our current state but concentrate on deltas to the mean.

Another technique is filtering. In most cases, your subconscious, especially your "lizard brain," has already decided what to focus on and how to think about it. This includes the biases, fallacies, and perception distortions we discussed. Because of the limited bandwidth, anything that could potentially pose a threat or is classified as dangerous by the pattern-recognition algorithms scanning your sensory information must be prioritized. This is why we overweigh risks and negative thoughts. They all get through the perception filter at the expense of more positive thoughts weighted to upsides and opportunities. As this risk bias increased our chances of survival, we are the direct descendants of the most risk-averse of our ancestors.

Apart from the limitations of the physical world and our imperfect cognition, all other barriers to improvement are imagined and can be reframed. At least based on my personal experience even though this might constitute post-rationalization. In any case, my choices have often led to positive outcomes. I enjoy a diverse and fulfilling life with health and mobility. I've also achieved financial independence early on and work because I want to. I'm confident that if I lived my life a thousand times over, I would be successful in at least 950 of them.

My journey hasn't always been easy. At times, I've prioritized wealth over my well-being and happiness. Other times, I've simply been fortunate rather than deserving of success. But overall, I've achieved my goals through effort and self-improvement. Throughout most of my life, I've been striving to become a better, more emotionally stable, and compassionate individual towards others. While I have made progress over the years, the process has been slow, frustrating, and even painful at times. Despite the many positive aspects of my life, I'm still working towards becoming more human.

I attribute my life satisfaction to a fundamental assumption that has allowed me to progress. It is the ultimate reframe that gave me access to more options in life:

1. It's all imagined.
2. Anything you want to accomplish is theoretically possible as long as it does not violate a law of nature.
3. If you cannot do it today, it is because you don't have the knowledge or resources yet.

But what is a reframe anyway? According to encyclopedias, cognitive reframing is a psychological technique that identifies and changes how situations, experiences, events, ideas, or emotions are viewed. It is the process by which such situations or thoughts are challenged and then changed.

You can reduce this to a shift in perspective ("changing the way something is viewed"). Shifting perspective enriches your data and gives you another dimension to work with. The simplest example is your vision. Each eye sees the world from a slightly different angle, and the brain combines both views into a much richer, three-dimensional picture.

Scientists have long debated why the brain is divided into two hemispheres. The brain's power is directly linked to the number of connections it can form between synapses. The more, the better. Yet, there is a massive divide down the middle of the structure. It is not for redundancy reasons, as the specific build of each half is somewhat different from the other. This phenomenon is not limited to humans, by the way. Any animal species, if it has a brain, will have a divide in the brain with slightly asymmetrical halves.

Research on this question is ongoing, but we believe that the two hemispheres process the world from different perspectives. The simplification that the left side does logic and the right side creativity is just that, a simplification. To a certain degree, both sides can take over tasks from the other side, as seen in split-brain patients. But the lens that each hemisphere applies to the information it processes seems to be different. The right hemisphere appears to take a broad field view associated with creativity, situational awareness, and peripheral vision. The left half is more associated with focus, rational, linear thought, but also focus in vision.

Many new and unexpected things can be discovered if you shift perspective. But identifying other viewpoints is hard without clues pointing you to those angles. When you are in an elevator, you think you are standing still. You don't see yourself zooming up or down vertically. If you drop a ball in a cabin moving upward, in your view, the ball moves downward. However, if the elevator shaft was transparent, and a person on the ground could see you, to them, the ball would still be moving upward.

When you lie in bed and enjoy the stillness of the night, you don't realize that the Earth is rotating and moving around the sun at an average of 107,000 kilometers per hour. In the 7.5 hours you sleep, you move more than 800,000 kilometers through space. Relative to the sun, to be precise. The sun and the solar system orbit the center of our galaxy, the Milky Way, at around 220 kilometers per second. It takes 240 million years for our solar system to go around the galaxy's center once and arrive at the same spot again. It isn't the same spot because the Milky Way and neighboring galaxies are thought to be moving at a rate of 630 kilometers per second. Not sure what this is relative to. Motion, for all practical purposes, only exists in relation to something else.

There are many mental models to broaden your view and unlock different perspectives but let me focus on my favorite one — first principle thinking.

To test someone's prevailing view on a topic, it is helpful to surface their underlying assumptions and biases. These can remain hidden and be heavily influenced by their subconscious mind. In first principle thinking, you move back in the chain of reasoning and continue to ask "Why?" until you get to the endpoint in a string of arguments. Why is the conclusion as you describe? Why do you make this assumption? Why do you think that? You want to get to the basis of the belief system.

Elon Musk famously did this when creating SpaceX. The common belief at the time was that space travel was so expensive and complicated that only the world's largest economies could afford to develop it. Hidden assumptions driving this narrative were that rockets could not be reused and needed customized computer components and guidance systems to function reliably. SpaceX upended this by figuring out how to reuse the largest first stage of the rocket and employ readily available consumer electronics. The cost of taking payload to Low Earth Orbit is currently around US$ 1,600 per kilogram with a SpaceX Falcon Heavy rocket. Compare that to US$ 6,500 per kilogram with a Russian Soyuz rocket or more than US$ 50,000 per kilogram with the retired Space Shuttle program.

Children intuitively apply first principle thinking. They don't take any narrative for granted and keep asking, "Why?" This can frustrate grown-ups as they often haven't thought about it and short-cut the conversation with "Because I say so." If the end point of your reasoning is a fact that you can verify or falsify by the scientific method, then you have your implicit answer for the whole chain. If your journey ends in dogma ("because this is what I believe"), at least you know that your assumptions are based on opinions, beliefs, or social conditioning and, therefore, can be changed if you want to.

When applying this consistently, I noticed how many of my firm views were based on very little hard evidence. It isn't surprising if you think about it. Where do all of our convictions come from? We have some genetic disposition in how we weigh risk and opportunity, how much energy and intrinsic motivation we have, and how curious, emotionally stable, and susceptible to other people's influence we are. The rest is conditioning. Outright brainwashing by our friends, family, social circles, schools, communities, and the corporate world of consumerism.

One of the oldest reframes is the stoic mindset. Stoicism is a school of philosophy founded in Athens in the early third century BCE, building on logic, physics, and ethics. It is a broad and encompassing philosophy that provides a sort of instruction manual for what a virtuous and, consequently, happy life looks like.

Marcus Aurelius, who ruled the Roman Empire for nearly 20 years until 180 AD, was a devout follower and practitioner of the Stoic philosophy. In his private diary, later published as "Meditations," he captures a core concept of the stoic mindset: "You have power over your mind — not outside events. Realize this, and you will find strength."

It means we cannot always influence or change the external events affecting us, but we can certainly decide how to deal with them. The stoic will exercise self-control not to let destructive emotions take over. If applied consistently, the stoic would become resilient to any misfortune. One of the mental reframes to achieve this is to visualize the worst case of the situation you are upset about. If you are unhappy about something your spouse said or did, picture that they had an accident and died, and you would never again be able to talk to that person. How upset are you really compared to how much you love your spouse? Isn't it better to forgive and move on rather than harbor these negative emotions? Make the time you spend with your spouse meaningful, and be grateful for the remaining time you have together, which might end at any moment.

All of that happened in your head. Instead of anger pumping adrenaline and cortisol through your body, increasing your heart rate, blood pressure, and respiratory rate in preparation for fight or flight, the opposite happened. Your heart rate and blood pressure lowered, and endorphins were released, acting like a natural painkiller and making you feel good. You changed your body's physiology by reframing the situation and putting your spouse's perceived transgression into perspective. That is mind over matter.

Although your brain is full of negative biases, it can also be fooled to the positive. It easily responds to primers that you can influence. Think of the word "**EAT**" and then complete the missing letter in the following word "**SO__P**." Did you complete the word "soup"? If you had thought of the word "SHOWER" before, you might have thought of "soap."

Cues and primers around us constantly influence the brain. Priming is even a negotiation tactic called anchoring. When you start a sales process with an unrealistically high anchor price, any reduction from that point suddenly seems like a good deal. We all know this tactic from price tags with "was €x, now €y".

In an experiment conducted by John Bargh and others in 1996, subjects were implicitly primed with thoughts of older people like nursing homes, wrinkles, or forgetting things. When exiting the test booth, they walked slower than others who received neutral stimuli.

To effectively prime your mind, you need to be aware of its natural preferences and biases. Humans are wired to prioritize short-term outcomes. A bias known as "future discounting" or "present bias" makes us select from alternative courses of action based on how we judge their consequences in the short term. Something that feels good today is more appealing than a potentially more considerable benefit in the future. Our pleasure-seeking brain will naturally try to optimize for the short term. Overcoming this natural instinct requires delayed gratification, which goes against our biology. But ultimately, it is necessary to achieve long-term happiness.

Because unfortunately, many things that are enjoyable in the moment can be detrimental in the long run if repeated over and over. One donut will not kill you, but having one every day will lead to insulin sensitivity, metabolic syndrome, type-II diabetes, and ultimately a higher risk of all-cause mortality. We decide one donut at a time, and it always seems like a good idea.

While drinking alcohol and disrupting a night of sleep won't cause dementia, doing so regularly over time might. Many leading causes of death don't have a singular trigger event, such as the number one global killer, ischaemic heart disease, which accounted for 16 percent of all deaths globally in 2019. Heart disease is caused by the compounding effects of small, unhealthy habits over the decades, often starting in your 20s and 30s when you feel invincible. Since heart disease kills one in six people, the long-term benefits of forming better habits early in life to avoid atherosclerosis is clear. Many things that are good for our long-term health simply don't seem appealing in the moment, whether it's waking up early to go for a run, a grueling workout, or declining a second glass of wine in social situations.

Unsurprisingly, it is difficult for humanity to significantly reduce carbon emissions, despite the drastic impact our actions are having on the biosphere. Climate change, which will cause displacement, poverty, and even death for millions of people and species, is a catastrophic outcome that we should be working to prevent. However, it can be challenging to make small sacrifices now to prevent a theoretical but potentially devastating outcome in the future.

Of course, you can reframe these situations and overcome the powerful "present bias." But it requires willpower and commitment. You can mentally prime your thinking toward the benefits of the future reward. You can reframe the unpleasant short-term effects of good habits to make them more enjoyable. You can educate yourself on the scientific evidence that unmasks justifications and social narratives driven by people trying to resolve their cognitive dissonances. And you should discount the judgment from others if your method works and leads to better outcomes in terms of health, wealth, and happiness.

A reframe should not make you a pariah to be effective. We are social creatures and need to live in the fabric of society. Realizing that it is all imagined allows you to keep some distance and unlock new perspectives hidden or forgotten by most. But if your life choices start impacting your ability to collaborate effectively with others, I would question if you have genuinely optimized for the best outcome. Some life choices can take you to the edge of societal consensus, which is fine as long as you stay on the tolerable side. Judging where that line lies precisely is an art — and dependent on the social circles you move in. Always expect some pushback and ridicule. Regarding my life choices, I often hear comments like:

- I find your regime too extreme; I am more 80:20 and try to be balanced by living by this rule I will tell you about now in detail.
- I wish you knew how much I enjoy my red wine, pizza, salami, donut…
- What you do seems sensible, but where is the fun in that?
- Doing (self-destructive behavior) XYZ is part of our culture. Unthinkable in country x, company y, or group z to abstain.

I am always willing to explain my choices to others if people ask and are genuinely interested. However, I am not a missionary and do not claim that my choices are right, and others are wrong. It depends on what you are solving for. If life to you is all about hedonism, then that is your choice. The truth is that most people haven't thought about it. They have been on autopilot for most of their lives and have gradually ended up in their current matrix of habits and desires. Shaped by their social environments, they have become accustomed to certain conventions reinforced daily by their peers. Even if they feel unease, they still try to convince themselves that this is who they are. Changing would mean giving up the essence of their existence.

Conversations about my choices are usually initiated by others. They notice that I do not drink alcohol, wear a continuous glucose monitor, stay away from processed food, or leave a party early to preserve my sleep — and feel the urge to say something about it. First, they ask innocent questions: "Are you taking medication? Are you a diabetic? Are you doing a (temporary) health challenge? Are there special religious or ethical reasons?" An affirmative answer to any of these questions would be satisfactory and leave their world order intact.

When I explain that this is a permanent life choice I made, people perceive it as a personal challenge. To the conventions they use to justify their behaviors, their inability to change, and their very existence. If someone else can live that way, what does that say about them? Many of the comments and rebuttals I have heard over time are driven by fear and insecurity. What some of them, in my view, are really saying is:

- I feel the need to justify why I stick to this self-defeating behavior, so I don't look inferior next to you.
- You remind me of the fact that I am trying to change but don't have the energy to do so.
- Your behavior threatens my self-image of being in control and intelligent — I will now discredit your life choice as wrong or outlandish in return.
- My main aim is to maximize pleasure in the moment, so I don't understand why you are punishing yourself so much.

The cognitive dissonance between behavior and self-image makes people develop creative ways to explain and justify themselves. It is a conversation that cannot be resolved rationally. If you applied first principle thinking and tested underlying assumptions, the reasoning chain would likely end in beliefs and convictions, not facts. However, everybody should define their path and make their own choices. No one changes their behavior by being proven wrong or stripped of the narratives they hold deeply. People change their behavior when their purpose and passion align with a new set of goals.

Reframing is difficult when you need to overcome your "future discounting" and "negativity bias." Following through on your reframe is even harder because, in some instances, you need to be resilient in the face of the social conventions and narratives that justify the behaviors of others. To succeed requires willpower. And conventional wisdom has it that only a finite amount of willpower is available to you every day. Like a muscle fatigues over time with use, the mental power of inhibition and discipline supposedly vanishes when you exercise it too much. In the 1990s, psychologist Roy Baumeister conducted experiments that laid the foundation for what we call "ego depletion." People who resisted the temptation of eating cookies sitting right in front of them later had less mental energy to solve a puzzle and gave up earlier than the ones who were only tempted by a plate of radishes. The conclusion was that willpower depends on a limited amount of mental energy that, once used up, will jeopardize our self-control.

Recent studies could not replicate Baumeister's findings of ego depletion. A study by psychologist Carol Dweck discovered that signs of ego depletion were only found in subjects who also *believed* that willpower was a limited resource. Subjects who saw willpower as something unconstrained did not experience the same mental fatigue or loss of self-control.

This more closely resembles my experience. For instance, I am very motivated to exercise every day. I enjoy the workout and how it makes me feel afterward. I see a strong link between my daily exercise and energy levels, further motivating me to hit the gym. There will be days that I don't feel fit or able, but willpower is not the constraint. On the contrary, I feel bad if I cannot exercise due to lack of time or an injury.

Steven Kotler, director of the Flow Research Collective, would probably agree with the concept of limitless willpower driven by motivation. In his book "The Art of Impossible," he explores what drives flow, a mental state of increased focus and heightened productivity. He talks about autonomous motivation as one of the key drivers. This is a motivation that was not forced on you but that you came up with freely on your own and that aligns your inner drive (passion) with the outcome you want to affect in the physical world (purpose).

In conclusion, reframing your life becomes more manageable if you are motivated. There is an infinite amount of willpower available to those who want it. Willpower will drive confidence, commitment, consistency, and, lastly, the compounding effects of the good habits you introduce. When I talk about improving your existence in the following chapters, these mental reframes are no quick fixes or shortcuts, like a diet or a detox weekend. They describe a lifestyle that generates a lifetime of benefits. Some will come naturally to you and will be easy to implement. Others might feel more foreign. Focus on these and build the motivation and cognitive reframe to improve.

Remember that you are accountable for your own life. Not your parents, children, the state, society, or anyone else. We are not victims of the imagined order, be it consumerism, status anxiety, hedonic adaptation, or stress eating. You can shape this life for the better. But only you can. No one else. And only if you want to.

> *You cannot create*
> *what you cannot imagine*
>
> — *Lucille Clifton*

HEALTH

*The physical world, all of it, only
ever has one destination: equilibrium.*

— Helen Czerski

Have you ever thought about the acidity of your blood? You might have noticed the pH value of your blood plasma when you last got your blood work done. But if you are like me, you have probably never worried much about it. It rarely gets out of control because your body regulates it so tightly.

Søren Sørensen invented the pH scale, which describes the hydrogen ion concentration in a solution (pH = potential of Hydrogen). The higher the concentration of hydrogen ions, the more acidic the solution and the lower the pH. Pure water is neutral at a pH of 7 on an inverse logarithmic scale from 0 to 14. To stay healthy and alive, your blood must remain within a pH range of 7.35 to 7.45. This is a narrow band. Your stomach fluids can have an acidity between 1.5 and 3.5, but your blood plasma must remain at 7.4 with a tolerance of only 0.05 up or down. If your pH drops below 7.35, you will suffer symptoms of acidosis, including headache, lethargy, muscle seizure, unconsciousness, and eventually coma. Similar symptoms would be experienced with alkalosis above 7.45, including confusion, muscle spasms, vomiting, and also coma. At a blood pH below 6.8 or above 7.8, you would be dead.

This rarely occurs because your body has several feedback and intervention mechanisms. Besides chemical buffers in the cells, the lungs and kidneys are the two main organs regulating your blood pH. Your lungs provide an instantaneous corrective by regulating the amount of acidic carbon dioxide you exhale. The kidneys remove acids by excreting them in urine, but they can also produce bicarbonate to make the blood more alkaline if needed.

Hundreds, if not thousands of similar processes are at work right now to keep your body alive. If your core temperature, normally at 37 degrees Celsius, drops below 35 or rises above 39, you risk hypothermia or a fever respectively, which can both be life-threatening. The set point of 37 degrees itself fluctuates slightly with the circadian rhythm or women's menstrual cycle. Your oxygen saturation, blood pressure, hemoglobin and glucose levels, melatonin, sodium, potassium, and calcium ion concentrations, your iron and copper levels, your energy balance and metabolism, and many lesser-known processes, for example, in your cerebrospinal fluid or neuroendocrine system, are regulated around the clock to keep you going. Some regulators also exist to keep you sane. In your sleep, you don't merely maintain and repair your physical constitution but also restore the balance of your emotions. Staying overly sad or euphoric for too long is not helpful for survival and procreation, so your brain will seek to restore equilibrium to your feelings and emotional state.

This state of balance is called homeostasis. Keeping all the different variables in their homeostatic range is essential to sustaining life, which is something we share with all organisms. If we fall out of homeostasis, we experience illness. This can happen acutely through trauma, infection, or some other environmental change that needs to be addressed immediately. But an imbalance can also build up gradually over time. High blood pressure or decreased insulin sensitivity do not destabilize the body overnight but are the triggers that deregulate other related systems, ultimately leading to poor health.

Whether large and acute or small and chronic, in any case, we must restore homeostasis to become healthy again. If the body's defense and restoration systems cannot achieve this on their own, we must resort to medication or other medical interventions. If we permanently fail to achieve homeostasis, it is ultimately game over, and we die.

There are various acute or chronic impacts that can disrupt homeostasis. Our actions and behaviors are foremost to blame. But even if we lived a perfect life, we would still struggle to maintain homeostasis. This is because our bodies exist in the physical world, which is governed by the laws of physics, and everything naturally deteriorates over time.

According to the second law of thermodynamics, entropy increases in every closed system. Entropy is a measure of disorder and, in physics, is understood as energy no longer available to do any more work. When maximum entropy is reached in a closed system, we call this a thermal equilibrium. There are no more heat flows between objects. To avoid entropy and maintain order, you need to expend energy in some form. Take a cup of hot coffee. If you leave it sitting out, it will radiate heat to its surrounding, raising the temperature in the room but lowering its own until both are the same. If you want to maintain the coffee's temperature, you have to insert energy in the form of heat. Energy is a finite resource. So, when no energy is left to stave off entropy, everything, the universe itself, will eventually reach equilibrium.

Entropy is the driving force behind deterioration, degradation, corrosion, decay, and any form of wear and tear. The laws of physics mandate that the entropy of the universe only increases over time. Without energy from the sun or food, all organisms move away from order and fall apart. This is true for any system of order, even inorganic ones. A house left on its own will get dirty and needs to be cleaned regularly. A glass with water can maintain its current state for some time. But eventually, the chances of moving to disorder by falling, breaking, and spilling the water on the floor will materialize, no matter how low the probability. Systems tend to become disorderly because there are more paths to disorder than to maintaining the existing order. What can go wrong will go wrong — eventually. The probability is stacked in favor of chaos and entropy for any system, organic or in-organic.

Our bodies encounter entropy in many situations, such as breaking down food molecules to extract energy. This process results in an increase in entropy as food molecules are highly ordered structures that break down into less ordered products. Aging and disease are natural consequences of the second law of thermodynamics. To maintain homeostasis, we constantly need to expend energy to offset entropy. Whether it's an acute injury, chronic illness, or the gradual decline of aging, they all represent deviations from homeostasis that can negatively impact our ability to live a full and vibrant life. Entropy ultimately wins. Every system that can break down will break down. The question is whether we can slow it down or reverse some of its effects.

Strangely, a large part of the medical field still treats aging differently from what we traditionally think of as illness, even though the underlying mechanism of how it affects health is the same. The US Food and Drug Administration, FDA, has so far avoided classifying aging as a treatable condition or even a disease on the basis that it is a natural process. This makes it difficult to get regulatory approval for drugs that can slow or reverse the biological aging process. With the approval of the TAME study (Targeting Aging with Metformin), the FDA at least opened up the possibility of a future policy change. The study investigates if off-label use of Metformin, a common drug to lower glucose in patients with mild type-II diabetes, can protect against age-related conditions such as cancer, dementia, or cardiovascular disease. If positive, this would establish an indication of aging. In that case, aging itself can be a suitable drug target and could lead to the FDA finally classifying aging as a disease.

In the context of health, we aim to improve both its quality and duration. For quality, there is no objective, absolute measure that applies to all of us equally. It depends on the individual circumstances. For instance, if someone plans to run a 3-hour marathon, they require a higher level of fitness compared to those who only engage in occasional hiking. The baseline fitness level for most individuals allows them to lead an active life, feel invigorated, enjoy all senses, and carry out daily tasks without pain or hindrance. Moreover, having some buffer and resilience enables people to perform strenuous tasks and recover quickly from illness or injury. However, individuals should aim to go beyond the baseline fitness level to counteract the effects of aging. Although many people may not realize their health is inadequate, they certainly appreciate good health when it's missing. My parents often tell me that getting old is no fun. What they really mean is losing mobility and enduring pain is no fun, and many of the conditions they suffer from today could have been prevented.

This directly relates to the concept of healthspan, which refers to the length of time we enjoy good health. Most of us desire to maintain the baseline health described above for as long as possible. Therefore, we must differentiate between lifespan (how long we live) and healthspan (how long we remain in good health).

> *A person who has their health has*
> *a thousand dreams, while the person*
> *that had lost their health has but one.*
> — *Unknown*

The last two centuries have afforded us significant advances in human lifespan. Global life expectancy at birth has more than doubled from around 29 years in 1850 to 72 years in 2016. In industrialized nations, life expectancy at birth often exceeds 80 years. These improvements are mainly attributed to drastically lowering infant and child mortality rates and curbing bacterial infections with antibiotics. Excluding these effects, the increase in lifespan attributable to all other medical advances is much more modest. Case in point, a 70-year-old in England could expect to live another nine years in 1850, while in 2016, the remaining years rose to 16 years on average. For those who reached 70, 166 years of scientific advancement only improved their remaining life expectancy by seven years.

This is because the main risk factor for death from any disease in the later years of life is aging. Be it cancer, cardiovascular disease, Alzheimer, or diabetes, the root cause of death is the absence of homeostasis due to aging. Indeed, your cardiovascular disease risk also increases from high blood pressure. But this only represents a 3-fold risk on average. Aging carries a 5,000-fold risk of cardiovascular disease in your later years. Scientists have estimated that if we cured all cancers, it would only extend the average lifespan by four years, as other diseases would take their place. If you understand what aging is and how it affects your system, you can imagine how the integrity of the body and its processes get compromised to the point of failure.

Aging already starts at birth. Scientists have grouped the deterioration processes into so-called hallmarks of aging to describe what it does. A defining scientific paper from 2013 describes nine of these:

Genome instability — Oxidative stress and environmental factors like radiation continuously bombard and alter molecules in your DNA, a classic example of the second law of thermodynamics in action. Your body has molecular repair processes to restore the original information, but these don't work perfectly, so damage and mistakes accumulate over time. Too much DNA damage causes premature aging.

Telomere shortening — Telomeres are protective caps on the ends of your chromosomes. With each cell division, these caps shorten a bit. After 40-60 divisions, they run out, and the cell becomes senescent or dies. This cell division limit (called the Hayflick limit after the person who discovered it) protects you from uncontrolled tumor growth and limits the cell's lifespan. An enzyme called telomerase can lengthen telomeres again if activated. However, lifestyle factors such as bad diet, obesity, smoking, or lack of exercise can shorten telomeres prematurely, leading to illness and death.

Epigenetic alterations — Genes are not always actively expressed. They get turned on and off as needed over your lifetime. So-called histones can temporarily spool unnecessary gene sequences into a lump, making them inaccessible for transcription. The ability to switch relevant genes on and off as needed (epigenetics) declines with age. One reason is that the coenzyme NAD is required for sirtuins to bind the histones (off-switch) to particular genes. As the production of NAD declines with age, you don't have enough material to fabricate the off switch. Unfavorable genes stay turned on and accelerate aging.

Loss of proteostasis — Your body makes more than 20,000 protein molecules that carry out various functions, from metabolic conversions, holding your cells together to making your muscles work. Maintaining all these proteins is a homeostatic process necessary for your survival. Dysfunctional or toxic proteins can accumulate in the cell through misfolding, oxidation, and other modifications. The ability to remove and recycle these protein fragments declines with age leading to a buildup of potentially dangerous garbage in your cells. Caloric restriction (fasting) is one way of reversing this.

Deregulated nutrient sensing — Your cells can sense how abundant nutrients are in your body and stimulate growth when plenty of glucose, fat, and protein are available. One of the pathways regulating this is mTOR. Because nutrients are abundant all the time in our way of life, this sensing ability diminishes over time. So, mTOR never turns off, and you are continuously in an anabolic (growth) state accelerating aging and promoting cancer. Again, fasting (or taking fasting-mimicking substances) can help inhibit the mTOR pathway.

Mitochondrial dysfunction — Mitochondria are tiny organisms (organelles) with their own DNA that convert carbon and oxygen into ATP, the fuel your cells run on. Depending on the cell type, there can be from 20 to thousands of them at work in a single cell. Their origin is unknown. They either were a different lifeform at some point and became symbiotic with cell-based organisms. Or some of our ancient DNA split off to form these separate energy converters. At any rate, mitochondria are exposed to the same problems as the rest of the cell, with damage to mitochondrial DNA, misfolding of their proteins, and other dysfunctions piling up over time.

Cellular senescence — Instead of dying and getting cleaned out, a cell can sometimes become senescent. This is a dormant state in which the cell doesn't function any longer but remains in the tissue and even sends out inflammation markers that keep your immune system busy. Telomere shortening, DNA damage, and stress can lead to a cell adopting this zombie state. The more zombie cells accumulate in the tissue of an organ, the less the organ can function correctly. At some point, the organ fails, and you die of "old age." Removing senescent cells from the tissue through substances called senolytics has extended lifespans significantly in animal trials.

Stem cell exhaustion — Once cells reach their Hayflick limit and die, they must be replaced so the body can continue functioning. Stem cells can create new cells indefinitely and replenish cell types with high turnover rates, like red blood cells, immune cells, or cells in your lungs and intestines. Over time you lose stem cells, and their division speed slows down. Both factors lead to a decline in your cells' replenishment rates, which are prominent causes of aging. Stem cell rejuvenation can slow down this effect.

Altered intercellular communication — Cells communicate with the organism by secreting signaling molecules into the blood. One of the most prominent signals is inflammation, which brings your immune system to action. As the number of senescent cells grows over time, inflammation signals chronically flood the system wearing down your immune system. Senescent cells also start sending signals that lead to senescence in neighboring cells. All this causes a breakdown of your typical defense mechanisms against external intruders like viruses and bacteria.

In 2022, scientists discussed adding at least four more hallmarks of aging to the list. One example is the loss of autophagy, which is the ability to clean up cells and covers repairs beyond just cleaning out misfolded proteins. Other examples are the increasing dysregulation of RNA processing, disturbances in your microbiome, or a vast array of mechanical properties which are altered with time. Undoubtedly, the various manifestations of aging will further get expanded and clustered differently as we learn more about the biochemistry of our bodies.

The exact number and descriptions of these hallmarks are of no consequence here. Key to note is that they all describe a loss of homeostasis. Conceptually, they represent the same phenomenon:

- There is a process that is vital to maintaining life.
- Keeping this process running is ensured by homeostatic regulators.
- These regulators are either not perfect, so small mistakes accumulate and compound over time. Or the

efficacy of the regulator decreases, leading to lasting imbalances. Both accelerate aging.

- The main contributors to all hallmarks of aging are entropy and the passage of time. Bad lifestyle choices accelerate, while better habits slow down these detrimental developments.

The dream of the longevity movement is to halt these hallmarks altogether. Despite all the technological advances of our modern era and the prophecies of sages in this field, I am still doubtful that we will see dramatic changes impacting our lifespans soon. We have yet to fully understand the complex network of systems that keep us alive for over 80 years on average. And this multitude of systems, genes, and pathways are all under siege by increasing entropy. Some interventions like fasting seem to promote broader repair mechanisms that tackle various hallmarks of aging at once. But organisms depend on thousands of systems. Repairing all cognitive, sensory, metabolic, and other physiological processes on an ongoing basis still seems out of reach. Bryan Johnson, a mid-40s entrepreneur who reportedly spends US$ 2 million annually on a rejuvenation regime he developed, has so far been able to turn back his biological clock by an underwhelming four years. The regime he follows seems brutally strict and hard to maintain for ordinary people.

Of course, research and investments in this field are increasing exponentially. And there is no reason humanity shouldn't be able to "solve" the problem of aging and death at some point. Ultimately, our bodies are just biological machines. We can live much longer by exerting enough energy and reversing all entropy accumulating in different places. Just because the oldest recorded human lived to 122 years does not mean this is the ceiling. We don't see any reason for a cap on our lifespans. Many animals and plants live much longer than we do, and at least one species, the tiny jellyfish called Turritopsis doohmii, is known to be technically immortal. If injured or sick, it can return to its polyp stage over three days and then grow into adulthood all over again.

Think of newborn babies. Despite all the damage and aging in people's bodies, parents create a new being in which everything is set back to zero. There is practically no DNA damage or oxidation; all stem cells are fresh, and telomeres are as long as they get. If you can reset the clock for your offspring, why not also for yourself? Indeed, we don't yet have the knowledge or the resources to achieve this. But it is just a matter of time until we figure it out.

With our existing knowledge and resources, we can already improve our healthspan considerably. We can move the period of physical and mental infirmity further out with simple interventions. We can now spend more time in excellent health and enjoy vibrant lives before a brief phase of deterioration and death. This sounds quite appealing in contrast to the long, slow decline over decades and inevitable end of life in hospitals that we seem to regard as the norm today. Given the impact of aging on the second half of our lives, it seems absurd that 86 percent of all healthcare costs in the US are directed at treating the effects of chronic disease rather than trying to delay the onset of aging in the first place.

Frame

Take a step back and examine how you think about your health. How well do you treat yourself and this one precious life you have? Which dominant narratives run in your family and social circles? Do you invoke the famous grandfather who smoked and drank all his life until he died peacefully at age 90 in his favorite armchair? What is your cognitive dissonance and which story do you tell yourself to resolve it?

Societal belief maintains that the medical field exists primarily to cure illness. We treat conditions as they arise, almost no matter the cost. According to the OECD, the annual healthcare cost per capita of those aged 85 years and above is six times higher than those aged between 55 and 59 years.

When we debate health insurance or universal healthcare, we imply that the cost of treating illness should be shouldered by society or the community of the insured. However, the cost of maintaining your health and preventing disease is something we consider a personal expense. Likewise, there is no penalty for neglecting your health. You can smoke as much as you like, choose not to exercise, or literally shoot yourself in the foot. Your health insurance will pick up the tab in many countries if you have one. Car, property, or other insurance would typically exclude damages that were your fault. However, for health, different standards apply.

The underlying belief is that everyone is free to do what they want as long as it isn't harmful to others. Society seems to value and encourage potentially self-harming behaviors to express one's personality. Medically obese people are celebrated as "curvy" or "plus-sized" propagators of a confident body image. Risky and sometimes deadly surgeries and other interventions are undertaken to achieve a different aesthetic or gender. Practitioners of "extreme sports" like free climbing, BASE jumping, or wingsuit flying are admired for the risks they take. Without judging any of these choices, they imply a lower value of good health versus our freedom to do whatever we want. Why is health such an afterthought for many people?

It starts with the fact that we consider self-harm "fun" and sometimes even heroic. The workaholic will actively brag about how little sleep she gets and how much of her children's lives she misses due to work. The social animal will proudly recount how late it got yesterday and how many bottles of wine he consumed. Being healthy is considered mainstream and boring, while stepping outside the norms and inflicting self-harm is cool. Outlaws don't worry about tomorrow; rebels live in the moment. They ride motorcycles and live on the edge.

This inclination to test boundaries is something our hormones establish in our teenage years. As adolescents, we start taking risks to form our identities and become independent young adults. It is part of our learning process to discover where our limits lie. Sometimes this behavior is also driven by a desire to belong to a social group. As a teenager, health is not a big concern, and aging is abstract. However, we never stop glorifying those times and pretend we can live like this forever. We extrapolate the adolescent lifestyle into the future. At the same time, we don't notice how the rate of decline accelerates. In our 20s and 30s, our bodies' repair mechanisms still work well, and the cellular damage has not accumulated to any worrying degree. This changes in our 40s and even more so in our 50s. It becomes increasingly hard to get back into homeostasis. Look at how fast kids recover from cuts and bruises and how much that changes in mid-life.

Even if you want to make a healthy choice, the cards are stacked against you. As explored earlier, we tend to favor the option that increases pleasure and avoids pain in the moment, disregarding the long-term consequences. This future discounting tends to underestimate the cumulative effect of a bad behavior repeated many times. We look at one glass of wine at a time, one cigar to smoke, one bag of chips, and one night of sleep to forfeit. And because of our narrow processing bandwidth that focuses on quick and sudden changes, we don't notice our gradual shift into illness over time. I believe nobody wants to be obese. Being out of breath and tired all the time, having difficulties performing routine tasks, and living with an elevated risk of cardiac arrest, among others, is not desirable. However, due to reasons within or outside of their control, people consistently consume more calories than their body needs, leading to weight gain. The change in body composition happens gradually, and we may not notice a significant difference when we look in the mirror each day. Being overweight has become normalized, and we don't recognize it as a problem.

Like the allegoric frog in the pot of water that does not notice the gradual temperature rise and eventually gets boiled to death, we slip into a sedentary, drug-reliant, work-dominated life of stress on autopilot. This life becomes the new norm and the status quo that is not challenged. The story about the frog is a myth, by the way. As the water gets warmer, the frog will actually jump out in time, while we seem to willingly surrender to the gradual decline of aging and bad habits.

To make matters worse, society does not support you but, instead, even helps you justify your dysfunctional state. To relieve you from the cognitive dissonance you experience, your lifestyle is post-hoc rationalized as your free choice. Something you should feel comfortable with. Something, even, that you should be proud of. Benign descriptors for obesity, like "curvy" or "queen-sized," are euphemisms for a disease that, according to any medical publication, decreases the quality and length of life and increases individual, national, and global healthcare costs.

Because everyone has their vices, solidarity with and support of others is low in health. You are on your own. Everyone has their demons to battle. In demanding tolerance for people's self-destructive behavior, we want to avoid being called out ourselves. But by doing so, we justify these behaviors and give people even less reason to change. Worse, we imply that self-destructive behavior is encouraged as a matter of expressing your personality. It is a collective delusion that self-harm is fun and that risking your health is a great thing to do in exchange for social currency or other perceived benefits. It is an imagined order that exists to protect the peace of everyone but ultimately ends up limiting and hurting you.

I don't think it is human or fair. Not to the individuals suffering from a deterioration of their life quality, premature aging, and unnecessary pain. And not to society which is bearing the cost. A life of stress, sugar, alcohol, sedentarism, sleep deprivation, and so forth leads straight to depression, dementia, diabetes, cancer, cardiovascular disease, and so on. The suffering for the individual, their families, and the cost for society is nothing we should tolerate and accept.

Of course, everyone should live their lives as they see fit. Stepping over boundaries and putting yourself at risk is part of life and generates valuable experiences. But the existing frame is too narrow and stacked in favor of the lazy. Many people don't even get the chance to improve because their so-called friends are dragging them down with them. This has nothing to do with intelligence, social status, or other forms of privilege. We are all subject to powerful narratives and social conditioning that often make it hard to form habits in favor of a better life.

Reframe

The easiest way to maintain your health is not to get sick. The concept of prevention is surprisingly un-derrepresented in people's minds. Preventing death is obviously impossible, at least not with our current knowledge and resources. What we can prevent or delay is premature death meaning a termination event that could have been postponed if another course of action had been chosen in the past.

Circa 155,000 people die every day, and it isn't clear how many of these deaths were premature and could have been prevented. The definitions for which causes of death are preventable vary widely. The most apparent form of preventable death is when it was solely caused by the victim (suicide). Less obvious is a death that could have been prevented with the current standard of care, which wasn't available generally or specifically to the victim for some reason. Something like cancer lies in between and needs to be differentiated by those types brought on by lifestyle choices (smoking) versus those of hereditary or other origins. Death certificates capture the physiological reason for the demise (heart failure) but not what led to this condition (obesity). The underlying cause needs to be obtained from the victim's medical records if available.

With these uncertainties in mind, estimates for preventable deaths vary from 20 to 40 percent of all incidents. The top four reasons for premature death usually include smoking, obesity, lack of movement, and alcohol abuse. In the US, accidental poisoning has recently reached the top 10 because of the misuse and accidental overdose with opioids like fentanyl.

Over many years smoking has been the uncontested, leading cause of preventable death in all studies, but more recently, obesity seems to have gained the upper hand. In the US, the rise in obesity rates, with now more than half of the population considered obese, has established it as the leading cause of death, preventable or not, making smoking number two. The World Obesity Foundation's 2023 Atlas predicts that by 2035 more than half of the global population will be obese.

Why do people smoke or become obese then? One answer is that they are still young and healthy when they pick up the underlying habits. They lack awareness of the consequences and do not appreciate the need for prevention. Secondly, there is an unhealthy notion that you can always start (re-)acting once you detect the first signs of illness. That is what medicine supposedly is for. But that is dead wrong.

Even in the US, with one of the best levels of healthcare, 12 percent of those experiencing their first heart attack died in 2017. A few decades ago, more than half of first heart attacks were fatal in the US, which is probably the rate in many countries today. Worse, your life expectancy drops dramatically once you experience and survive your first major health event. According to recent data from Germany, 10-20 percent of strokes are fatal. Of the rest, more than half will die in the five years following the event. A 2019 study in Acto Orthopaedica found that the one-year mortality rate after a hip fracture was 21 percent on average. So, one in five people who break their hip dies within 12 months. This statistic is for patients whose hip fracture was surgically repaired. For all others, the mortality rate was 70 percent. Another study from 2017 found that for adults in the US and Europe, the all-cause mortality rate for people with a hip fracture doubled over 12 years.

Avoid getting sick. Not only because sickness carries a risk in itself, but because you rarely fully recover again. Your ability to reach homeostasis is permanently impaired, and the chance of subsequent adverse health events increases. As a result, your remaining timeline is shortened. If all of this sounds obvious, ask yourself how much energy you invest in avoiding getting sick. When people discover that I wear a continuous glucose monitor and take 1 gram of Metformin daily preventatively without being a diabetic, they think I am crazy. According to the US Center for Disease Control (CDC), life expectancy for a 50-year-old diagnosed with type-II diabetes is six years shorter than for people without it. So, what is crazy? Taking a proven, cheap, and benign preventative drug that consistently lowers blood glucose and prevents insulin resistance starting in your mid-40s? Or watching your glucose levels rise from test to test until they are too high seriously impacting your remaining life- and healthspan?

It amazes me how much we trust ranges and thresholds provided by labs and doctors we don't actually understand. Take lipid panels. For total cholesterol, any value below 200 milligrams per deciliter is considered "normal," and values from 200 to 239 are "borderline high." What we are trying to determine is the risk of atherosclerosis. This buildup of fatty deposits in your blood vessels can cause heart attacks and strokes and results from lipoproteins in your blood vessel walls. Causes differ by genetics, anatomical specificities, or lifestyle choices.

Atherosclerosis is not necessarily related to cholesterol in circulation at all, certainly not to total cholesterol. It starts building up already in childhood. Autopsies of young adults who committed suicide consistently showed the presence of atherosclerosis already in their 20s and 30s. The lesions that finally lead to a blockage of an artery usually start developing in your 40s. In your 50s, you would typically begin receiving statins or other drugs to lower your blood cholesterol. But this might be too late, as half of all strokes and heart attacks occur before the age of 60.

The understanding of which metric indeed indicates your risk of a major cardiac event (HDL, LDL, Lp(a) or most likely apoB), what the presence of calcifications tells you, and whether you should apply a 10-year or a 30-year risk perspective is still in development. Despite all the simplifications (HDL is not universally "good" cholesterol) and outright nonsense (dietary cholesterol has hardly any impact on your blood lipids, so don't worry about eating eggs), what surprises me most is that people are satisfied if some arbitrary metric like total cholesterol is within a range that is labeled "normal."

A normal value isn't necessarily an optimal one. The normal range for blood pressure goes up to 120/80 mm Hg (millimeters of mercury). Still, a recent study in the New England Journal of Medicine found that your risk of cardiovascular disease is already elevated if you consistently measure within the upper end of the normal range. The official recommended daily intake for Vitamin D is between 600 and 800 IU (International Units), but recent studies suggest that this may only be a minimum. The optimal dose is currently placed between 1,000 and 2,000 IU a day. Both recommendations fail to take into account highly individual factors such as metabolization rates of oral Vitamin D supplementation or exposure to sunlight. It would make more sense to recommend a target blood concentration, which the Endocrine Society puts at 30 to 100 nanograms of Vitamin D per milliliter of serum.

Of course, as laypeople, we cannot be expected to second-guess official recommendations and guidelines by medical professionals. But we should remind ourselves of the fundamental premise that most healthcare operates under — "Don't fix it if it ain't broken." Your doctor is trying to find defects but won't spend time on getting you into the best possible state that will prevent or delay the onset of defects in the future. Why? Because they don't know, and there is hardly any research on the optimal state. It is easier to identify when the system breaks down versus when it will run as long as possible.

We know that no movement is terrible for you and can probably identify how much movement is necessary at a minimum to prevent the worst outcomes. But we have no idea how much movement would be optimal. For something as fundamental as exercise, no study tries to determine the minimum effective dose, a standard procedure in any drug development.

Hence, don't be satisfied if all your values are within range. That just means that no damage can be identified yet. But it doesn't mean you are taking good care of your body. Keep track of the results from previous examinations and look at trajectories rather than individual values. Your glucose might be fine now, but has it been creeping up over the last ten years? If the dentist didn't detect caries or gum disease at your last appointment, it doesn't mean you can stop brushing your teeth either.

It doesn't take a cunning reframing mind to realize how insane it is to actively and willingly shorten your life expectancy for trivial things such as smoking, drinking, overeating, or not moving. You might argue that there is pleasure in all those and that they have value to you. Do they? Let's reframe your narrative!

Warren Buffett, the famous investor, is worth US$ 108 billion as of February 2023. Would you want to trade places with him knowing that he is 92 years old? No? Wouldn't it be great to have all that money and be the fifth most wealthy person on the planet? I am sure you wouldn't make the switch unless you are over 90 years yourself. Because your remaining years, how many there might be, are worth more than US$ 108 billion to you. Why are they worth so much less when you are satisfying your nicotine addiction, seeking social approval by drinking alcohol, or silencing the stress and mental demons by binging on unhealthy food?

The age during which you lay the foundations for a healthy second half of your life is in your 40s and 50s. It is probably not too late to do good things in your 60s and 70s. But it will be much harder to prevent conditions already accumulating in your body over decades. The truth is that with age, everything gets worse. We continuously degrade unless we find some miraculous restoration technique using nanobots, stem cells, genetic modifications, or other ways of turning back the clock.

Until then, your muscle strength, grip strength, leg strength, bone density, gait speed, lean mass percentage, cardiorespiratory fitness, metabolic rate, and so on all decline with age. Cellular and genetic damage cumulates over time, and dysfunctional cells and cell fragments harm the optimal flow of information and micronutrients across the organism.

Logically, if you cannot change the slope of the curve, you need to elevate the starting point and parallel shift the declining curve upwards to reach a higher target in the future. Try to reframe what level of health you are solving for. Adequate health today is fine but will degrade to frailty over time. If you want to enjoy a similar level of fitness in your 90s, you have to be in the top decile of healthy people today. Only the strongest and fittest 40-year-olds will decline to the level that they can still walk up five flights of stairs and lift their grandchildren in old age.

Imagine a bathtub that is constantly leaking. The water level in the tub represents your health and fitness level, and the rate of the leak represents the natural decline due to aging. Filling the bathtub only halfway will make you run out of water soon. If you cannot fix the leak (i.e., slow down the rate of decline), you need to start with more water in the tub. This means filling the bathtub to the brim. Yes, the bathtub will still leak, and the water level will decline over time. But because you started with more water, you'll still have a substantial amount left when you reach your 90s.

You need to think about the glide path more than what you consider good enough today. Peter Attia calls this the "Centenarian Decathlon" and recommends defining the ten things you want to be able to do in the ninth decade of your life and working backward from there. I, for one, want to easily hike 10 kilometers with a backpack, carry and lift a suitcase for air travel, get in and out of cars with ease, walk uphill and up a couple of flights of stairs, pick up my dog, take a sauna bath, and get in and out of swimming pools. Regardless of the concrete list, each activity is linked to a specific functional exercise I can practice and measure my current ability against. Respiratory fitness for hiking, motion control and stability for getting in and out of a swimming pool, overhead press strength for lifting a ten-kilogram suitcase into a plane's overhead bin. Given sarcopenia, it does not suffice to be able to do these activities today. I need above-average shoulder and arm strength today to get to an acceptable amount for the activity I prioritize in 45 years.

Prevention starts with avoiding unnecessary risks from self-harming behaviors. Most of us would probably not engage in BASE jumping, an activity where you hurl yourself off a building or cliff and have to deploy a parachute almost immediately to avoid killing yourself. It is one of the most dangerous recreational activities. The injury rate for BASE jumping is 0.2-0.4 percent, and the death rate is 0.04 percent per jump.

According to the US Actuarial Life Table, 0.04 percent is also the risk of dying of all causes at age 53. However, according to a 2016 Harvard School of Public Health study, being obese increases your all-cause mortality risk by 45-93 percent against the base rate. So, if you are 53 years old and have a body mass index (BMI) over 35, your all-cause mortality risk doubles to circa 0.08 percent. In other words, being obese elevates your risk of dying by the same amount as BASE jumping, one of the most dangerous things you can do for fun. If you are 62, a BMI over 35 carries a two-fold risk of dying compared to BASE jumping.

Of course, people shy away from jumping off a building but are more relaxed and joke about having "a few pounds too many" because of the differently timed feedback loops. A few seconds after jumping, you will be either dead, injured, or unharmed. For being overweight, both the buildup of the condition and the onset of the illness happens gradually over time. By the time you notice the effects of the condition, you have already failed to prevent it.

So, prevention needs to consider long-term risks and cannot rely on short-term feedback loops. Prevention is also not just avoidance but involves building up resiliency and strength to take on unknown injuries and diseases at a later stage. Prevention creates a health buffer for an involuntary decline in ability over time. Prevention needs to elevate your starting point and adjust the slope of decline for you to reach a higher target level in the future.

The good news is that prevention and the levers for excellent health are simple and mostly free. According to a Harvard School of Public Health study, merely adopting five healthy habits during your adult life can add 12 years of life expectancy for men and 14 years for women. These habits are eating a healthy diet, maintaining a body mass index between 18.5 and 25, daily moderate to vigorous physical activity of at least 30 minutes, consuming little alcohol, and not smoking.

I am surprised sleep is not mentioned. Nevertheless, long before you will receive 3D-printed organs or have nanobots repair mitochondrial DNA, maintaining your health today is simply a matter of common sense. The things they discovered at Harvard that add more than a decade of life expectancy are all very ordinary states of the human condition. Moving about, maintaining a standard ratio between fat and lean mass, and avoiding toxins such as bad food, alcohol, or smoking, are what we were built for. So, conversely, keeping your body in a state that it wasn't built for apparently wears it down prematurely and makes you lose 12-14 years of life on average. Your body did not evolve to deal with toxins chronically, carry excessive amounts of fat squished between your organs, and then remain idle for most of the day. The expectation that this kind of behavior would have no consequences is absurd.

Let's take movement. We are not talking about structured exercise or strength training (yet). Our body has evolved to move. We are not built to work out in a gym but to walk, run, carry, and throw things out in nature. No one knows for sure, but ancient humans supposedly walked between 6 and 16 kilometers per day. The recommendation to take 10,000 steps daily is based on nothing but adds up to about 8 kilometers and fits into this historic range well enough. Our body relies on us using this ability to move. Following the principle of "use-it-or-lose-it," skeletal muscle tissue atrophies quickly if not used to conserve energy. A 2008 study estimated that you lose 12 percent of muscle strength per week of bed rest in a hospital. After 3-5 weeks, you would have lost half of your overall strength.

Consequently, the WHO recommends moderate to vigorous physical activity, such as walking, running, carrying something, climbing, playing a sport, or cleaning the house. According to them, insufficient physical activity is the fourth leading risk factor for mortality overall. This is quite ironic in a world where human progress is almost defined by ways of eliminating physical activity. With elevators, escalators, cars, chairs, tools, and machines, there is no need to move anymore.

Unsurprisingly, the WHO reported in 2008 that 31 percent of persons aged 15 and above were insufficiently active, which means they engaged in less than 150 minutes of moderate physical activity per week. The WHO's standard is already lower than the 30 minutes per day recommended by the Harvard study. There are 10,080 minutes a week, so a third of all people do not even move 1.5 percent of the time. Even if you account for the eight hours of recommended sleep in the denominator, 150 minutes a week still only represents 2.2 percent of your waking time.

In a 2022 update, the Global Status Report on Physical Activity, the WHO found that 1.4 billion adults (28 percent of the global population) did not meet the recommended level of physical activity to maintain their physical and mental health. So, the global "inactivity pandemic" has stayed at the same level. More worryingly, more than 80 percent of adolescents (boys and girls aged 11 to 17) spend less than an hour of moderate physical activity daily. Apart from the individuals suffering from chronic diseases and premature death, the WHO estimates the economic burden of inactivity alone to be US$ 68 billion due to healthcare expenditures and productivity losses.

The reframing thought is that your body does not need extraordinary interventions to stay healthy. You don't need expensive supplements, unique treatments, or costly exercise equipment. Most benefit derives from giving your body what it naturally wants — movement, rest, and good fuel. You can spend money on additional things, which might improve your health further. But the foundation is to just treat your body according to the user manual. You wouldn't leave your car in the rain with the windows down or leave your home without locking the door. Just treat your body with the same common sense and care. If you have too much fat mass, restrain your calorie input until you get back into shape. If you have no strength, work out until you can do your daily activities without pain or discomfort. If you cannot concentrate or are fatigued, prioritize your sleep more. You are most familiar with the user manual of your body. It is what your body naturally wants to get back into homeostasis.

And the point of homeostasis does not stay the same all your life. If you picture a scale, the balance point sits in the middle. The scale is level if you put the same weight on either side. However, if the balance point were off center, let's say somewhat to the right, you would have to put more weight on the left side of the scale to restore balance. The more the balance point moves to the right, the higher the weight needed on the left side to keep the scales level.

Homeostasis, your life's balance point, works the same way. When you are young, the effort required to remain stable is low. You hardly notice recovering from a hangover, giant pizza, or sitting in a classroom all day. As you age, the balance point of your life's scale moves to the right. With time, you need to add more and more effort to keep your scale level. The cost of that pizza or inactivity goes up. And if you keep piling on those detrimental events and don't exert enough energy on the other side, you know the story: entropy, decay, death.

I don't want to imply that health is only about blindly extending your time on the planet. Some people say that the additional years you gain get added to the end of life when you are already old and miserable. This is obviously not the aim. The better your body can achieve homeostasis, the shallower your glide path of decline, and the longer you can enjoy your life in good health. If you died tomorrow, the effort wouldn't have been wasted. You would still have been able to enjoy your life in excellent health until the last moment.

Like homeostasis, your efforts to maintain and improve your health must be balanced with everything else. You get it wrong if you spend 16 hours a day just working on your health. The objective is not to become obsessed and create new obstructions that prevent you from leading a life of fulfillment and contribution.

Fortunately, the foundations for being healthy are straightforward and not at all time-consuming. Activities like physical movement or recovery will add to your enjoyment, and avoiding bad habits will free up time and energy if you are willing to say no to them.

Admittedly, this is the hardest part. You will have to say no to things you might enjoy today. Things that give you shallow, short-term pleasure but nonetheless are things you like. Your glass(es) of wine in the evening, the big cuts of meat and sausages on the grill, the late-night binging on some mindless series or computer game. You will have to cut back on the bad habits you keep justifying to others and yourself.

You might even think those are things that define your very existence. "If I can live longer but not do the things I enjoy, what is the point of that?" is something I can hear you say. Let's bring Warren Buffett into the picture one more time. There are many stories about the mental models he employed to become one of the most successful investors. One of them is the 25/5 rule. Buffett gave career advice to his pilot and instructed him to create a list of the 25 most important things he wanted to achieve. Once the pilot had compiled the list, Buffett advised him to cross out numbers 6 to 25 and only focus on the top 5. The distraction potential of your secondary priorities is immense precisely because you desire them to a certain degree as well. Completely ignoring them is a tough choice to make. However, they will get in the way of achieving what you truly care about.

Confronted with the story, Buffett denied having had this conversation or inventing the 25/5 rule. Regardless, you will have to make choices and build habits that will feel like you are giving up something you consider essential or pleasurable — wrongly so, as we have established. Suppose you take a step back and reframe the situation intellectually. In that case, you should realize quickly that your beliefs were grounded in social conditioning by the imagined order and your (sub-conscious) rationalization attempts to resolve cognitive dissonance. But it is one thing to realize something, and it is something else entirely to act on it.

We are complex organisms comprising thousands of biochemical processes, all subject to the laws of nature. We live in the physical world. All our sensory input, consciousness, and sense of being derive from the physical environment. Even if we could upload our minds into a computer someday, I think the result would be pretty disappointing. Our minds are dynamic and rely on constant interaction with other organisms and the natural world. Our self is far more than our brain and the collection of thoughts. Our physical state directly impacts our mind, how we feel, and what we experience. Conversely, our cognitive function and mental health would quickly deteriorate without sensory stimuli.

Therefore, my number one priority on the imaginary "Warren Buffett list" of 25 things is my physical health. Nothing is more important to my existence. Let me, therefore, take you through the six elements I consider vital to health:

- Welcome well-dosed **stress**
- Avoid **toxins**
- Engage in **recovery**
- Periodically undergo **overhaul**
- Provide the right **nutrients**
- Apply rigorous **governance**

Stress

In the late 1980s, scientists built an artificial Earth to understand how our planet's living systems work together. Compared to the actual Earth, it was a relatively modest undertaking. They constructed a dome of steel tubing and glass frames and sealed it off to make it self-sustaining. They called the dome "Biosphere 2" and included various plants and trees to study how they could mimic our planet's life-support systems on a smaller scale.

The experiment lasted four years and yielded many interesting insights. One of the more unexpected findings was that trees couldn't grow properly in this artificial environment, even though they were exposed to the same nutrients and gravitational forces as outside the dome. Once they reached a certain height, trees snapped under their weight or toppled over. Researchers subsequently discovered the root cause. It was the absence of wind in the dome.

When saplings grow into trees, wind plays a vital role in their development. The external forces of getting hit by wind, from ever-changing directions and with different intensities, make the sapling develop what is now called "stress wood" that replaces the regular, softer wood in the stem and partially in the roots. As a response to the mechanical forces, a tree forms stronger wood fibers along its vulnerable parts to fortify the structure. Without the stress induced by the wind, the tree would be weaker and wouldn't be able to mature into an actual tree. What made the trees fall over in "Biosphere 2" was a lack of stress.

Stress, as the first recommendation in a chapter on improving your health, will probably strike you as odd. Stress is usually considered something bad. Understandably so, as stress represents, by definition, a negative impact. If it were pleasurable, it would not be stressful. A stressor in the context of health and physiology usually implies pain or, at least, some form of discomfort.

As Peter Atia put it, if you knew nothing about exercise and I described its effects, you would likely avoid it at all costs. If I told you that you would be doing something that elevates your heart rate, raises your blood pressure, and increases your inflammatory markers, free radical production, and hepatic glucose output, you would probably get worried. But these are only first-order effects. Applied thoughtfully, stress has such positive second-order impacts that they are often worth the short-term discomfort. People who exercise regularly have a lower resting heart rate, lower blood pressure, and lower levels of inflammation markers.

What is stress, then, and why am I recommending it? A stressor is something that deliberately and temporarily disrupts homeostasis. Stressing a system leads to an overcompensating response by the body called hormesis aimed at restoring homeostasis. Hormesis makes your body adapt further to ensure it can handle the stressor better next time. It works like a vaccine. You administer a controlled dose of a stressor, and your body adapts by getting better at handling it. A low amount of stress leads to a high inhibition response.

Stressing your muscles to hypertrophy will make them grow and fortify themselves to better deal with the same load next time. As a result, the system becomes more resilient. We know this intuitively. If you want to get stronger, you must exercise harder than before. To lose fat, you must be hungry to a certain degree. If you want to learn something, you have to put in the work.

This concept is captured in the term "antifragility," coined by Nassim Taleb. Unlike fragile items that break under stress, antifragile systems benefit from volatility and shock. They are not just resilient to the shock; they become stronger and better because of the stressor. Antifragile systems mostly consist of individual units that itself remain fragile but this fragility benefits the overall system. Small and frequent forest fires clear out the undergrowth providing light and nutrients for new growth, aiding the entire forest. The stock market or the culinary scene in your hometown is antifragile. Their constituent units, companies and restaurants, are fragile and can go out of business due to shocks like economic developments or customer behavior. But that also weeds out the less adapted elements, which are less resilient, offering less relevant goods and services. The stressor helps clear out the lower quality units like the forest fire clears the undergrowth.

Two things are common to all antifragile systems and, therefore, also apply to your body. Firstly, the stressor must trigger an adaptation. To be beneficial, some kind of learning process is required, a feedback loop that gets inserted into the system as new information. Secondly, it takes some time for the adaptation to happen, which is why recovery is essential.

Working a muscle at a higher load than before is new information to that muscle. It learns that it must create extra capacity to manage this new level. Regular exposure to heat or cold expands the thermal range your body expects and prepares for. Your physiological and nervous response to cold or hot temperatures adapts, making you more resilient in different climates.

Evolution is the ultimate example of an adaptive and hence antifragile system. A random mutation in the gene code represents new information. If it turns out to be beneficial to the survival and procreation of the species, it will get copied more widely and persist. If it is less helpful, the fragile carrier will vanish from the germ line. If humans were immortal, there would be no adaptation to new information. Death and offspring are nature's feedback loops. Because each member of a species is fragile and dies, evolution can constantly adapt to new environments by incorporating new information.

The other defining characteristic of antifragile systems is that a stressor's effect depends on its intensity. Too much of a good thing can become harmful. If you load too much weight, you can injure your muscle tissue or even a bone. An excessive dose of a stressor can cause damage to the overall system. For example, potassium is essential for muscle contractions, nerve function, and fluid balance. We need about 2.5 to 3 grams per day to function well. A dose of 18-20 grams, however, is considered lethal. So, if you consumed the recommended weekly amount of potassium all in one day, you could die.

A stressor can also be damaging at a low dose if it is applied chronically without a chance for the system to recover. This is where stress gets its bad reputation from — chronic stress. Continuous, repetitive application of a stressor overloads the system at some point. If you don't get a chance to recover and adapt but continuously are exposed to the same burden, you don't strengthen but weaken the system.

This is true for almost anything. If you have your favorite meal every day of the year, you will begin to loathe it. If you only run at full speed every day without any recovery in between, you will injure your joints and bones from the strain. You will become seriously ill if you are constantly overwhelmed by the demands of your work and private life. If you are always unhappy at work or in your relationship, you will suffer mental problems and maybe even a breakdown.

This is the kind of stress you need to avoid. I remember working with a company that makes elevator doors. An essential part of their customers' requirements was that new door models had to pass a stress test. A robotic apparatus called the simulator would open and close the test door automatically over and over to mechanically induce wear and tear. The new model would only receive certification once it demonstrated that it could withstand one million cycles; for some customers, two million cycles. Even with modern simulators, the one-million-cycle test took about two seconds per cycle and hence about three weeks. So, the lifetime of the elevator door, which could generally last ten years and more, got condensed to three weeks. You don't want to be that door.

But that does not change the fact that acute, well-dosed stress is beneficial and essential to us. Our tendency to seek comfort and avoid stress is not doing us any favors. Quite the opposite. It makes us weaker and less resilient. An unforeseen event like a fall can then seriously harm us.

You need to embrace stress. The adage "What doesn't kill you, makes you stronger" is nonsense. Excessive and chronic stress makes you weaker long before it kills you. But the reverse is true: "No pain, no gain." Temporary pain and discomfort are positive. Exhaustion from exercise makes you stronger. Practice makes you better at a skill. Having a challenging conversation can save your relationship. Pain leads to learning, adaptation, and, ultimately, improvement. These principles apply almost universally. For your health, I recommend the following stressors.

Mobility Training

Start with mobility training, which is similar to stretching but different in meaningful ways. Stretching typically involves holding a particular position to lengthen a muscle or muscle group and also improves the range of motion and flexibility and can help eliminate muscle tension. Mobility training focuses more on the movement quality of different joints and contributes to balance, coordination, stability, and better functional movement patterns.

The physiological effects of mobility training include increased blood flow to the muscles and joints, enhanced flexibility, and range of motion. Additionally, mobility training can help increase the production of synovial fluid, a lubricant that helps reduce friction between the joints. This can help to reduce the risk of wear and tear and improve joint health over time.

Especially if you are new to exercise and haven't moved much in the past, mobilizing your joints and muscle groups will help you transition into more meaningful forms of exercise without hurting yourself. An injury is the most frustrating and habit-breaking event in the context of exercise. It takes long to heal properly, particularly for tissue that doesn't metabolize actively, such as joints and cartilage. But the rate at which you lose fitness is high, so people tend to restart their routines while not fully recovered yet, leading to new and sometimes worse injuries. With proper mobilization, you can usually prevent this from happening.

Resistance Training

Resistance training, which involves using weights or other forms of resistance, has enormously positive effects on the body. One of the most important ones is increased muscle mass, as the repeated contractions and load on the muscles stimulate muscle growth and hypertrophy. Resistance training also helps to increase bone density, which helps prevent osteoporosis and other bone-related conditions. Additionally, it can increase the body's metabolism, helping to burn more calories and improve overall body composition. It also helps improve cardiovascular health by reducing blood pressure and improving cholesterol levels. There is no downside to becoming stronger. If there is anything I urge you to do — at any age — it is to take up regular strength training. Just 30-40 minutes, two to three times a week, will significantly improve your fitness and health.

Particularly women sometimes worry they might become too muscular performing resistance training. They argue that bulging muscles would negatively impact their physique. So, instead of adequately stressing their muscles, they often revert to low-intensity cardio or use tiny weights in the 1-2 kilogram range. I travel often and see people in gyms around the world. It amazes me how many do the equivalent of walking on treadmills or gently cycling on bikes while constantly staring at their phones and typing messages. Their necks are strained looking at the screen, the stimulus to the body is very low, and that time is effectively wasted. One person I encountered in a gym in Querétaro, Mexico, seemed to recognize this and didn't even bother changing into sports clothes. He walked on the treadmill in a suit and dress shoes.

From my own experience, I can assure you that there is no such thing as spontaneous, bulging muscle growth. It takes some time to become strong. The rate at which muscle mass can be gained varies depending on training volume, intensity, and frequency, as well as individual factors such as age and genetics. Women can generally expect to gain about 250 to 500 grams of muscle mass per month with consistent strength training and a balanced diet. Most of that would not be immediately visible, so the worry is unfounded. Even if you accumulate more muscle mass than you aesthetically prefer, just back off on your training. Without continuous exercise, you lose your gains quickly. I wish you could somehow build strength and then magically keep it. But that is not how it works.

One of the reasons people resist resistance training is that they don't do it effectively. Even people who have been going to the gym for years don't improve because they perform the same routine repeatedly and don't challenge their muscles to hypertrophy. If you could have done four more repetitions of your movement after you stopped, you are not experiencing enough stress. On the other hand, the load is probably too high if you struggle to do at least four repetitions in one set. Aim at a weight that you can safely do 5 to 10 repetitions at and feel like you have at most one or two reps left in the tank when you stop. Don't go to failure regularly, nor leave money on the table.

There are various philosophies and approaches to stimulating strength improvements that differ by which outcome people hope to achieve. Some want to optimize for lean mass growth, others for endurance, explosive strength, etc. Some might recommend many repetitions with light weights or few with heavy weights. Some might focus on the speed of the movement, while others just want to tense the muscle without moving (the dreaded wall sitting exercise or plank). Ultimately, they are all doing the same: stressing a system to the point that triggers adaptation and then resting to let that adaptation happen biophysically. The repetition range I recommend here targets a middle ground between these approaches.

Whether for all-purpose strength or a specific functional target, keep up your strength training until you die. Older adults say they are too weak to handle weights. It's the other way around. They are weak because they don't handle weights. The leading cause of accidental death in the elderly is falling. Without the strength and stability to prevent the fall, or at least cushion its impact, your chances of dying subsequent to the injury increase substantially from the base rate. In old age, the hazard ratio of not being strong to strong is 3.2. The hazard ratio of smoking at that age is about 2.

In humanity's history, no one has likely ever wished for less strength. I imagine no 90-year-old has ever yearned to be weaker. Being old will have its challenges, I have no illusions about that. But wouldn't I rather be old and strong than old and frail?

The University of Illinois, in a 16-week study, was able to build muscle mass in 80-year-olds through simple squat and weightlifting routines that started softly but successively added weight. At the end of the study, the participants added lean body mass at the same rate as a 20-year-old. It's never too late to start resistance training.

High-Intensity Cardio Training

What resistance training is to your skeletal system and muscles, high-intensity cardio training is to your heart and cardiovascular system. This type of workout involves short bursts of intense exercise followed by periods of rest or lower-intensity movements. You try to elevate your heart rate quickly by sprinting, hill cycling, running, or rowing. The goal is to push the body to its maximum capacity for a short period, followed by a rest period to allow recovery before the next burst. The duration and intensity of the intervals typically range from 10-60 seconds for the high-intensity intervals, followed by a rest period that is equal to or longer than the high-intensity interval.

High-intensity interval training (HIIT) has numerous benefits for your health. Of course, it helps your anaerobic fitness and increases functional threshold and reserve capacity for most sports. HIIT also increases aerobic fitness as measured by VO_2 max, the maximal rate of oxygen your body can attain during physical exertion. To improve VO_2 max specifically, you would probably train at longer intervals of about four minutes.

The short, high-intensity stress on your cardiovascular system increases cardiac contractility, muscle capillary density, and cell mitochondrial adaptation. While also improving insulin sensitivity and reducing blood pressure, a great benefit of high-intensity training is fat loss caused by increased fat oxidation and elevated hormones that drive lipolysis and reduce appetite. Studies have shown that HIIT raises your metabolic rate for hours after exercise.

However, it is a misconception that HIIT is a substitute for other types of cardio training. Research indeed suggests that HIIT achieves similar physiological benefits in one-tenth of the time compared to traditional car-dio training. While it may be tempting to focus solely on high-intensity exercises, it's important to remember that life occurs at various intensity levels, and training for all of them is necessary for good health. Strength training provides stability, force, and functionality in all situations, static or dynamic. HIIT improves your ability to recruit a lot of energy quickly to chase your dog, cycle up the hill, or walk up five flights of stairs. But what about endurance?

The body can metabolize different forms of energy into adenosine triphosphate (ATP), which generally fuels the cellular processes. The fastest form of energy available is the ATP already in your cells. At an all-out effort, you will deplete it in seconds before your cells start replenishing ATP from glucose in your blood and glycogen in your liver and muscles. However, the chemical process of transforming glucose takes time and cannot backfill ATP fast enough if you go at full speed. That's why all-out intervals only last around 10 seconds, roughly the world record for the 100-meter sprint. With the amount of glycogen available, the average person can carry on for about 30 minutes at a moderate intensity. When glucose stores deplete, you need to ramp up a third energy source abundant in most people's bodies: fat.

Low-Intensity Cardio Training

Low-intensity cardio training involves more extended periods of steady-state exercise at a lower level of exertion, such as brisk walking, jogging, or cycling at a moderate pace. Many people have trouble finding this zone and go too slow or fast. The most accurate way to determine the right level would be measuring lactic acid in your blood, but this is not practical. If you can easily breathe through your nose, you are probably not going hard enough. You are going too hard if you cannot speak more than a few words before taking a breath. If you can hear yourself breathing, you are going much too hard. The sweet spot is where you can speak in complete sentences, interrupted by the occasional breath, and maintain this level for an hour or longer.

This type of training is beneficial because it relies on the aerobic system, which oxidizes fat. Fatty acids, primarily triglycerides, yield the most ATP on an energy-per-gram basis as they completely oxidize into CO_2 and water. Fat is ideal for storing energy. If you only had glycogen, you would weigh twice as much with the same energy reserve because carbohydrates require additional water to be stored.

Fat oxidation is slower than glucose conversion and requires adequate oxygen to operate. However, it enables you to keep going for extended periods. A man in his 40s would be considered athletic if he had a body fat percentage of 16 percent. Anything below 8 percent of body fat would be dangerously low. Therefore, at a weight of 75 kilograms, this person could safely burn six kilograms of fat before running into trouble. That amounts to 46,200 kcal of energy. In general, a person burns about 60 kcal per kilometer of running. So, six kilograms of fat should theoretically provide enough energy for 750 kilometers of running or over 17 consecutive marathons.

Welcome to the endurance level. Because of the slower rate of transforming fat into ATP, your body adapts to low-intensity cardio training by increasing the number of mitochondria in your cells and their efficiency. This is a game changer for your metabolism and energy production systems. Consuming fat more efficiently as an energy source preserves glycogen for more intensive efforts. This increased stamina further lowers heart rate and blood pressure, which allows you to perform even more efficiently at an endurance level.

Try performing 80 percent of your cardio training at low intensity, consistently aiming at a minimum of two to three hours per week with at least 30 minutes per session. When you leave the aerobic zone and go too hard, even briefly, your mitochondrial physiology switches from fat oxidation to glycolysis. This creates lactate that your body must remove before you can get back into the beneficial fat oxidation process. Consequently, one high-intensity session will be enough for most people per week if you get in your low-intensity work regularly.

Hot and Cold Exposure

Leaving the thermoneutral zone, in which the body can easily regulate its core temperature, leads to adaptations of several systems. While the scientific evidence for the benefits of heat therapy (mostly dry sauna) is rock solid, the same cannot be said for cold exposure. I still recommend it for psychological reasons, as I will explain.

Both hot and cold temperatures, particularly in succession, help improve circulation and lead to better cardiovascular health. As the blood vessels dilate, blood flow improves, and inflammation reduces. There is some evidence that ice baths improve metabolism by activating brown adipose tissue (brown fat), which increases the metabolic rate of the body by burning fat for heat. Wim Hof, the world record holder for the longest ice bath and nicknamed "The Iceman," created an entire business around breathing exercises and cold immersion. He says ice baths help reduce muscle soreness, improve your immune system and sleep, and speed up your metabolism.

What undoubtedly improves sleep and decreases muscle soreness is a sauna bath in the evening. In a comprehensive study on heat exposure, called the Finland sauna study, over 2,000 individuals with varying sauna habits were observed for 20 years. The control group used the sauna once a week, while the most active group used it four to seven times a week for 20 minutes at 80 degrees Celsius. Interestingly, they couldn't find a control group in Finland that used the sauna less than once a week. Nevertheless, the results were impressive. The most active group had a 40 percent lower relative risk and an 18 percentage points lower absolute risk of all-cause mortality after 21 years compared to the control group (31 versus 49 percent). Additionally, the active group had lower risks of sudden cardiac death, fatal coronary heart disease, stroke, and Alzheimer's disease. Experts noted that it is rare to find such significant benefits from a single intervention. Researchers believe that sauna baths have positive effects on the body because it reacts to heat exposure similarly as to exercise, which is a well-known health intervention. So, if you cannot exercise, a sauna bath may be a good substitute.

Heat and cold exposure are thought to impact even more systems. Studies mention an increase in immune function through the stimulation of white blood cells and improvements in mental health, especially a decrease in depression and anxiety symptoms. From personal experience, I can add that a succession of hot and cold immersions leads to better sleep quality (measured with an Oura ring) and improved overall mood and cognitive function (as noticed subjectively).

While the benefits of cold therapy might not yet be confirmed scientifically, I see value in proper cold exposure. Due to the low conductivity of air, cryotherapy is quite tolerable, despite extreme temperatures of -160 degrees. However, exposing yourself to the initial shock of a 10-degree Celsius ice bath and just sitting in your discomfort, learning to tolerate it, will teach you much about what you are capable of and where your boundaries lie. You will notice how it gets easier every time as you build resiliency. Not only towards the cold but towards most adversity. If you can sit in ice water for ten minutes or even five, your perspective changes on other challenges. An ice bath is a reframe in itself. Not the most pleasant one, I admit.

Fasting

The concept of fasting involves restricting your food intake in one of three ways: by limiting certain types of foods (such as keto, vegetarian, or low-fat diets), by restricting the times you eat (such as with 18:6 time restricted feeding), or by reducing your overall daily calorie intake. Each of these methods has its own unique benefits, and people usually combine them to suit their different motivations, such as ethical, religious, allergic, metabolic, or performance-related concerns. By narrowing your feeding window to four or six hours a day, you might want to increase insulin sensitivity without limiting the calories you consume. By prioritizing particular macronutrients like protein or fat, you might try to induce a metabolic effect, like stimulating protein synthesis for muscle growth or shifting your body into a state of ketosis. If you are trying to lose weight, which is mostly synonymous with reducing fat mass, you will likely exercise caloric restriction.

It can be confusing to label these different interventions as "fasting." Especially the term "intermittent fasting" can mean various things and most often refers to simply skipping breakfast. To me, caloric restriction comes closest to the actual meaning of fasting. Medically speaking, you are fasting when your body switches from an anabolic (breaking down nutrients from the food you ate) to a catabolic state (mainly relying on stored nutrients). Depending on genetics, lifestyle, metabolism, and more, this happens 4 to 24 hours after your last meal.

In the context of stress, I will focus on a multi-day fast. In this scenario, you consume nothing but water, tea, and maybe some black coffee for at least 24 to ideally 72 hours. You basically don't eat anything for three days. Most people can safely fast for seven or even up to ten days. But, as with all other recommendations and ideas in this book, you should always consult a medical professional before attempting any kind of prolonged fast. If you are new to this, start skipping a few meals and fast for 24 hours before attempting several days.

The extended fast is aimed at transitioning your body into a metabolic state that is not commonly used. It triggers a clean-up and recovery protocol known as autophagy, which I will cover in more detail later. Due to the abundance of food available to us nowadays and how regularly we consume it, we typically never leave our default, glucose-based metabolism. However, our ancestors often went without food for days and, like many other animals, developed metabolic strategies to deal with scarcity. When we're starving, we can recycle material and nutrients in our cells and suppress any additional demand from coping with illness or procreation. These processes incidentally repair some of the deterioration described in the hallmarks of aging, especially those from misfolded proteins and other waste in cells. It's unclear to what extent but going without food occasionally may improve your health and increase your lifespan. So, why do I recommend three days of fasting?

When the glucose from your last meal is cleared from the bloodstream, and your insulin levels drop, you start consuming glycogen stored in your liver and muscles. Depending on your reserves, these typically last for 24 to 72 hours, after which you enter a state of ketosis. Your primary energy source becomes ketone bodies made from fatty acids in your liver. Your brain still requires some glucose, but your body can make the required amounts from amino acids or fat. Your body now shifted its primary fuel from carbohydrates to fat.

If you have never or rarely entered ketosis, it can take some time in the beginning, and you might feel a bit weak during the transition (called the "keto flu"). You can speed up the depletion of glycogen and the onset of ketosis by exercising in or before the fasted state. The more frequently you fast, the easier and quicker it will be for your body to transition into ketosis, which is known as metabolic flexibility. While some sources claim that ketosis can be achieved 12 or 16 hours after the last meal, my personal experience indicates that it usually takes a full day of fasting after reducing carbs and exercising. If you're interested in learning about your metabolic flexibility, there are affordable finger-prick tests available that can determine the level of ketone bodies in your blood. An ideal ketone level for autophagy falls within the range of 1.5 to 3 mmol per liter.

There is much hype surrounding intermittent fasting regimes, such as the 18:6-hour schedule, but I remain skeptical about their benefits. While they may help decrease insulin sensitivity, the fasting window is generally too short to have a significant impact on cellular health. Most studies on the supposed longevity benefits of fasting have been conducted on laboratory mice, which typically only live two to three years and starve after two to three days without food. An 18-hour fast for a mouse would probably correspond to a multi-day fast for a human.

Entering ketosis on a prolonged fast has various benefits. The most obvious is burning fat for fuel. It stimulates autophagy, improves gut health, enhances brain function, reduces inflammation, and positively impacts some hormone levels. For example, insulin-like growth factor 1 (IGF-1) levels are significantly reduced during a prolonged fast. Like mTOR, this hormone promotes growth and development and is an autophagy inhibitor. During the refeeding phase after the fast, IGF-1 levels rise again and seem to contribute to the proliferation of stem cells, addressing another of the hallmarks of aging.

The exact effects of fasting, especially prolonged fasting, are not yet fully understood. As with exercise, there is no scientifically evidenced recommendation for a minimally effective fasting dose. In animal studies, caloric restriction by about 50 percent has generated sheer unbelievable lifespan extensions between 50 and 300 percent. These are not automatically transferable to humans, and we cannot conduct analogous trials on humans for ethical and practical reasons. It would take decades to detect any changes in healthspan, and if they existed, these would have been denied to the control group.

Studies with monkeys, our closest relatives, have been inconclusive. A study in Wisconsin showed healthspan advantages for a group of monkeys that reduced their food intake by 30 percent versus another group that could feed without restriction. A similar study in Maryland, however, did not. Later analysis showed a significant difference in the quality of the diets that the monkeys received. Both groups in Wisconsin ate processed monkey feed that contained up to 29 percent of added sugar, while both groups in Maryland received natural foods. So, the real conclusion is that eating less of a bad diet makes you live longer, but not necessarily eating less of a good one.

People from the island of Okinawa consume about 40 percent fewer calories than Americans and live four years longer on average. Women in the US consume about 25 percent fewer calories than men and live five years longer. While these correlations do not imply causality, periodic fasting is believed to have positive health benefits that accumulate over time and may be most effective when practiced for three to five days. A reward in terms of healthspan is very likely because the documented effects are known interventions preventing major chronic diseases, like increasing insulin sensitivity and lowering blood lipid levels and inflammation. With this reward in mind, the risk of fasting occasionally is close to zero.

This contradicts our societal norms, which place a strong emphasis on regular eating. Apart from the standard three meals, some dietitians have recommended five or even seven smaller meals throughout the day. Eating is also a social activity. Not having dinner at an evening gathering would strike many as peculiar. Sharing dinner is a significant social affair that expresses a sense of community. Although different diets are becoming more accepted, not eating anything can still be perceived as odd.

I prioritize my health and consider myself psychologically resilient in the face of what other people think of me. In this case, however, there is no need to confront the imagined order too much. You wouldn't do a prolonged fast more than every other month or once a quarter, so there are ways to time your fasting window to not overlap with your social obligations.

Many people cannot imagine not eating for three days and consider this an immense challenge. A psychological challenge at best, as the physical effort is hardly worth mentioning for a healthy person. Your body has enough energy reserves to keep running for many days without significantly impacting your ability to work out, do your daily chores, and more. I maintain my resistance and other cardio training during fasts, except for high-intensity training that relies on glycogen.

I admit there is a mental challenge. Much of our day revolves around food. According to the American Time Use Survey, US adults spend 67 minutes daily on eating and drinking as "primary activity" and another 23 minutes on eating while conducting other activities like watching television. This does not include the time to buy groceries, prepare the food, and clean up later. So, fasting frees up significant time. And when you get hungry, drink a glass of water and wait 15 minutes. In most cases, the feeling of hunger passes quickly, and you forget that you were hungry before. But the first time you attempt a prolonged fast will nevertheless feel difficult. Good. Welcome to the next chapter.

Leaving the Comfort Zone

Prior to venturing into private equity, I had been a corporate executive for nearly a decade. I was happy, and my performance had caught the attention of the Group CEO, who considered me for a spot on the Group Executive Board. When I received an invitation to join a private equity firm, I was curious but hesitant. It wasn't until months later that I ultimately decided to leave behind my flourishing career and take a chance on the unknown.

Had I known how hard the transition was going to be, I would have declined immediately. For the first two years, I struggled with my new role until I learned to embrace it. Previously, I had been the boss, leading teams and receiving public recognition. But in my new role, I felt like a shadow man and had to learn everything from scratch. Not just investing, governing companies, and partnering with senior managers but also recruiting talent and creating value at scale. My ego was bruised, and I considered returning to the industry I knew. I felt uncomfortable, vulnerable, and self-conscious. But with time, I adapted to the private equity culture and regained my confidence. I began to see the opportunities and impact that my new job offered and realized how vast and fascinating this world was. Instead of merely playing a game, I suddenly saw the opportunity to influence its rules.

Looking back after nearly eight years, I am glad I persisted. Returning to my old world would have been the more comfortable choice in the short term. But I would have missed out on a tremendous personal development journey that profoundly changed me. This kind of growth wouldn't have been possible without the pain and discomfort of transitioning to a new career in middle age. The discomfort forced me to adapt and learn, and as a result, I improved. Hormesis as the overshooting adaptation pathway of stress applies physically as well as mentally.

At all costs, we avoid pain, discomfort, anxiety, shame, sadness, and other things we fear. But the truth is that everything we value and love exists only in contrast to these negative emotions. You cannot appreciate joy if you don't know sadness. We've talked about how to stress your body to adapt and improve physically. The same applies to your mental state. Embracing a challenge that, obviously, should not be dangerous but carries significant odds of failing makes you better. If you fail, you learn something about yourself and understand where your limits lie. If you succeed, you learn something about yourself and understand where you can stretch to next.

Toxins

The year was 1898, and the German pharmaceutical company Bayer had just released a new cough syrup that promised to relieve those suffering from respiratory ailments. The company marketed the syrup as a miracle cure, claiming it was safer and more effective than comparable products. One year before, Bayer had developed aspirin and quickly gained a reputation for high-quality medications throughout Europe and the United States. News of the effectiveness of the cough syrup spread, and doctors started prescribing it liberally to patients of all ages, especially children. An advertisement from around 1900 stated, "The Sedative Cough Cure. Relief follows the first dose. The soothing effect of heroin makes coughs subside at once. This preparation does not constipate or leave bad after-effects."

Whether the medication did cause constipation or not, I couldn't find out. What we know for sure is that the cough syrup turned patients into heroin addicts. Heroin, it became increasingly apparent, was highly addictive and could cause serious harm to those who used it regularly. A dose as low as 30 milligrams is lethal to humans without a tolerance to the drug.

Despite mounting evidence of the drug's toxicity, Bayer refused to take it off the market, continuing to sell the cough syrup as a safe and effective treatment for coughs and colds. It wasn't until the early 20th century that governments worldwide began to crack down on the use of opioids like heroin. But the pharma company continued marketing heroin syrup until 1912 for conditions like bronchitis or "irritation." In 1914, World War I broke out, and the company's factories were seized by the German government to produce chemicals for the war effort. As a result, Bayer was forced to stop making its heroin cough syrup.

Over time, people have frequently attributed all kinds of health benefits to toxic substances. The use of mercury, lead, and arsenic in various ancient health remedies is well documented. These practices can be excused to a certain extent from today's perspective. The scientific method was unknown then, and cures were more driven by hope than by understanding how the body works. The active sale of toxins by corporations, in full knowledge of their harmful effects, is less excusable. Bayer was aware that heroin was highly addictive and dangerous to their patients but kept on selling the product for nearly 20 years until finally, the German war mobilization effort stopped them. Equally, tobacco companies aggressively marketed cigarettes as healthy and "doctors recommended" until the 1950s, even though they knew about the devastating health effects of smoking. A 1952 advertisement for the Camel brand featured a physician wearing a stethoscope claiming that "more doctors smoke Camels than any other cigarette."

The greed of corporations and their unwillingness to back down from selling harmful products is a practice that sadly continues until today. Oil and gas companies knew that their products fueled the economy but also a detrimental rise in global temperatures. Exxon conducted its own research and reached these conclusions already in the 1970s. Despite this knowledge, Exxon and other oil companies continued to invest heavily in fossil fuel development while downplaying the risks associated with their products. Many oil companies also funded think tanks and organizations that denied the existence of climate change.

Today, tobacco companies like Philip Morris, alcohol companies like Diageo, and sugar companies like Mondelēz are no better than Bayer at the beginning of the 20th Century. They know how addictive and harmful their products are but shift the accountability to consumers who should "drink responsibly" or "consume in moderation." But this requires a keen understanding of the toxicology of these substances coupled with a fair amount of discipline and self-control by consumers. The default state of our brain (pleasure-seeking, post-hoc rationalizing, cognitive dissonance-resolving) makes it all too easy for us to latch on to claims, arguments, and "studies" that purport the benefits of these substances. Nowadays, simple facts like the efficacy of vaccines are disputed by a body of made-up evidence that people willingly adopt and internalize. The movie "Don't look up" is a wonderful caricature of this self-defeating tendency.

While there are benefits in stressing your body to trigger adaptation and improvement, toxins should be avoided as much as possible. For many of the substances I mention in this chapter, there is a safe amount that does not cause immediate or significant harm. In the broad sense of my definition, there are also toxins, like radiation, that you cannot practically avoid. The exposure of taking a flight, getting an x-ray, or just living under the sun must be accepted for all intents and purposes. However, in my philosophy, I avoid all toxins to the extent possible. Many think they can balance their exposure to toxins with rules and discipline, like not drinking alone or only on particular days. Some might succeed at this practice, but to me, the constant tension and exercise of willpower feel exhausting. And, if I am being honest, I would constantly fool myself and keep inaccurate accounts.

In my mental frame, I am clear that I will avoid toxins as much as possible. I flip the burden of proof. Instead of generally allowing myself access but trying to control frequency and dose, I generally don't allow myself access but recognize necessary or practical exceptions. Especially for addictive substances, I don't think the concept of "opt-out" most people employ works very well. If you generally allow yourself to use addictive substances, by the time you want to actively "opt-out," you are already hooked and less capable of making a rational decision. My concept is "opt-in." I generally avoid a toxin unless for deliberate exceptions that I choose in a rational state of mind.

In this chapter, I will first cover toxins that are lethal above a particular dosage. I call them "overdose toxins." A decision to avoid them is simply a matter of knowledge. As soon as sufficient scientific evidence identifies something as harmful, stay away from it. For instance, we know how carcinogenic asbestos is, so it is straightforward to avoid it. You wouldn't be tempted by its superior insulation quality and heat resistance because the health risks are not worth it. Avoiding overdose toxins is merely a matter of awareness and information.

Avoiding "addiction toxins," which I will cover after, is more challenging as it requires additional willpower and resolve. Awareness and information often aren't the issue. Even if they are fully aware of the dangers involved, people will turn a blind eye or otherwise rationalize their behavior. Insightful books like "Dopamine Nation" or "Never Enough" have been written on the nature of addiction, which I refer to for further reading. Let me merely point out that the underlying driver of addiction, again, is homeostasis. Your brain seeks to achieve mental balance. Any departure from homeostasis triggers an opposing reaction to regulate your mood back to mean. When activities or substances stimulate the release of dopamine, a neurotransmitter responsible for pleasurable feelings, the brain immediately starts producing neurotransmitters whose effects are the exact opposite. The homeostatic regulator attempts to balance the internal systems. If you stayed euphoric indefinitely from one positive experience, you would be less alert going forward. Your mood must be reset after each incident. So, whatever end of the spectrum your emotions lean towards, positive or negative, your brain will react with the opposite stimulus to level you again.

However, when homeostasis downregulates the dopamine, it overshoots and pushes you slightly to the negative. Instead of feeling balanced after the high wears off, you feel a bit worse than before. The higher and faster the positive spike floods your emotions, the more of the counteragent gets released, and the more you dip towards the negative afterward. This is a normal process quite analogous to how glucose gets regulated. Moderately increasing glucose levels get lowered by gentle secretion of insulin. However, if you gulp down a Coke, your glucose spikes massively. In response, the pancreas floods your blood with insulin to curtail the sugar high. In doing so, it overshoots, and you end up with lower glucose than before. This makes you crave more sugar to revert to the homeostatic mean, an effect we are familiar with. A sweet treat makes you want more shortly after.

Worse, you get used to the positive stimulus over time, a process called habituation or tolerance. As you repeat taking the substance, less dopamine gets released every time. So, you need more substance to get your mood back to the happy place you liked so much initially. And with each subsequent crash below the homeostatic line into a negative state, you learn that you feel bad when you are not taking the addictive drug. You fool yourself into believing the drug is net positive, while all it does is make you feel normal again.

Avoid Poisons

Heavy metals, such as lead, mercury, and cadmium, pesticides, and industrial chemicals, such as polychlorinated biphenyls (PCBs) and dioxins, are all toxic to humans and can cause a range of health problems, including cancer, neurological damage, and reproductive issues.

The effects of other substances like aluminum salts in deodorants are still under investigation, and the FDA continues to allow their use. However, I would err on the side of caution and consult scientific studies. The negative impact of electromagnetic radiation from high-voltage electricity lines, for example, or "electrosmog" from smartphones, has never been proven. Conspiracy theorists claim this is due to governmental or corporate interventions. I don't blame them, given the many cover-ups, like in the recent diesel scandal. Your individual risk appetite will guide you, but I would try to inform your choices with credible scientific evidence before making any major lifestyle changes. This can be onerous as you would have to research biases of the publishing organization, peer review, methodology, and many other aspects. As a rule of thumb, I would discount any source or platform whose main objective is to keep your attention and expose you to advertisements. I would prioritize information sources that are in the .edu or .org domains.

At a minimum, you should test your home environment for known toxins. Get your tap water tested occasionally and buy a device that tests for volatile organic compounds (VOCs), carbon monoxide, nitrogen oxides, ozone, and other particulate matter in the air you breathe. Consider installing a filter for the water you drink from the tap and setting up an air filter in the rooms you spend most of your time in. This will also help you to ...

Avoid Pathogens

Pathogens are not toxins in the strict sense. They are microorganisms such as bacteria, viruses, fungi, and parasites that can cause disease in humans and animals.

The awareness and sensitivity to pathogens have fortunately increased since the Covid-19 pandemic, so it would be wise to maintain some of the common-sense hygiene protocols that were established then:

- Get vaccinated
- Wash your hands frequently when traveling
- Wash your food before consumption
- Keep a distance from people who are visibly ill. Ask them to wear a face mask if you cannot avoid their presence. As a last resort, wear a face mask yourself.
- Strengthen your immune system.

Avoid Radiation

Harmful radiation typically refers to ionizing radiation, which alters molecules in your cells by knocking out electrons. This can affect and damage your DNA, proteins, or essential lipids. When DNA gets damaged, this can lead to mutations and, ultimately, cancer. Ionizing radiation includes alpha particles, beta particles, gamma rays, X-rays, and neutron radiation.

Protect yourself from overexposure to UV rays from the sun, particularly UVB. When sunny outside, wear sunglasses, protective clothing, and sunscreen. UV radiation has the same effect as other forms of ionizing radiation, albeit generally less damaging.

Naturally, limit the number of X-rays, CT scans, and other forms of radiation you expose yourself to. Magnetic Resonance Imaging (MRI) uses a strong magnetic field and radio waves but does not expose you to ionizing radiation.

Similarly, I wouldn't worry about flights much, although they carry some radiation load. On a round-trip flight from New York to Los Angeles, you would probably absorb 30-40 microsieverts (μSv) of radiation. In contrast, a person in the United States would be exposed to about 3.1 millisieverts (mSv) per year from natural sources like the sun and the earth. One millisievert equals 1,000 microsieverts.

However, the risks cumulate over a lifetime. Exposure to 1 sievert of ionizing radiation (equals 1,000 millisieverts) in a short period would cause acute radiation syndrome. A long-haul flight only represents about one twenty-fifth thousandth of that amount. However, a life of constant air travel and frequent exposure to the sun will increase your chances of a harmful gene mutation and potential cancer. It is a game of Russian Roulette with one bullet and many thousand chambers. You will get lucky most of the time, but the more you play the game, the higher your chances of incurring a cell defect that can lead to a severe illness.

An unfortunate ionization event can happen anytime, even during your first X-ray. You cannot entirely shield yourself from radiation and its cancer risk. As we saw, constant molecular damage is one of the sources of aging. Your aim here is to limit the exposure to the unavoidable amount.

Avoid Drugs

Don't take drugs unless medically necessary and under a medical professional's supervision. Harmful drugs include:

- Opioids like heroin, fentanyl, oxycodone, hydrocodone, or morphine are highly addictive and can cause respiratory failure and overdose deaths.
- Stimulants like cocaine, methamphetamine, or amphetamines (Adderall) can lead to addiction, heart problems, stroke, and severe mental health issues.
- Hallucinogens like LSD, PCP, psilocybin mushrooms, or ketamine can cause unpredictable psychological effects, including hallucinations, delusions, and psychosis.
- Synthetic cannabinoids like spice or K2 attempt to mimic the effects of cannabis but can be far more potent and harmful with a real risk of death.
- Depressants like barbiturates or benzodiazepines (Xanax, Valium) can lead to addiction, overdose, and death, especially when combined with other substances like alcohol or opioids.

- Inhalants like solvents, aerosol sprays, or gases can cause brain damage, organ failure, and sudden death.
- Anabolic steroids like testosterone and other synthetic hormones can lead to liver damage, heart problems, and aggressive behavior if used excessively.

Even over-the-counter medication like acetaminophen (Tylenol) or ibuprofen (Nurofen from the third chapter) can be harmful if taken in high doses or over a long period.

Don't Smoke

Banning smoking is considered one of the most impactful public health interventions of the past decades. A study published in The Lancet in 2013 estimated that tobacco control measures have prevented eight million premature deaths globally in the five years after 2008. The measures included taxes on tobacco products, advertisement bans, cessation programs, and outright smoking bans.

Yet, about 20 percent of the global adult population continues to smoke tobacco, according to a WHO report from 2021. The rate has decreased over the past decades due to the aforementioned anti-smoking policies. But these have mainly been adopted in high-income countries. In low- and middle-income countries, the tobacco industry can often still aggressively market its products. Therefore, the annual death rate due to smoking-related diseases remains high at approximately eight million people worldwide. This includes smokers but also those exposed to secondhand smoke.

Smoking must be one of the most irrational things people do. On average, smokers die ten years earlier than non-smokers. Smoking is the leading cause of lung cancer, responsible for almost 85 percent of all cases. It also increases the risk for several other types of cancer, like mouth, throat, esophagus, pancreas, bladder, and kidney. It causes heart disease, stroke, reduced fertility, and chronic obstructive pulmonary disease (COPD), leading to progressive lung damage. As mentioned earlier, smoking was the leading cause of preventable death until obesity took over recently.

It doesn't even give you much pleasure in return. I know because I started smoking when I dated a girl who smoked. She never suggested I smoke or otherwise is to blame. She was very pretty, and many guys were chasing her, so to fit in, I started smoking mostly out of insecurity. The relationship didn't last, but the nicotine addiction did for some time until I quit. I maintain that smoking is one of the most irrational self-harming behaviors, but I say this with all humility as I know how easy it is to slide into the habit and how hard it is to escape once your homeostatic level includes the drug.

In my professional circles, it is rare to find any cigarette smokers anymore. Nor many people with obesity, for that matter. Some environmental factors like long working hours or frequent travel are incompatible with 10 to 20 smoking breaks a day, which often involves having to leave the building. There is also a strong bias in these professional communities that smoking or obesity is visible evidence of a lack of discipline and self-control. "If they cannot look after themselves, how can they look after a business unit, division, or company?" is the underlying notion. "Never trust a fat CEO" is something I heard more than once.

Many of the people who frown upon their smoking and overweight colleagues are hypocrites. They don't take good care of themselves by not sleeping properly, eating bad food, and indulging in fine wines and cigars. Particularly cigars are seen as the worry-free embodiment of sophistication and celebration and, for some reason, as something entirely different from cigarettes. However, the fermentation process and larger quantity of tobacco in cigars produce much higher levels of toxins and carcinogenic substances than cigarettes. While a cigarette contains 8 milligrams of nicotine on average, a cigar can have 100 to 200. Smoking one cigar typically exposes you to the nicotine and toxins of a whole pack of cigarettes. In the Zutphen study, which followed 1,373 men born between 1900 and 1920 for 40 years in the Dutch city of Zutphen, the negative impact of cigar or pipe smoking on life expectancy was estimated at 5.2 years, so roughly half that of cigarette smokers.

There is not much better news for those who use e-cigarettes. While probably less harmful than smoking, the long-term effects of inhaling heated e-liquids are not yet fully understood (or disclosed by the companies producing them). What is known is that the vapor of e-cigarettes contains formaldehyde and acetaldehyde, which are both toxic. Vaping, like smoking marihuana, is also considered a gateway to smoking tobacco. Children and young teens, in particular, will find the many flavors of e-cigarettes more accessible than smoking tobacco. Once they get addicted to nicotine, it is a small step to start using other tobacco products.

How dangerous it is to smoke is evidenced by the courageous policy adopted by New Zealand. As of 2023, the legal smoking age will increase yearly by one year. Those under 15 in 2022 will never be allowed to smoke as they will perpetually be underage. So, the next generation in New Zealand will forever be banned from smoking, even as adults.

Don't Drink

The word "alcohol" has its roots in the Arabic language. It is derived from the word "al-kuḥl" (الكحل), which initially referred to a fine powder of antimony sulfide used as a cosmetic eyeliner in ancient times. The term later evolved to mean any substance obtained through sublimation or distillation, and eventually, it came to be associated with the intoxicating component in fermented drinks.

When we speak of alcohol, we mean ethanol, a specific kind of alcohol known as ethyl or grain alcohol. Ethanol is toxic. Consuming it in its pure form is life-threatening, even in tiny amounts. As little as a few milliliters can cause immediate intoxication and central nervous system depression leading to unconsciousness, seizures, respiratory depression, coma, and death. Due to chemical burning by pure ethanol, you wouldn't want to induce vomiting if swallowed accidentally, as this could further damage the esophagus and airway. You would need immediate medical attention.

When ethanol is consumed in alcoholic beverages, it is instantly registered by the body as a toxin. Accordingly, the liver starts metabolizing and removing it from the system. The enzyme "alcohol dehydrogenase" converts ethanol into acetaldehyde, another highly toxic and reactive compound. The chemical industry uses acetaldehyde to produce resins and solvents, and it has been classified as a Group 1 carcinogen by the International Agency for Research on Cancer (IARC). Fortunately, acetaldehyde is further metabolized into acetate, a less harmful substance. However, the metabolic process can sometimes struggle to keep up if you consume large quantities of alcohol in one sitting, accumulating toxic acetaldehyde in the body.

Alcohol has been around for a long time. Humans have been consuming it for thousands of years, with the earliest evidence of intentional fermentation and production of alcoholic beverages dating back to 7000 BCE. Traces of a fermented drink made from honey, rice, and fruit were found in China in pottery jars.

Despite all this history, alcohol consumption is by no means commonplace in the World but dependent on the cultural and religious context. Today, only about half of the global adult population consumes alcohol to any degree. The other half abstains. According to the WHO, circa 46 percent of people aged 15 and older reported not drinking alcohol in 2016.

In the past decades, the consumption of alcohol has declined, particularly in European countries. Spain, France, and Italy have traditionally been known for their wine-drinking cultures, but wine consumption per capita there has declined steadily since the 1970s. According to a data set collected by the WHO, Italian adults consumed 7.1 liters of pure alcohol from wine in 2000. In 2009, the consumption rate had decreased by a third to

4.8 liters annually. France continues to have the highest per capita consumption and lowest rate of decline, from 8.5 to 7.4 liters of pure alcohol per annum. In Spain, however, consumption fell from 4.5 to 2.3 liters during the same period.

These rates of decline are attributed to a statistical cohort rather than a period effect. Studies suggest that younger people are more health-conscious than previous generations and more interested in alternative forms of socializing and entertainment that don't involve drinking. For example, the National Institute on Alcohol Abuse and Alcoholism in the United States discovered that the percentage of high school seniors who reported drinking alcohol in the past month declined from 70 percent in 1991 to 41 percent in 2018. According to the Office for National Statistics in the United Kingdom, the percentage of young people aged 16 to 24 who reported drinking alcohol in the past week declined from 61 percent in 2005 to 48 percent in 2018. In Europe and North America, consuming alcohol is, therefore, the trademark of the older generations. They will often claim that drinking wine, in particular, is deeply rooted in their cultures. The data, however, shows a strong trend away from alcohol and wine consumption that has been unfolding for decades. Sensibly so, as alcohol is a toxin that the body tries to rid from its system the second it enters the bloodstream.

Some species have evolved to consume alcohol as a regular part of their diet. The long-tailed macaque, a Southeast Asian monkey, eats naturally fermented fruit and consumes the equivalent of several alcoholic drinks per day without any ill effects. The pen-tailed treeshrew, another small mammal from Southeast Asia, consumes even more alcohol from fermented fruit without experiencing any negative consequences. It has adapted to metabolize alcohol so efficiently that it does not experience any impact on its judgment or motor skills. Even fruit flies can handle alcohol better than humans. They may have evolved a tolerance to high levels of alcohol from rotting fruit to protect themselves from harmful microorganisms on the fruit.

In hundreds of thousands of years of evolution, humans have not adapted to alcohol, so clearly, there is no evolutionary benefit to be derived for our survival or procreation. Alcohol does not benefit us in any way. It negatively impacts inhibition and reasoning, motor control, and risk tolerance and systematically shuts down one part of the brain after another with every additional drink. This leads to violence, domestic abuse, automotive accidents, and many other bad outcomes.

Alcohol follows the same mechanics of addiction we covered earlier, and (Western) society makes it particularly easy for people to develop a psychological or physical dependence. The imagined order currently characterizes alcohol as a culturally accepted social lubricant associated with fun and pleasure. Drinking "in moderation," a vaguely defined quantity that most people would claim to adhere to, is encouraged and even thought to have health benefits.

I am regularly surprised that companies provide uncapped amounts of alcohol to their employees at firm events but blame the individual if they drank too much and vomited or passed out at the same event. It is schizophrenic first to encourage the consumption of high-percentage drinks like cocktails and then to frown on the lack of self-control of an individual whose rational thinking ability was significantly reduced by that same cocktail. Firm festivities with free liquor are anachronistic examples of our imagined order and will undoubtedly change. In the mid-20th century, companies used to hand out free cigarettes at parties. It was seen as a gesture of hospitality, and it was not unusual for cigarette companies to sponsor events or even supply free samples to promote their products. Today, it would be unthinkable for companies to provide free cigarettes at corporate events. It is equally inappropriate for companies to serve alcohol ad libitum.

The effects of alcohol have been thoroughly researched, and there are many reasons to avoid it. Alcohol (ethanol) is classified as a Group 1 carcinogen by the IARC, part of the WHO. A Group 1 carcinogen is an agent with sufficient evidence of carcinogenicity in humans and includes asbestos, radiation, and tobacco. A

2018 study published in The Lancet (volume 392, issue 10152, pages 1015-1035), titled "1990–2016: a systematic analysis for the Global Burden of Disease Study 2016" and financed by the Bill and Melinda Gates Foundation sums it up:

Alcohol use is a leading risk factor for global disease burden and causes substantial health loss. We found that the risk of all-cause mortality, and cancers specifically, rises with increasing levels of consumption, and the level of consumption that minimizes health loss is zero. These results suggest that alcohol control policies might need to be revised worldwide, refocusing on efforts to lower overall population-level consumption.

An extensive 2018 study by Angela Woods demonstrated that just one drink a day could increase the risk of cancer or heart disease. A 2019 study published in BMC Public Health tried to compare the cancer risks of alcohol to smoking. They found that consuming one bottle of alcohol per week is equivalent to five cigarettes per week for men and ten for women.

Many think that the health risks of alcohol are confined to heavy drinkers and therefore do not apply to them. They are wrong. The WHO published a report in The Lancet in 2023, specifically on the health and cancer risks associated with low levels of alcohol consumption. They found that in Europe, the region with the highest consumption per capita globally, half of all alcohol-attributable cancers are caused by "light" and "moderate" alcohol consumption. The headline of their news release reads, "No level of alcohol consumption is safe for our health," stating that risks start from the first drop regardless of the price or quality of the alcoholic beverage.

In light of these findings, governments are reviewing and revising their recommendations as to which levels of alcohol are safe to consume. The Canadian Center on Substance Abuse and Addiction has lowered the recommended consumption of alcohol to zero. In its report, it found that zero is the only safe amount. Consuming one to two standard drinks per week (not per day) was considered low risk, and anything above that was a moderate to high health risk.

In their research, the WHO explicitly discounts reports suggesting any positive or protective health benefits from low to moderate alcohol consumption. Jürgen Rehm, one of the senior scientists working with the WHO, says that "potential protective effects of alcohol consumption, suggested by some studies, are tightly connected with the comparison groups chosen and the statistical methods used."

Studies have exposed these confounders and biases where moderate wine consumption has been linked to a reduction in the risk of heart disease (for example, Do "Moderate" Drinkers Have Reduced Mortality Risk? A

Systematic Review and Meta-Analysis of Alcohol Consumption and All-Cause Mortality, in Journal of Studies on Alcohol and Drugs, 2016). One common confounder is the inclusion of the "sick quitter." This person abstains from alcohol for health reasons but gets included in the non-drinker group. Because of the prior illness, the "sick quitter" unfairly impacts the comparison of non-drinkers to moderate drinkers without these prior health issues (for example, Selection biases in observational studies affect associations between "moderate" alcohol consumption and mortality, in Addiction, 2017).

In a 2014 study published in the British Medical Journal, scientists used Mendelian randomization to eliminate these confounding factors. Mendelian randomization uses genetic variants, in this case related to alcohol metabolism, as proxies for alcohol exposure. The results suggest that the cardioprotective effects of moderate alcohol consumption observed in some observational studies seem to be overstated due to confounding and other biases. Even if these findings were incorrect, the WHO concluded in 2023 that no studies demonstrate that the potential beneficial effects of light and moderate drinking on cardiovascular diseases outweigh the cancer risk associated with these same levels of alcohol consumption for individual consumers.

Apart from these risks, I avoid alcohol mainly because of its detrimental effects on sleep and metabolism. We will cover sleep in more detail later, but I want to point out a common misconception about how alcohol affects it. Most people will assume that a glass of wine or two promotes sleep. Having a "nightcap" before bed is universally seen as helpful. Nothing could be further from the truth. Alcohol is a sedative and works like a sleeping pill. You might lose consciousness faster, but you are lowering your sleep quantity and quality. Alcohol interrupts the neurotransmitters that keep you sleeping, as confirmed in a study on "Alcohol and the Sleeping Brain" published in the 2014 Handbook of Clinical Neurology. The body is busy processing the ethanol and removing it from your system. Consequently, you wake up often at night and cycle between non-REM light sleep and brief phases of being nearly awake. You won't remember these episodes most of the time, as you do not reach full consciousness.

Alcohol also blocks your REM sleep, so you miss out on a critical restoration phase in charge of memory consolidation and emotional regulation. Over time, this is thought to cause several mental health issues, from depression and anxiety to cognitive decline, to potentially even Alzheimer's disease. Alcohol also inhibits a hormone called vasopressin, an antidiuretic which prevents you from having to go pee. As vasopressin gets suppressed, you need to go to the bathroom more frequently at night, further interrupting your sleep. You might discount the cancer risk of ethanol, but even one glass of wine leads to lighter and more fragmented sleep as long as your body metabolizes the toxin. Unfortunately, this impact cumulates over the decades and is linked to the prevalence of widespread depression in old age.

Lastly, alcohol makes you fat. Not only does it trigger appetite, in particular for unhealthy foods. As a toxin, it also slows down your metabolism. Your liver prioritizes removing ethanol from your body and breaking it down into harmless acetate. Meanwhile, fat oxidation is significantly reduced, and glucose metabolism is altered. At seven calories per gram, alcohol is highly dense in calories compared to other macronutrients, such as carbohydrates and protein, at four calories per gram. And to make things worse, alcoholic beverages often contain a lot of sugar.

In conclusion, there is no reason to drink alcohol. Like tobacco, it has been used by humans for millennia and has shortened their life- and healthspans throughout history. Because of their addictive and psychoactive effects, both drugs have persisted in societies that have not banned them outright. While the first to outlaw cigarettes, administrations are finally starting to act on alcohol. We saw that one glass of wine equals roughly one cigarette (two for women). The softer benefits of alcohol, helping you relax, especially in social settings, can all be achieved by other means. Children don't need alcohol to interact with others, nor do half of the adult population globally. It is a sign of underlying insecurity and immaturity if people need a substance to be social.

Lastly, the taste. For beer and cocktails, alcohol-free variants are very similar to their original counterparts and leave nothing to be desired. For wine and spirits, the higher percentage of ethanol does influence the taste significantly, and I have not found any non-alcoholic versions that have come close. However, alcohol is an acquired taste. Wine and spirits taste terrible to anyone trying them for the first time. Ethanol is fuel and has a bitter and astringent flavor that people need to get used to. Over time, exposure to the taste and the social contexts in which alcohol is consumed can lead to an increased appreciation of alcoholic drinks. When you stop drinking them, you also lose appreciation. After three years of abstinence, I tasted wine at a Christmas party. Not any wine, but a US$ 500 version. To me, it tasted like gasoline with grape juice.

Limit Sugar

It would go too far to classify sugar as a toxin, even though there seems to be a lethal amount that leads to hyperglycemia. The exact dose varies with age, weight, health, and tolerance but is estimated to be over 1.4 kilograms of sugar consumed at once. This is an improbable amount for anyone to eat in one sitting, and even oxygen and water can turn toxic at extreme levels.

But more seriously, regular sugar intake can result in chronic toxicity, surpassing the body's natural ability to maintain homeostasis. Overindulging in sugar can lead to obesity, type-II diabetes, heart disease, and tooth decay.

We naturally crave sugar. Our primary energy source is glucose, a single sugar molecule (monosaccharide), the simplest form of carbohydrate in nature. Together with other monosaccharides like fructose (found in fruits or honey) or galactose (found in milk), they can be combined into disaccharides (two sugar molecules like in sucrose, lactose, or maltose) or polysaccharides (many sugar molecules like in starch, glycogen, cellulose). Table sugar is sucrose, a disaccharide containing one glucose and fructose molecule each.

When we eat carbohydrates, we mostly get a mix of monosaccharides, disaccharides, and polysaccharides. Everything that isn't already glucose needs to be broken down and converted into it by the digestive tract. The resulting monosaccharides are absorbed through the wall of your small intestine into the bloodstream and, with the help of insulin, get moved into the cells to be converted into ATP.

When there is more glucose than the cells need right now, the excess amount gets converted to glycogen and stored in the liver and muscles for later. When glycogen stores are full, the rest gets converted to triglycerides and stored in your fat cells. Other monosaccharides, like fructose, are primarily metabolized in the liver and converted into glucose or fat.

We need glucose to survive, so how can sugar be unhealthy? The problem is that we had to work hard for carbohydrates in our ancestral diet. Hunter-gatherer tribes consumed animal products like meat and plant material like roots, tubers, vegetables, seeds, nuts, and fruits. Except for ripe fruit and honey, all these contained protein, fat, and complex carbohydrates, which first had to be extracted, broken down, and converted into glucose. Even if they wolfed down a meal hastily, the chemical processes in their bodies would need time to convert and extract the glucose from the food. Blood glucose levels would have increased gradually, met by a corresponding response by the pancreas in the release of insulin. This is how we evolved to be. As a default, our bodies do not expect vast amounts of glucose and fructose to arrive already broken down and ready for consumption.

Of course, the body can deal with a one-off tsunami of monosaccharides. Given how infrequently this would have occurred during our evolution, our bodies genuinely love and encourage it. Naturally so. If the body can get its glucose ready to go, not having to convert it from other sources, this saves a lot of energy. As said, we evolved for a world of scarcity and value any shortcut. In functional MRI, we can visualize how our brain rewards us for sucrose. Sugar triggers the same brain activity and dopamine release as after consuming heroin or cocaine. Pure forms of sugar are highly addictive and make you want to eat more.

It wasn't until the 18th and 19th centuries that sugar, as we know it, became widely available. Table sugar was a scarce and costly resource. In the Middle Ages, it was mainly imported from the Middle East and the Mediterranean, and only apothecaries, royal households, and monasteries had access to sugar supplies. It was used as a medicine in various treatments and was considered a suitable gift for royalty. The royals, in turn, showed off their wealth by displaying sculptures made of pure sugar to impress their guests at banquets.

In ancient Rome, sugar was so rare, they used "sugar of lead" as a substitute. Lead (II) acetate was used to sweeten wine and other foods. Being lead-based, this sweetener was highly toxic and led to neurological damage, kidney failure, and even death. Along with lead-containing water pipes and cookware, "sugar of lead" is believed to have contributed to many health problems in Roman society. It may even have played a role in the empire's eventual decline.

All that changed when production processes and global logistics allowed large quantities of sugar cane to be converted into sucrose, primarily by exploiting enslaved people for the hard manual labor. Consequently, cheap sugar became widely available in Europe and North America. In the 1960s, high-fructose corn syrup was developed from cornstarch as a sweeter and easier-to-process alternative that could be produced domestically.

While our ancestors consumed about 15-20 grams of sugar a day on average, mostly from complex carbohydrates in the plant foods they consumed, the latest figures for the United States show approximately 94 grams of added sugar consumed by the average American today. This far exceeds the 25 grams the WHO or American Heart Association recommend as a limit.

Today, glucose and fructose tsunamis keep hitting our systems constantly. Without the fiber in fresh fruit or the time-consuming need for extraction and conversion from natural foods, these monosaccharides enter the bloodstream and liver all at once when you down a cola, frappuccino, breakfast cereal, or most other processed food. The pancreas and liver were not designed to cope with these amounts of pure energy regularly. It is like filling up your diesel car with refined kerosene (RP-1), typically used as a liquid rocket fuel. The vehicle might still run for a while, but the wear on seals, gaskets, the fuel pump, and other components would significantly reduce the engine's lifespan.

Apart from the physiological consequences of insulin resistance and excessive fat storage, this sugar-heavy fueling of the body is highly inefficient and, ironically, leads to systematic overeating and constant hunger. A blood glucose level of around 90 milligrams per deciliter is considered normal in a fasted state. With five liters of blood in your body, there are less than 5 grams of glucose in your bloodstream at any given time as the homeostatic rate. That is the equivalent of about five grapes (glucose and fructose).

When you flood your system with sugar, most of it has to spill over into fat storage. There is no other place to go if the body has no immediate use for it. But despite all the storage piling up, you soon crave more food. In response to the sugar tsunami, insulin is secreted at an unusually high rate to reduce your blood sugar to the equivalent of five grapes again. As insulin overshoots, two things happen. One, the high insulin level signals that plenty of energy is available, so lipolysis, your ability to use the stored fat, is shut down. Two, because of all the insulin, the glucose level in your bloodstream crashes, making you crave more food. The higher and faster your intake of pure sugars, the less energized and satiated you will feel, the more fat you will store, and the less you can access that fat.

So, sugar is not toxic in the same sense as the other substances we have discussed. Alcohol has no function in the body and must be eliminated quickly, while sugars are vital for survival. However, we need to limit the amount and rate of absorption, particularly of simple sugars like table sugar, high-fructose corn syrup, and the thousand other substances the food industry came up with to disguise the addition of simple mono- and disaccharides. It all comes back to homeostasis. If the body can regulate it well (not too much, not too fast) and you build in extended periods without food exposure, you will be fine and can occasionally eat a dessert or other sweet food. The key is being honest with yourself and monitoring your blood glucose levels frequently. Subjective criteria only work for a few very disciplined or motivated people. The vast majority of us should monitor this closely, as I will describe in the chapter on governance.

Just a quick word on artificial sweeteners, synthetic or natural sugar substitutes used to provide sweetness without the calories of sugar. Examples are high-intensity sweeteners, such as aspartame, sucralose, and stevia, or sugar alcohols, like xylitol, erythritol, and sorbitol. There is no conclusive evidence that currently approved sweeteners are acutely or chronically toxic. Particularly cancer risks, partially found in animal trials, have not been confirmed for humans. While likely safe, some sweeteners like aspartame (Coke Zero) seem to increase appetite and create imbalances in the gut biome, which are not ideal for staying lean.

Limit Ultra-processed Food

Ultra-processed foods have gone through multiple processing stages, often containing artificial additives, preservatives, and high levels of sugar, salt, and saturated fats. Examples of ultra-processed foods are sugary drinks, snack foods, frozen meals, and fast foods.

The processing itself is not a concern. It makes the food safe to consume, convenient and affordable and extends the shelf life of the products. In many ways, our ability to produce cheap and convenient food has fueled population growth and the decline in undernourishment over the past decades. However, it has also been the driver of our obesity crisis. Food companies' desire to produce as cheaply as possible has led to a race to the bottom regarding the quality of ingredients. Therefore, you should keep a distance from ultra-processed foods and consume them only as an exception.

To reduce production costs and appeal to consumers, ultra-processed foods typically combine high sugar content with fat. Except for dairy products and some tropical fruit, this combination is rare in nature. The sugar makes us crave more, while the fat adds a lot of calories. It is a problematic concoction for our metabolism. High sugar levels, over time, increase your insulin levels because of reduced insulin sensitivity, and high insulin levels, in turn, shut off lipolysis, your fat metabolism. Fat and sugar together are the fastest way to make you fat. In other words, ultra-processed foods are your fast track to metabolic syndrome, including obesity, high blood pressure, blood sugar, and cholesterol.

At the same time, you are consuming low-quality ingredients devoid of nutrients. You might be getting the energy content, but beyond that, there is little value in ultra-processed foods. If there are vitamins or minerals, they typically have been added in their synthetic form. The lack of fiber can lead to digestion issues and the lack of nutrients to poor mental health. Some studies suggest a correlation between eating ultra-processed food and an increased risk of depression and anxiety.

So, while not toxic and generally safe to consume, I try to limit the consumption of ultra-processed foods as much as possible and focus on consuming whole, unprocessed foods.

Limit Red Meat

Some studies have linked eating large amounts of red meat, such as beef, pork, lamb, or venison, to colon cancer. Based on findings from observational studies, the IARC has classified the consumption of red meat as "probably carcinogenic to humans" (Group 2A). To date, there is no conclusive evidence that consuming red meat as such is harmful.

However, processed meats seem to be a different story. These include sausages, bacon, ham, salamis, and most deli meats. When transforming the meat through salting, curing, fermenting, or smoking, known carcinogens and other health risks are added to the meal. Processing commonly includes nitrates and nitrites, added as preservatives, color enhancers, or flavoring. These can form N-nitroso compounds (NOCs) during digestion which have been proven to cause cancer in at least 40 animal species, including monkeys. There is supporting evidence in humans that NOCs increase the risk for gastric, esophageal, and colon cancer. Consequently, the IARC has classified processed meats as "carcinogenic to humans" in Group 1, meaning they consider the evidence sufficient. In their review, the IARC concluded that consuming more than 50 grams of processed meat daily increases the risk of colorectal cancer by about 18 percent.

A risk common to processed and unprocessed meats is cooking them at high temperatures like grilling, frying, or broiling. This forms heterocyclic amines (HCAs) and polycyclic aromatic hydrocarbons (PAHs), which can alter DNA and cause cancer. Studies linking HCAs and PAHs to cancer are observational, so they don't establish a direct cause-and-effect link. However, they have shown a high correlation between diets high in grilled and fried meats and incidences of cancer.

Another risk attributed to meat consumption is raised blood uric acid levels due to organic compounds called purines that play a role in the synthesis of DNA. Purines are not specific to red meat. The highest concentrations are in organ meats and certain seafood (mackerel, herring, sardines, shellfish). Higher uric acid levels are a cause of gout, a form of inflammatory arthritis, and kidney stones. Some recent studies also seem to establish a connection with cardiovascular risk, but this remains controversial.

The three unhealthy foods — sugar, ultra-processed foods, and processed meats — are interrelated. They alter the state of natural foods. By adding sugar, we get too much high-octane fuel that wears down our system over time. By processing food, we inadvertently add chemicals and compounds that are harmful to our bodies. While not toxic per se, I would try to limit consumption of any of these and focus on food in its natural state. It's what our bodies know how to handle.

Recovery

When I worked at a global consulting firm in the early 2000s, we rarely discussed rest, sleep, or recovery. Work usually started at 8 AM and finished after midnight. We knew we had hit the halfway mark of our workday when it started getting dark and clients were leaving the building. We could finally process what we had learned during the day, build our Excel models, and draw the charts. When I say "draw," I mean we hand-drew graphs and scribbled text on yellow sheets of paper, faxed them to India, and got fully formatted PowerPoint slides back to our email. Ahead of steering committees or other important deadlines, this would continue until the early morning. Pulling an "all-nighter" was seen as something honorable. Even if you finished all your work early, say at 8 PM, you would not just get up and leave.

Staying late was part of the game. It demonstrated you were willing to go "the extra mile." This practice was so widespread that an author who conducted undercover research on consultancy firms in 2004 gave her documentary novel the telling title "We Never Sleep."

Though exhausting the first few weeks, you somehow got used to it. Your eyes felt like they were on fire, your breathing was short and choppy, and you'd get annoyed if your spouse told you a story and didn't get to the point quickly enough. But you started to believe that you somehow got away with less sleep than other people. You seemingly were more resilient, tougher, and had the energy to perform at the highest level. "I can sleep when I am dead" became a mantra.

Things are, fortunately, changing in the consulting world and elsewhere. Studies have shown that going without sleep for 24 hours can result in impairment equivalent to having a blood alcohol concentration of 0.1 percent, above the legal limit for driving in most countries. Pulling "an all-nighter" is nothing to be proud of, and young employees are less willing to exchange health for money. Companies start recognizing that downtime is not unproductive but leads to overall better outcomes. And science is beginning to generate evidence on how essential recovery is to adaptation and growth.

If stress is the Yin, recovery is the Yang. Recovery addresses imbalances in your body or mind, helps establish homeostasis, and promotes hormesis, leading to physical and mental improvements. It allows for the adaptation that makes stressors effective in the first place. Think of recovery on two levels:

- **Foundational recovery**, first and foremost sleep, is essential to maintain the physiological processes associated with being alive. Moving your body, processing sensory input, and metabolizing nutrition requires a base level of regular repair and maintenance for all the biochemistry in your body to keep functioning daily.
- **Contextual recovery** is mostly about stimulating the parasympathetic nervous system in response to and compensating for external stressors, such as exercise, work, mental stress, or other situational factors. Not surprisingly, the required intensity and duration of contextual recovery depend on the context.

Imagine cleaning your home to appreciate the distinction. Regular vacuum cleaning is a form of foundational recovery. All surfaces, like windows or floors, get dirty over time and need periodic cleaning. However, doing the dishes or cleaning up something that fell on the floor is like contextual recovery and needs an intervention customized to the event.

Foundational Recovery

Living is like running an engine. Operating it causes wear and tear, even if the machine is idling. The engine needs regular cleaning, lubrication, and the exchange of routine maintenance parts to extend its lifetime. The same is true for the body. We need nutrients, water, and oxygen to keep processes running smoothly, but we also need basic maintenance to stave off wear and tear. This is achieved by sleeping, our prime mode of foundational recovery. All living organisms rely on foundational recovery phases, although form and duration vary widely. Koalas, brown bats, and, famously, sloths easily sleep 20 hours per day, while humans require only 7 to 9. Even bacteria and fungi exhibit circadian rhythms with periods of reduced activity. Given how vulnerable sleep makes all living species, we intuitively grasp it must be crucial to survival.

Indeed, a lack of sleep is detri*mental*. After 24 hours of being awake, your cognitive performance starts suffering dramatically. Memory, attention, and concentration are impaired, mood swings become more likely, and basic motor skills and reaction times are impacted, making accidents and injuries more likely. As sleep deprivation persists, these effects become more severe. After 48 hours, your immune system starts shutting down, and your brain experiences involuntary bursts of microsleep. After 72 hours, you start hallucinating and suffer severe cognitive impairment. No wonder sleep deprivation is prohibited by the Geneva Conventions as a form of torture.

You can easily go without food for days, even weeks, but you cannot function properly if you miss just one night of sleep. Nevertheless, people still treat sleep as an annoying requirement they would rather get rid of. Most people have no idea what sleep does for them. They see it as an unproductive period of unconsciousness.

Researchers are still discovering the various processes unfolding during slumber. Matthew Walker's "Why We Sleep" is a must-read for anyone less familiar with the subject. It certainly has changed the way I think about rest and recovery and has ultimately led to my decision to abstain from alcohol altogether soon four years ago. The most important insight from Walker's book and other publications is that sleep is not a uniform state we must endure for a certain period. It is a sequence of activities your body needs to cycle through several times to be effective.

As you know, we can identify different stages of sleep by listening to the electric signals of our brain with an electroencephalogram (EEG). We distinguish rapid eye movement phases (REM), during which we typically dream, from non-REM sleep phases that are light (phases N1 and N2) or deep (phase N3). We cycle through these different stages four to six times during the night. Each cycle lasts between 90 and 120 minutes and starts with a few minutes of light N1 transition sleep. Then we go deeper, first into light N2 sleep (10 to 25 minutes), and finally into deep Non-REM sleep (N3), usually just referred to just as deep sleep (20 to 40 minutes in the first cycles). After reaching the deepest sleep stage, which has the lowest brainwave activity and is the hardest to wake up from, we cycle back to N2 and round off the cycle with ten minutes of REM sleep.

You can imagine your sleep being like a program on your washing machine. It performs distinct stages of soaking, agitating, rinsing, and spinning your laundry. Depending on the selected schedule, it might run through this cycle several times to ensure everything gets clean. While we cycle between dream and deep sleep stages, the composition of these cycles changes over the course of the night. Most, if not all, of your deep sleep typically occurs in the first half of the night, while most REM sleep happens in the second. Your last REM phase, containing the dreams you might remember, can last an hour before waking up. Again, think of your washing machine. It might do a couple of spinning stages between cycles to get rid of the dirty water, but the last spinning step is the longest to get your laundry as dry as possible.

When you drink alcohol, even just one glass, it will mostly impact your deep sleep. As noted above, the emergency protocol your liver performs to eliminate the alcohol interferes with your ability to stay asleep. Your sleep cycles constantly get interrupted, making reaching deeper stages difficult, as if someone keeps resetting your washing machine to start over again. You do a lot of soaking but never get to the rinsing.

However, when you get up before your natural sleep cycles have concluded, you cut off most of your REM sleep. Early morning flights, a change in time zone, or the desire to be part of the "5-AM club" that Tech CEOs seem to propagate prevent you from concluding the sleep program your body has evolved to perform. This is like interrupting the washing machine before its final spinning stage. Your laundry will be clean but dripping wet.

So, while people are aware of how many hours they sleep, they ignore sleep composition. Sleep quantity is just a function of the time it takes your brain and body to cycle through an evolutionary program in a specific order and intensity. These are guided by your circadian rhythm, a roughly 24-hour cycle controlled by a group of nerve cells called the suprachiasmatic nucleus in the hypothalamus. Several inputs, foremost (blue) light, help these nerve cells set the clock. However, it reacts conservatively to changes. If you cross several time zones, your circadian rhythm only adjusts by approximately an hour per day. So, if you fly from Frankfurt to New York, it will take about six days to experience regular sleep composition again. In the interim, some of your sleep stages will be underrepresented and replaced by light sleep.

Your circadian rhythm is not what makes you fall asleep. It is an internal biological clock that governs several processes, like the release of melatonin, that prepares your body for sleep by adjusting core temperature and other factors. You fall asleep because of a buildup of a molecule called adenosine. Again, this is a homeostatic process. While you are awake, adenosine builds up; while you sleep, adenosine is reduced. Caffeine has a similar molecular structure and blocks adenosine receptors. When you drink coffee, the buildup in adenosine is temporarily interrupted, and you feel more awake. A nap in the late afternoon, ironically, also keeps you awake. The natural buildup of adenosine during the day creates "sleep pressure." The nap reduces sleep pressure hours before your usual bedtime, making it harder for you to fall asleep.

Subjectively, you cannot assess whether you have had enough of either of these recovery protocols. You might have slept eight hours and feel fine. But sleep quality is hard to determine without data. You don't experience yourself sleeping and mainly judge your sleep quality based on the number of interruptions you remember and how you felt when you woke up. There is no direct way of knowing whether you had enough deep or REM sleep. This is why people easily believe they can get away with less sleep or underestimate the effects of alcohol and coffee. Without data, they don't know.

Deep sleep is associated chiefly with physical repair and recovery. Growth hormones are released to promote tissue growth, for example muscle growth after resistance training. Most crucially, deep sleep detoxifies your brain by activating the glymphatic system. Brain cells called astrocytes shrink by 60 percent to increase your brain's extracellular space and allow cerebrospinal fluid to flow more freely through the brain tissue. Like in a washing machine, the fluid flushes out metabolic waste products and toxins that accumulate in your brain during waking hours. Substances like beta-amyloid and tau proteins thought to cause Alzheimer's and other neurodegenerative diseases get cleaned out and absorbed into the bloodstream. This glymphatic system is nearly ten times more active during deep sleep than during waking times. Reducing your time in deep sleep effectively reduces an essential clean-up protocol in your brain.

REM sleep, on the other hand, is characterized by vivid dreams and rapid eye movements. Brain activity resembles wakefulness during this stage, so researchers have called it "paradoxical sleep." A key feature of REM sleep is muscle atonia, or temporary paralysis, which prevents individuals from physically acting out their dreams. All mammals have muscle atonia, but some twitching and movement might still occur, as you will know if you have a dog.

REM sleep consolidates procedural and spatial memories. That is to say, new information you gathered throughout the day on skills or the location of objects is transferred to your long-term memory and made more accessible for later. This is a crucial part of learning and one of the adaptions that make us continuously improve. REM sleep also enhances creativity and problem-solving by facilitating the formation of new neural connections between unrelated concepts. This is why people wake up and suddenly see the solution to a problem they have been wrestling with. REM sleep also helps process and manage emotions experienced during waking hours. This can contribute to the vivid and intense dreams in this stage.

REM sleep is a critical component of your cognitive function, memory, creativity, and emotional health. As most of your REM sleep occurs right before your natural waking time, Matthew Walker estimates that if you consistently reduce your sleep by one hour, you lose about 60 percent of REM sleep. That is 60 percent less memory, creativity, and emotional health.

So, deep sleep makes you stronger and cleans out waste, while REM sleep keeps you sane and makes you smarter and more creative. Can you afford to miss any part of this? Each part of your sleep serves a purpose; you cannot arbitrarily cut off pieces. You also let your washing machine cycle through its entire program, why not your recovery program? To harvest the benefits of optimal foundational recovery, consider the following advice.

- **Cool temperature**: your core temperature naturally declines as you transition from wakefulness to sleep. Being too warm will make it harder for you to fall asleep. Try keeping your bedroom cool at 18 degrees Celsius. A warm bath or sauna two hours before bedtime initially raises your core temperature, but as you cool down, it helps with sleep onset.

- **Distractions**: anything that prevents your body from cycling down into deep sleep and back up again is problematic. This includes any form of irregular light or noise in your bedroom. Constant light or sound curtains like pink or white noise will be less distracting, though total silence and darkness are preferred.

- **Metabolic processes**: if your body is busy with digestion or processing alcohol, it will be hard to experience complete sleep cycles. That is why a large meal or alcohol before bedtime is not conducive to good sleep. If you must, have them as early as possible, at least three to four hours before bedtime.

- **Adenosine**: you need sleep pressure from adenosine to fall asleep. Caffeine has a half-life of four to six hours in your bloodstream. Stop drinking coffee at 4 PM latest and try to avoid naps in the afternoon or evening. Limit naps to 20-25 minutes to avoid cycling into deep sleep. If you must have an espresso after dinner, go for decaf.

- **Sleep schedule**: Try to be as consistent as possible with your sleep and waking times. If you frequently travel between time zones, stay in your habitual time zone for short trips. If you want to switch over to a new time zone, try adjusting your sleep schedule in the days leading up to your trip by 1-2 hours per day. Once at your destination, commit fully to the new time zone and get as much natural light as possible in the morning to reset your circadian rhythm.

Contextual Recovery

Foundational recovery is what your body naturally requires just to maintain base functionality. But life exposes us to many mental and physical stressors that require specialized recovery protocols. These either get the affected system back into homeostasis. Or if new information was available, the recovery triggers hormesis and adapts your homeostatic balance point to a higher level.

There are a million ways to relax and recover, many of which depend on the stress you are trying to address. Exercise can significantly improve mental well-being and reduce stress. Meditation and mindfulness exercises come in more ways than I can attempt to cover. Deep breathing, progressive muscle relaxation, autogenic training, therapeutic massage, yoga, social time with friends and family, psychological therapy, traveling, hobbies, leisure activities, nature immersion, and simply doing nothing. As there are so many common ways to decompress, I thought I would assemble my top ten list of unconventional ways of recovery.

1. **Wall staring**: Focusing on a blank wall or staring at a fixed point can help to quiet the mind and promote a meditative state.

2. **Belly laughing**: Engaging in forced or spontaneous laughter can release endorphins, reduce stress, and improve mood.

3. **Coloring or doodling**: Engaging in simple creative activities like coloring or doodling can be meditative and relaxing.

4. **Autonomous Sensory Meridian Response** (ASMR): Some people find listening to soft-spoken voices, gentle sounds, or watching repetitive tasks calming and relaxing.

5. **Earthing or grounding**: Walking barefoot on natural surfaces like grass, sand, or soil is believed to help promote relaxation.

6. **Watching fish swim:** Observing fish in an aquarium or a pond can be calming, similar to watching flowing water or a flickering flame.

7. **Chewing gum**: The repetitive motion of chewing gum can help to reduce stress and promote relaxation.

8. **Inversion therapy**: Hanging upside down or using an inversion table can help to relieve muscle tension, reduce stress, and promote relaxation.

9. **Dancing**: Engaging in spontaneous or structured dancing can help to release pent-up energy, reduce stress, and improve mood.

10. **Finger tapping**: This involves tapping on specific acupressure points on the body while focusing on an issue or emotion to release stress and promote relaxation.

You need to find out what works for you. Personally, I have experimented with various methods of meditation, including with a teacher, an app, and even a high-tech gadget that measures brainwaves and provides sensory feedback. It isn't for me. Instead, I prefer to unwind by playing the piano, taking a sauna bath, going for a run, or cuddling with my dog.

It doesn't matter what form of recovery you engage in. What is common to these techniques is that they stimulate the parasympathetic nervous system (PNS). When we are stressed, our sympathetic nervous system (SNS) is triggered into "fight or flight." However, activating the PNS induces a "rest and digest" state resulting in a decrease in heart rate and blood pressure, reducing the workload of the cardiovascular system. Breathing becomes deeper and more regular, and digestion and salivation are stimulated. There is no magic to stimulating the PNS; it is merely the counterprogram to the SNS. If we are in "fight or flight" mode constantly, our cardiovascular, immune, digestive, and other systems can suffer from the one-sided stimulus. Activating the PNS occasionally restores balance.

Our world is filled with stimuli. While a hundred years ago, humans would have had books, newspapers, radio, and interpersonal communication at their disposal, today, with the internet and connected devices, the amount of information available at any moment is orders of magnitude higher. Everything is trying to grab your attention, and the more emotionally charged advertisements and news pieces are, the more successful they are at getting it. This is why watching television, streaming content, or doom scrolling through social media feeds is not included as a form of recovery. They only add additional stimuli and trigger your SNS.

The dose and form of PNS activation depend on the context and your prior exposure to stressors. The rule of thumb is to respond in kind. If you stress your body physically, try to recover by not adding additional strain and engaging in light activities that increase blood flow and restorative protocols. Massage, light yoga, a sauna bath, and an easy walk can help your muscles and other tissue heal and regenerate. For mental stress, reduce additional stimuli and try to activate your PNS. You can enlist many different triggers, such as warmth, physical touch, deep pressure, deep breathing, stimulating the vagus nerve, slow rhythmic music, exposure to nature, positive social interactions, etc. You have to experiment and find out which technique works reliably for you. Plan and prioritize regular recovery time in your daily or weekly schedule to allow yourself to recharge and relax. Several apps and gadgets can help you maintain this balance. But make sure you avoid additional stimuli, especially from screens, to get a break from the constant bombardment with information.

Overhaul

One of the most influential scientists of all time was born in Woolsthorpe, a small hamlet in Lincolnshire, England, on January 4, 1643. His name was Isaac Newton, and during his lifetime, he formulated the Law of Universal Gravitation and the three fundamental Laws of Motion. He created calculus, a mathematical framework that allows the user to solve complex mathematical problems involving change and motion, discovered that white light is composed of a spectrum of colors, and invented the reflecting telescope. Newton served as a professor of mathematics at the University of Cambridge, was Master of the Royal Mint, and for 24 years President of the Royal Society, one of the most prestigious scientific academies until today.

Most people don't know that Isaac Newton was also deeply interested in alchemy, especially in the Philosopher's Stone and the Elixir of Life. He wrote more than a million words discussing alchemical topics, particularly how the Philosopher's Stone could be created and had the power to transform metals, prolong life, and provide spiritual enlightenment. He wrote about his attempts to create the Stone and his challenges in deciphering and understanding the ancient alchemical texts he studied. Newton believed he could make the Elixir of Life once he had created the Philosopher's Stone. He could mix a potion with other ingredients such as mercury, sulfur, and antimony that, he believed, would grant immortality or, at least, significantly extend the human lifespan.

Sadly, Newton did not succeed, at least not as far as we know. Creating a magic potion that reverses aging and grants eternal youth has been the dream for many civilizations. The oldest surviving work of literature, the Gilgamesh Epic, already deals with this topic. The Mesopotamian poem dates to 2100 BCE and tells the story of King Gilgamesh, who embarks on a quest for immortality after the death of his close friend Enkidu. After many challenges and battles, he finally accepts his mortality and learns about the value of life.

So, neither King Gilgamesh nor Isaac Newton has figured out how to overhaul our bodies to a more youthful state. Evolution has not selected our species for an indefinite lifespan. There is no evolutionary benefit to keeping us around after 40 to 60 years, enough time to have offspring and provide for their offspring as grandparents. No biological processes have developed to promote rejuvenation beyond that. On the other hand, there is no evolutionary necessity to kill us off, either.

Achieving a longer healthspan comes down to basics: a healthy diet, sufficient sleep, regular exercise, strong social connections, and avoiding toxins and chronic stress. While unhealthy habits accelerate aging, these interventions slow it down. But at present, there are no proven overhaul protocols that can truly turn back the clock. Several attempts and ideas are in the making, but they are largely unproven and experimental. Many hope we will discover and develop such protocols in the next 10 to 20 years, but this hope has persisted for over four millennia since the Epic of Gilgamesh.

Our best bet is to address aging at the cellular level. The human body consists of roughly 30 to 40 trillion cells. Everything that constitutes life happens in our cells or as an interaction between them. Every illness is an illness of cells. When we die, it is because of malfunction or damage to cells. Many of the hallmarks of aging, consequently, describe a deterioration in the function of a cell or its inability to produce new, fresh cells. If we can maintain good functionality of existing cells and a steady supply of new ones, we could significantly delay the effects of aging.

Autophagy

A few of the hallmarks of aging deal with the garbage accumulating in cells over time. Misfolded proteins, dysfunctional organelles, and other cellular debris impair the smooth functioning of the cell and need to be removed occasionally.

Similar to deep sleep being a cleanup program for your brain, cells have a program called autophagy, during which they consume and recycle waste products. Autophagy means "consume yourself" and is one of the many homeostatic processes your body has developed, among others, to survive in times of scarcity. As our ancestors periodically faced hunger or starvation, autophagy's primary function is reusing materials. The cleanup is likely an additional benefit.

In times of abundance, autophagy is significantly reduced. It is a catabolic process and therefore suppressed by mTOR when the body is in an anabolic state. In times of abundance, cells have enough energy and building blocks to maintain their normal functions without recycling components. By suppressing autophagy, cells can allocate their resources to growth, replication, and other energy-demanding processes.

If you spend most of your life in an anabolic state, i.e., eating three meals a day, you suppress autophagy, a vital homeostatic process. Switching to a catabolic state can take up to 24 hours of not adding nutrients to your body. Intermittent fasting can help maintain a base level of functionality, but from an overhaul perspective, I believe you need to run a more intensive version of autophagy periodically. A water-only fast of at least 72 hours has been shown to increase autophagy significantly. The resulting cell renewal is thought to protect against age-related diseases like neurodegeneration, cardiomyopathy, diabetes, and cancer.

One way of stimulating autophagy seems to be through a drug called sirolimus. It is based on the natural compound rapamycin. It was first discovered in a soil sample collected from the Easter Islands (Rapa Nui) in 1972 and used primarily for its immunosuppressive effects alongside organ transplants. But rapamycin seems to have many more potential uses. It inhibits mTOR, which therefore stands for "mechanistic Target of Rapamycin." As we saw, inhibiting mTOR promotes autophagy and has several other longevity benefits. Rapamycin would qualify as a fasting-mimicking drug, but research on the minimal effective dose is still ongoing, so we currently don't have an established protocol at our disposal.

Senolytics

One of the hallmarks of aging is cells becoming senescent. Above a certain threshold, these so-called zombie cells can impact the functioning of the tissue or organ they comprise. Senolytics are compounds that selectively target and remove these senescent cells. Natural substances with potential senolytic properties include quercetin (in apples, onions, and berries) and fisetin (in strawberries and cucumbers). These findings are based mainly on animal models and cell cultures, and there is currently no established effective dose or recommendation for use in humans.

A promising chemical senolytic compound is dasatinib. Originally developed and approved for treating certain types of leukemia, dasatinib seems to target and eliminate senescent cells selectively. In mouse studies, a combination of dasatinib and quercetin has been reported to improve cardiac function and reduce cardiovascular disease, alleviate frailty and muscle weakness, decrease osteoporosis, enhance running endurance, mitigate fatty liver and lung disease, reduce Alzheimer's-like dementia, and extend the lifespan of these mice by up to 36 percent.

In 2019, a human study at the Mayo Clinic administered a short-term treatment of 100 milligrams of dasatinib combined with 1 gram of quercetin for three consecutive days to patients with diabetic kidney disease. The study showed a reduction in the senescent cell burden of these patients. While promising, more research and extensive clinical trials are needed to confirm these findings and establish the safety, efficacy, and optimal dosing of senolytics for various age-related diseases and conditions in humans.

Telomere lengthening

Beyond the typical lifestyle factors of sleep, exercise, diet, etc., no established protocols exist to lengthen telomeres safely. The caps on your chromosomes shorten every time the cell divides. Some compounds, such as TA-65 and cycloastragenol, have been marketed as telomerase activators (an enzyme that lengthens telomeres), but studies have not yet supported this. A study in 2020 found hyperbaric oxygen therapy to be effective in lengthening telomeres. However, the study comprised too few participants to be indicative.

The problem with resetting the Hayflick limit, the number of times the cell can divide, is that you don't want to inadvertently promote cancer. If cell division gets out of control due to a mutation, the Hayflick limit can help contain the runaway process. Indeed, some cancer cells have learned to bypass the Hayflick limit by activating or upregulating telomerase.

Rather than lengthening telomeres medically, i.e., beyond the typical good lifestyle factors, it is probably safer to concentrate on senolytics and replenishing stem cells once safe and effective interventions have been established. When cells reach the Hayflick limit, they become senescent or die. If you can eliminate zombie cells and provide new cells from your reservoir of stem cells, you don't need to manipulate telomere length, which seems to be playing with fire regarding cancer.

Stem cell therapy

Stem cells have the potential to differentiate into various cell types and repair damaged tissues. If we could use stem cells to replace old or dying tissue, this would come closest to the Elixir of Life. Harnessing the power of stem cells would even allow us to treat conditions out of reach currently, like spinal cord injuries.

While a few forms of stem cell therapies have been in use for some time, for example, in conjunction with chemotherapy for certain types of leukemia, safe and effective treatments for rejuvenation purposes are still in the early stages of research. Online, many offers claim to harvest and multiply the patient's stem cells and reinject them for anti-aging benefits, but I would approach these claims with extreme caution.

Again, the only course of action safely available to us is to preserve our existing stem cells as much as possible by adhering to the good lifestyle practices we have encountered numerous times: sleep, diet, exercise, etc. While potentially in development in some lab somewhere, the Elixir of Life continues to elude us for now.

Nutrients

The question of what kind of fuel to feed your body seems to be one of the most complex. At least, there are tens of thousands of different dietary approaches and philosophies out there. From scientifically backed to completely made-up, diets come in every shape and form. On the paleo diet, you supposedly eat as our hunter-gatherer ancestors did. In Ethical Fruitarianism, you only eat the fruit, nuts, and seeds that have fallen naturally from plants without causing harm or disturbance to the plant itself. If you are a Raw Vegan, you cannot heat anything above 48 degrees Celsius; while on the Ice Diet, you consume at least one liter of frozen water daily to burn more calories. When it comes to diet, it's clearly all imagined. More than 90 percent of dietary advice is on what foods you can or cannot consume, and people become zealots as to these nutritional dogmas. My favorite is the Seafood Diet: I eat when I see food.

The truth is nobody knows for sure. When you test a drug for efficacy on a specific indication, you can run a controlled clinical trial. When it comes to food, it remains guesswork. Firstly, you never consume just one substance but a broad mix of molecules, so it is very difficult to isolate the effect of one nutrient on a system as complex as the human body. Secondly, you cannot reliably control what people eat over any significant time.

People are not laboratory mice. Especially in long-term studies, they will report what they eat from memory, an unreliable source of information. And lastly, for food, we can only run observational studies, which makes it hard to distinguish correlation from causation. For example, during the summer months, we see an increase in ice cream consumption and drowning incidents. There is a strong correlation between the two. But eating ice cream doesn't cause drowning. The underlying cause for both is the warmer weather.

Safely disregard all studies and news articles that tell you that eating this amount of nuts or broccoli will do anything. It's all imagined. The fact is that diets can vary widely due to environmental and personal factors. Depending on climate and available flora and fauna, humans have adapted to sustain various compositions of macronutrients. Aside from your personal preferences, ethical or religious requirements, age and life stage, or weight management goals, what you eat doesn't matter much as long as you follow a few simple guidelines.

Calories

You cannot outrun a bad diet. In his book "Burn," Herman Pontzer found that human energy expenditure seems relatively constant across different populations and activity levels. When studying the Hadza, a modern hunter-gatherer population in Tanzania, he found that their daily energy expenditure wasn't significantly higher than that of people in Western populations. While physically more active individuals burn more calories than sedentary ones, this increase in calorie expenditure plateaus at a certain point. He calls this "constrained energy expenditure," which suggests that the human body adapts to higher activity levels by reducing energy expenditure in other areas, such as resting metabolic rate and immune function. This does not diminish any of the health benefits we have attributed to exercise, but if you are physically active, it should not serve as an excuse to open the floodgates on your diet. Regardless of what you read, you need to be in a caloric deficit to lose weight.

You can easily approximate your total daily energy expenditure (TDEE) by estimating your basal metabolic rate (BMR), how many calories your body needs to maintain its essential functions at rest, and then multiplying your BMR by activity level. The Harris-Benedict Equation is a widely used formula to estimate your BMR.

- For men: BMR = 88.362 + (13.397 x weight in kg) + (4.799 x height in cm) - (5.677 x age in years)
- For women: BMR = 447.593 + (9.247 x weight in kg) + (3.098 x height in cm) - (4.330 x age in years)

Once you have your BMR, multiply it by your activity level:

- Sedentary (little to no exercise): BMR x 1.2
- Lightly active (light exercise or sports 1-3 days a week): BMR x 1.375
- Moderately active (moderate exercise or sports 3-5 days a week): BMR x 1.55
- Very active (strenuous exercise or sports 6-7 days a week): BMR x 1.725
- Extra active (strenuous exercise, physical job, or training twice a day): BMR x 1.9

I consider myself moderately active, weigh 88 kilograms, and am a 195 centimeters tall male. My TDEE is roughly 3,000 kilocalories based on the calculation method. I can eat this on average per day to maintain my weight, irrespective of the precise composition between fats, carbs, and protein. I emphasize *on average*, as switching things up is probably a good idea for your metabolism. If you do prolonged fasts or maintain a calorie deficit consistently for a more extended period, your body adapts your BMR downward, which further limits the number of calories you can consume without building excess fat. This phenomenon is known as adaptive thermogenesis or metabolic adaptation and is a survival mechanism. Periodic refeeds ("cheat days") can help during a more prolonged phase of caloric deficit. In my experience, allowing for one or two days per week with more calories than your targeted average helps prevent lowering your basal metabolic rate.

Macronutrients

People harbor nearly religious beliefs on the exact composition of their macronutrients. I have seen it all, from breakfasts with six eggs to panicked outcries at the sight of the breadbasket. In the United Airlines lounge in Los Angeles, I once witnessed a woman stack an entire plate with at least 30 or more bacon strips. I am guessing she was on a ketogenic diet (or a huge fan of bacon).

Neither carbohydrates, fats, nor proteins are bad for you. They all help support vital functions in your body. Mix them as much as you like, especially if you follow my advice on exercise (mobility, resistance, high-intensity, and low-intensity cardio). To simplify, I have thought of only one thing to remember in the context of each of the three macronutrients.

Plentiful Protein

We consume protein not primarily for its energy content but for its components, the amino acids. There are 20 amino acids, which the body uses as building blocks to form any of the more than 20,000 protein chains it needs to function daily. Proteins are critical to nearly any process in your body, from the actin and myosin in your muscles to the collagen in your skin and cartilage, the proteins that transport oxygen, lipids, and other substances through the body, the enzymes, hormones, immunoglobulins, and so many more.

11 of the 20 amino acids can be synthesized by the body. The other nine cannot and must be consumed through the diet, which is why they are called essential amino acids: histidine, isoleucine, leucine, lysine, methionine, phenylalanine, threonine, tryptophan, and valine. Sources that contain all nine essential amino acids are called complete proteins and include most animal-based foods such as meat, poultry, fish, eggs, and dairy. Plant-based sources, like soy, quinoa, and buckwheat, are also considered complete proteins. Other plant-based foods like nuts, legumes, or grains are considered incomplete proteins as they don't contain the full range of these vital amino acids. It is easiest to get all your amino acids from animal-based foods, but if you prefer a plant-based diet, you need to eat a variety of foods to get the composition right.

What people don't appreciate, however, is how much protein you need to consume. Depending on size and activity level, your body synthesizes 250 to 300 grams of protein daily. You would have to eat 1 kilogram of chicken breast or more than 80 eggs to provide that much protein through your diet alone. Fortunately, your body reuses and recycles most of its amino acids. It is estimated that around 70-80 percent of the amino acids required for protein synthesis are derived from the breakdown and recycling of existing ones. This process, known as protein turnover, helps to maintain a constant pool of free amino acids that can be used for new protein synthesis. The missing 20-30 percent have to be provided through your diet, which equals around 60-90 grams of protein per day. As a proxy, you should at least consume 1 gram of protein per kilogram of body weight to provide enough amino acids to the body.

As we get older, our body's ability to break down used proteins and create new ones slows down. To offset this, we need to consume more external amino acids. Recent studies suggest that individuals over 50 should aim for 1.5 to 2 grams of protein per kilogram of body weight each day. For someone who weighs 75 kilograms, this would mean consuming up to 150 grams of protein daily or 50 grams per meal if they eat three times a day.

It can be challenging to consume that amount of protein without including animal-based foods in every meal. You must plan and track your protein consumption, especially if you are on a time-restricted feeding schedule. Eating 50 to 100 grams in one sitting is not without challenges, particularly on a plant-based diet. For 100 grams of protein, you would have to consume 1 kilogram of cooked soybeans, an impractical (and undesirable) amount.

In his book "Should We Eat Meat?" Vaclav Smil explores the complexities surrounding meat production, consumption, and sustainability. He acknowledges its role in human evolution and highlights the environmental, ethical, and health concerns of excessive meat consumption. The current scale of meat production, particularly in industrialized systems, clearly is unsustainable and contributes to various environmental issues such as deforestation, water pollution, and greenhouse gas emissions. Although he does not advocate for complete veganism, he encourages a more moderate and responsible approach to meat consumption that balances human dietary needs, environmental sustainability, and animal welfare.

Vaclav Smil argues that chicken and dairy products are the most sustainable options from an energy conversion perspective if you are going to have meat. Chickens and dairy cows convert feed into edible products more efficiently than other livestock animals, such as pigs and cattle. This higher conversion efficiency results in fewer resources being used, such as land, water, and feed, and lower greenhouse gas emissions per unit of food produced.

I will not argue for a particular diet, but I stress the importance of protein. From a health perspective, eating meat and dairy products is the easiest and most complete way of providing essential amino acids to your body. There are valid ethical and environmental concerns against our form of industrialized meat consumption. If you choose a plant-based diet, you must track your protein intake, as it requires more planning and attention. Protein in plant-based food is also less bioavailable as much of it is bound in the fibers that your digestion can-not access. As a vegetarian or vegan, you should consider supplementing your protein intake with (vegan) protein shakes.

Complex Carbs

Carbohydrates are beneficial for maintaining an ac-tive lifestyle as they supply glucose and glycogen. But you need to be mindful of the type of carbs you consume. Simple carbs can have an addictive effect on the body similar to crack cocaine. Therefore, opting for complex carbohydrates is a better choice as they consist of longer molecule chains that require more time to break down and digest. These carbs generally offer more nutrients and fiber than their simple counterparts. Here are some examples of complex carbohydrates:

- **Whole grains**: whole wheat, brown rice, quinoa, barley, bulgur, millet, and oats. Whole-grain bread, pasta, and cereals made from these grains are also good sources of complex carbohydrates.
- **Legumes**: Beans, lentils, and peas are all rich in complex carbohydrates, as well as protein and fiber.
- **Starchy vegetables**: Potatoes, sweet potatoes, yams, corn, and squash are all examples of starchy vegeta-bles that contain complex carbohydrates.
- **Non-starchy vegetables**: Although they have fewer carbohydrates compared to starchy vegetables,

non-starchy vegetables like leafy greens, broccoli, cauliflower, and bell peppers still provide complex carbohydrates along with essential vitamins, minerals, and fiber.

- **Fruit**: While fruit contain simple sugars, they also provide fiber and other nutrients, making them healthier than refined sugar. Examples include apples, pears, oranges, and berries. Avoid fruit juices, which often lack fiber and have a higher sugar concentration.

Again, have any carbohydrate you like, but try to incorporate a high rate of complex carbs. If you have metabolic syndrome, you should follow dietary advice specific to this condition, which would probably limit your intake of simple carbs even further.

Favorable Fats

From my perspective, you can have any kind of fat you like, with the exception of trans fats. Keep in mind that at nine calories per gram, fat is more than twice as calorie-dense as carbs or proteins at four calories per gram.

Unsaturated fats like monounsaturated fats found in olive oil, avocados, and almonds, as well as polyunsaturated fats including Omega-3 fatty acids found in salmon, walnuts, and flaxseeds, are beneficial for your health. Saturated fats in butter, fatty cuts of meat, or coconut oil have traditionally been considered a risk to cardiovascular health. In the 1950s and 1960s, researcher Ancel Keys published a number of influential studies, including the Seven Countries Study, which observed a correlation between saturated fat intake and heart disease rates. This led to the "fat-free mania," the adoption of low-fat dietary guidelines by health authorities. As a result, the food industry promoted low-fat products but vastly increased the sugar content in processed foods to compensate for the loss in taste.

The findings were based mainly on the assumption that saturated fat increased low-density lipoprotein (LDL) levels, considered a "bad" cholesterol. However, a meta-analysis published in 2010 combined the results of 21 studies involving over 340,000 participants and found no significant association between saturated fat intake and the risk of heart disease, stroke, or other cardiovascular events. The impact of dietary fat (the fat you consume) on your blood lipid composition seems much lower than previously thought. Furthermore, blood LDL concentrations don't seem to be the best risk indicator. Next to LDL, there are other atherogenic lipoprotein particles (VLDL, IDL) that contribute to atherosclerosis. They all have an apolipoprotein in common called apoB, which, more recently, is thought to be the better predictor of cardiovascular risk. The response of apoB levels to saturated fat seems to be highly individual. For many, there is no link; for some, there might be. Try to understand better how your body reacts to saturated fats by testing your blood after a couple of weeks on different diets. If you have a strong apoB response, limiting the amounts of saturated fats might be better for you.

Generally, saturated fats seem less unhealthy than previously thought. The evidence for trans fats, unfortunately, is solid, which is why many countries have banned their use. Examples of trans fats are partially hydrogenated vegetable oils, margarine, shortening, and some commercially prepared baked goods, fried foods, and snack foods. Since 2018, the FDA has banned their use in the United States, while in the European Union, the use of trans fats in processed foods is limited to 2 grams per 100 grams of fat.

Micronutrients

The WHO maintains that people obtain all their required micronutrients from a balanced, diverse, and healthy diet, as this is the best way to meet nutritional needs. They recognize that certain population groups or individuals with specific dietary requirements may benefit from supplements, such as iron and folic acid for pregnant women or vitamin A for children aged six months to five years in regions with high vitamin A deficiency. The general public, however, should be fine with getting all essential nutrients from their diet.

On the other end of the spectrum is Bryan Johnson, an American entrepreneur, investor, and futurist, who founded Braintree and sold it to PayPal for US$ 800 million. He developed a longevity protocol he calls the "Blueprint" and published it online. As part of his daily routine, he takes the following supplements.

- **Upon waking**: Acarbose 200mg (Rx), Ashwagandha 600mg, B Complex .25 pill M/Th, BroccoMax 250mg, C 500mg, Ca-AKG 2 grams, Cocoa Flavanols 500mg, D-3 2,000 IU, DHEA 25mg, E 67mg, EPA 500mg with vitamin E 5mg, Garlic 2.4g equivalent, Garlic 1.2g (kyolic), Ginger Root 2.2g, Glucosamine Sulphate 2KCL 1,500mg, Iodine as potassium iodide 125 mcg, Lithium, as lithium orotate, 1mg, Lycopene 10mg, Lysine 1g, Metformin ER 1,500 (Rx), Nicotinamide Riboside 375mg (6 x wk), N-Acetyl-L-Cysteine (NAC) 1,800 mg, Turmeric with piperine 1g, Taurine 1g, Ubiquinol 100mg, Zeaxanthin (20mg Lutein, 4mg Zeaxanthin), Zinc 15mg
- **With dinner**: Acarbose 200mg (Rx), BroccoMax 250mg, C 500mg, Ca-AKG 2 grams, Cocoa Flavanols 500mg, EPA 500mg, Garlic 2.4g equivalent, Garlic 1.2g (kyolic), Ginger Root 2.2g, Glucosamine Sulphate 2KCL 1,500mg, Hyaluronic Acid 300mg, Lysine 1g, L-Tyrosine, 500mg, Metformin ER 500 mg (Rx), N-Acetyl-L-Cysteine (NAC) 1,800 mg,

Nicotinamide Riboside 375mg (6x wk), Turmeric 1g

- **Before bed**: Melatonin 300 mcg
- **Other**: Extra Virgin Olive Oil, 30mL daily; Pea Protein, 29 grams daily; Dark Chocolate, 15 grams; Rapamycin 13mg, bi-weekly (Rx), Testosterone 2mg patch 6x weekly; B12 methylcobalamin 1x/wk

I will share my personal tactics in the last chapter, which lie between these two approaches. The reality is that supplementation regimes will always be highly customized as they are influenced by age, sex, genes, health, diet, and other lifestyle factors too numerous to list. Different stages in life (pregnancy, menopause), energy requirements (running a marathon, lifting weights), and dietary choices (vegan, keto) create different demands and deficiencies that you need to address.

In terms of strategy, I approach the question of micronutrient balance from three angles.

1. Where are you deficient at base level?
2. Which deficiencies are you creating by your lifestyle choices?
3. Which future deficiencies can you anticipate and prevent?

For the first question, you need to get tested regularly. As I will explore in the next chapter, regular broad blood panels will point to chronically or acutely low levels of vital nutrients. The resulting interventions should be discussed with a medical doctor specializing in preventative medicine. A traditionally trained doctor will usually just scan for parameters outside of standard ranges. The lab highlights these values in their report by using bold print. I prefer a doctor who looks at all parameters and checks whether they are optimal. I would deep-dive into parameters that are either close to one end of the range or have changed significantly from the last tests.

The answer to the second question is highly individual. The strategic approach is to understand where you are out of homeostasis. If you are sick, you need to support your body in different ways than if you are experiencing a lot of stress through exercise. There also might be functional targets that you are working on, like lowering blood cholesterol, sleeping better, or improving your digestion.

Nutritional interventions are numerous — and for a large part, completely made-up and unsubstantiated. Before following any regime, I would ask myself if taking too much of this micronutrient or supplement is harmful. Excessive amounts of common nutrients, such as potassium, vitamin D, vitamin B6, iron, zinc, and selenium, can cause serious health issues. Secondly, I would look at the supporting evidence, mainly in the form of clinical studies. Thirdly, I would always try to find out the minimal effective dose and if you can reach it through nutrition alone. Resveratrol, a polyphenolic compound, is thought to have anti-inflammatory and antioxidant effects. The minimum effective dose is believed to be somewhere between 50 and 150 milligrams. Red wine contains resveratrol and has gained a reputation as a good source. On average, a 150-milliliter glass of red wine contains about 1 milligram of resveratrol. So, to have any effect, you would have to drink 50 to 150 glasses in one sitting. Good luck with that.

On the third question, studies support supplementing specific micronutrients to compensate for age-related deficiencies. As with protein, the synthesis and metabolism of some nutrients decline with age, which can negatively affect cellular health.

Levels of the coenzyme nicotinamide adenine dinucleotide (NAD+) decline with age. This can cause issues as it plays a crucial role in various cellular processes, including energy metabolism, DNA repair, and cell signaling. There is a debate on how to compensate for this decline. NAD+ cannot be supplemented directly, but precursors like nicotinamide riboside (NR) and nicotinamide mononucleotide (NMN) are thought to boost levels of NAD+ in your cells. Research is ongoing, especially on the bioavailability of oral supplements, but from what I understand, there is no harm in taking them.

Similar declines are seen in levels of vitamin D (essential for bone health and immune function), magnesium (muscle and nerve function as well as sleep quality), and B-complex vitamins (energy production, brain function, and cell metabolism).

You will find many of these interventions in Bryan Johnson's protocol. I would not consider all of them to have scientific merit, but it is a complete list of what longevity experts are discussing currently.

It is advisable to consult with your physician before taking any supplements as they may have unintended consequences when taken with other medications or substances. It is always better to double-check for your safety.

Governance

Finally, we get to my favorite chapter of measuring and governing it all. What is the value of anything if it has no measurable impact? The word impact implies physicality, some change in the physical world. Thomas, my friend and mentor back in consulting, used to say that impact was defined as "concept quality multiplied by implementation probability." The world is filled with ideas, but very few actualize them. Go to a modern art gallery, seek out a painting with a few blobs of color on it, and listen to visitors moan: "What is so special about that? I could have done that." Well, they haven't, which is the crucial difference between them and the artist. It is the difference between no impact and impact.

It starts with the data. The Romans coined the proverb "praemonitus, praemunitus," which translates to "to be forewarned is to be forearmed." In a world where data is one of the most valuable currencies, I am surprised how many people find it strange and excessive to track their vital statistics. Often these same people cannot get enough visibility and control in their companies, but find it absurd to track their sleep, a key driver of their health that they have no objective data on. So many affordable gadgets are available that give you a wealth of information with minimal effort, but people still don't embrace these possibilities.

I can only speculate as to their motivations, but a large part is probably due to overconfidence on the one side (believing that they intuitively know everything there is to know) and fear on the other. Fear, their rationalizations and justifications for bad habits won't hold up in light of the evidence, finally tipping their cognitive dissonance in favor of objective data. And for some, it is simply ignorance.

Let's go back to why we are doing this. Our aim is not to get sick. As we saw, mortality risk increases dramatically as soon as you experience your first major health event. Once you are diagnosed with diabetes, hypertension, arteriosclerosis, cancer, or dementia — or simply break your hip — you are fighting an uphill battle. In many cases, reversing the underlying condition isn't possible anymore. All you can do is slow down its progression. Cancer might go into remission, but very few are ever cured once cancer metastasizes. Many forms of dementia, including Alzheimer's disease, are currently incurable.

Centenarians also die of these diseases, but they get them 20 years later on average. If you want to extend your healthspan, you need to be able to detect the big killers early. For example, your chances of surviving cancer are largely a question of timing. As a solid growth at the point of origin, removing cancer is a simple surgical procedure. Once it metastasizes, cancer cells can potentially get anywhere in the body. You then have to fire the big guns of chemotherapy at your entire body but can never be sure you have eliminated all dangerous growth. Like pulling weed, it can always end up popping up somewhere else.

It is critical to detect the first signs of serious illnesses early on. While a heart attack or stroke happens suddenly and can have tragic consequences, the prequel to the event has been in the making for decades. The art is picking up these gradual changes over time. How many people keep their medical records and compare them to newer results? Do you know if your sleep has improved or worsened over the past five years? How do you define how much exercise or recovery, what kind of nutrition, and what kind of preventative measures you need? This is your one life. People know every statistic about basketball players or the football league they watch but don't have any insight into their health.

You can claim that ignorance is bliss, and it would probably be true if every individual had a personalized death clock that would just shut us down when our time ran out. The truth is that we don't just shut down. In most cases, we gradually decline into a state of decrepitude that causes pain, suffering, frustration, depression, and a lot of cost. The last 20 years of many peoples' lives are devoid of dignity. With our current medicine, we can easily prolong this terrible suffering without improving the underlying quality of life. So, it is better to know and prepare even for hereditary risks that you might be unable to avoid entirely. Even here, early detection and focused preventative measures can often significantly delay the onset of these.

Governance, therefore, is about transparency, insights, and action. In psychology and social studies, the Hawthorne Effect is considered when conducting research on human behavior. It describes a phenomenon in which individuals change or improve their behavior or performance when they know they are being observed. Make the Hawthorne Effect your friend by sharing your goals and statistics with friends and family. Even if not, ensure you collect the data and make informed choices. Praemonitus, praemunitus.

Baseline risk

Get your genome sequenced and screened for known hereditary risks. Gene sequencing companies provide a lot of useless information (like which variant of the ABCC11 gene you have to determine whether your ear wax is dry or wet), but it often points to some areas you should monitor more closely.

I would not over-index the results. Companies try to sell you all kinds of insights, for example, how your metabolism supposedly functions and if you have fast-twitch or slow-twitch muscle fibers. Genes are rarely deterministic as they still need to get expressed through epigenetic processes in your cells, which environmental and lifestyle factors can influence. But they do influence probability. For example, Apolipoprotein E (ApoE) has different variants or alleles. Two to three percent of the population have two copies of the ApoE allele 4, so one from each parent. This increases their risk of developing Alzheimer's disease by a factor of 10 to 15. It doesn't mean they will get it. But if I had two copies of ApoE ε4, I would closely follow the research on early detection and prevention of Alzheimer's disease and get tested regularly.

A standard gene test only looks at specific gene sequences where established research exists, typically about 1 percent of your genome. I had a company sequence my entire genome, which yielded 220 gigabytes of data. Some analytics services let you upload this data to screen for genetic risks against databases that get updated more frequently. Clinical data on correlations between gene variants and diseases are, of course, increasing over time. In the future, we might sequence our genome periodically and compare these data sets to locate mutations and damage that need fixing. With gene editing technology advancing quickly, the idea of repairing the degeneration of DNA might become a reality in the not-so-distant future.

Annual screening for big killers

I recommend an annual checkup that includes lab work on all your fluids (blood, urine, stool), screening for skin cancer, cardiovascular risk, tumors, and organ size and functionality. Typically, this involves a questionnaire on habits and mental health changes and a full-body MRI scan which scans for tumors in your brain and organs. Next, a CT of your lungs and a stress ECG on a stationary bicycle can be used to determine heart problems and exercise capacity. An echo can be performed to visualize blood flow, the state of your main arteries, the health of your heart chambers, and other organs like the liver, kidneys, pancreas, prostate, etc.

Some checkups will also screen for eye health, vision and hearing, posture, mobility, and many other factors. A regular DEXA scan can also help you track your body composition and bone density. Similarly, tooth and gum health should be examined regularly.

The aim is to detect early signs of the big killers like diabetes, atherosclerosis, hypertension, or cancer. Age-related risks should be added at the appropriate times, like scanning for colon or prostate cancer or testing your hormone levels. Getting these tested at a younger age is beneficial to understand your baseline. For adult men, for example, the normal range of testosterone reaches from 270 to 1,070 nanograms per deciliter. The real question is not where you are exactly in that range but how it compares to your younger, healthier self.

Monthly assessment of health

Every month, I would check how slow-moving indicators have evolved. These are typically averages of your weekly and daily values and parameters that are less easy to measure frequently. Weight, body fat percentage, sleep quality, and many other factors vary daily due to different circumstances and inaccuracies in measuring them. Looking at trends over longer periods helps you understand underlying trajectories. While you might have lost weight due to a 3-day fast (mainly from the water released by a reduction in glycogen), it doesn't help in understanding your underlying body composition. Other factors, like blood lipids, don't change quickly, so measuring them daily doesn't add value.

I suggest capturing the following values in an Excel or Google Sheets table on a monthly basis.

- Average weight over the period
- Average fat percentage over the period (percentage of visceral fat, if you can get it)
- Average glucose or Hba1c
- Average resting heart rate
- Average heart rate variability
- Average respiratory rate
- Blood pressure
- Blood lipids (HDL, LDL, Triglycerides, ApoB, if you can get it)
- Uric Acid
- Screening for arterial fibrillation by ECG
- VO_2 max
- Functional threshold power (FTP) for running or cycling
- Sleep metrics (duration, deep sleep, REM sleep).

Create your own customized list that reflects what you care about. Some focus more on "output indicators" like measures of strength and mobility. For instance, how many push- or pull-ups you can perform in one go or how long you can dead hang (hanging your entire body weight from a bar), which gives you a sense of your grip strength, a proxy for overall strength.

Capturing the data will also give you a sense of ranges and the impact of your lifestyle choices. The feedback loop of understanding cause and effect is a valuable aspect of governance. Instead of just following some fitness advice, it is better to uncover how your body responds to the stressors and recovery techniques you employ. You learn about the underlying mechanisms and can apply them to build your own regime.

Weekly assessment of vitality

I track a subset of the above every week, especially when they are relevant to some target I am pursuing. I currently run two half marathons per year, so in preparation for these, I will closely monitor my VO_2 max and functional threshold power values and other fitness-related statistics like weight, heart rate at rest, heart rate variability, sleep, and so on. It depends on how quantitative and data-driven you are.

Daily tracking

Some metrics are more insightful if you capture them daily. Resting heart rate is a long-term indicator of fitness; however, it also indicates an acute infection. Before I notice a cold in my sinuses or lungs, my resting heart rate increases by 10-15 beats per minute as my body is dealing with the onset of the infection. Capturing this early helps me prioritize sleep and go easy on the exercise not to inadvertently weaken my immune system.

To monitor my blood glucose levels, I use a continuous glucose monitor (CGM) which provides me with up-to-date data on how my sugar levels react to various foods, exercise, and other external factors. Through this, I've gained valuable insights into how different foods, consumed at different times and in different orders, affect my body. With this knowledge, I feel confident in managing my carbohydrate intake and mitigating any risks associated with diabetes. This beats blindly following a restrictive low-carb diet. Wearing a CGM has been a liberating experience and I highly recommend trying it for a few months to learn how your body responds. Here are some examples of what I've discovered so far.

- **Glucose is individual** — Oats are whole-grain and have a low glycemic index, meaning they don't raise blood sugar quickly. However, my morning porridge spikes my blood sugar regardless of the type of oats, additions like berries, or milk alternatives. Steel-cut oats are less severe, but my usual porridge is like a sweet dessert to my glucose level.

- **Timing and sequence matters** — Starting a meal with simple carbs spikes my glucose, while eating something else first leads to a more muted response. Similarly, there is a big difference if I have a dessert right after the main course (good) or wait 30 minutes between courses (bad).

- **Bad sleep drives up glucose** — When I have too little sleep, I crave food more, and my glucose levels rise faster. This sets off an unhealthy chain reaction.

- **Detecting mental stress** — It is difficult to detect stress without measuring cortisol directly. However, if I see my glucose staying elevated during the night, this indicates I am wrestling with psychological stress. Cortisol stimulates the liver to provide more glucose to your blood as an energy reservoir for a fight-or-flight response.

- **Atmospheric pressure lowers glucose** — While using a hyperbaric oxygen chamber, which involves inhaling pure oxygen at increased atmospheric pressure, my glucose drops to half the typical value. According to research, this could be due to the extra oxygen stimulating cellular metabolism, which leads to repair requiring more glucose in the cells.

The key to all governance is generating insights and implementing the learnings. You need to visualize and contextualize the data to make sense of it. The most important question to ask yourself is, "Why?" If you see a deviation, what could explain it? Which other values moved simultaneously, and what could the underlying cause be for these developments?

During my data collection and experiments, I gained interesting insights. For example, a couple of years ago, I recorded the days I drank alcohol versus the days I abstained and analyzed the resulting impact on my resting heart rate. I found that drinking alcohol increased my resting heart rate by about ten beats per minute, probably because of the additional metabolic processing. Another data set I looked at showed that my respiratory rate decreased from 14 to 12.5 breaths per minute during a prolonged fast. Also, my resting heart rate was lowered. In the absence of digestion, the entire system seemingly can relax.

In summary, health is about becoming **STRONG**. Promoting well-dosed Stress and avoiding Toxins help you achieve and maintain life-preserving homeostasis for longer. Notably, the stressors you employ provide new information to your body. Allowing for subsequent Recovery and periodic Overhaul will incorporate this feedback into your system and drive adaptations that improve your resilience and strength. Finally, providing the necessary Nutrients and applying effective Governance to how you lead your life builds the platform on which everything rests.

> *Eat half, walk double, laugh triple, and love without measure.*
>
> — *Tibetan proverb*

HAPPINESS

It never ceased to amaze me: we all love ourselves more than others but care more about their opinions than our own.

— Marcus Aurelius, Meditations

In 2023, Finland was declared the world's happiest country for the sixth time by the United Nations in its annual World Happiness Report. The report ranks 156 countries based on various factors related to the well-being and happiness of their citizens.

I have been to Finland many times, and it is not immediately evident why they dominate this ranking. They don't seem very happy. In fact, until recently, Finland had one of the highest suicide rates in the world. If you look up the ten most popular sightseeing attractions in Helsinki on TripAdvisor, you'll find the tram system and the public library as numbers seven and eight. They also have an oddly specific word for getting drunk alone at home in your underwear: "kalsarikännit," which roughly translates to "pants drunk." A Finnish CEO once told me, as a joke, that the Finns were relieved when social distancing rules were lifted after the COVID-19 pandemic. During the Corona measures, they had to keep a two-meter distance from each other, but now they could finally go back to the usual three.

Finns are stereotypically characterized as introverted or reserved. It is, of course, wrong to generalize personality traits. Finnish culture tends to value silence and privacy, which can be mistaken for introversion by people from more expressive or talkative cultures. But it shows that happiness is not a clearly defined term, and our superficial image of Finns does not immediately square with their seemingly satisfied state of mind.

But is it really happiness that the report measures, or rather a high standard of living? There are six criteria, most of which are sourced from the "life evaluation" section of the Gallup World Poll. These are self-reported estimates collected from the adult population of 160 countries across six criteria.

- Gross Domestic Product (GDP) per capita: A country's economic output.

- Social support: Having someone to count on in times of trouble, which is usually assessed by having friends and family members who can help.

- Healthy life expectancy: The average number of years a person can expect to live in good health.

- Freedom to make life choices: The extent to which individuals feel they have the freedom to make decisions about their lives.

- Generosity: A measure of the willingness to help others, often through charitable giving or volunteering.

- Perceptions of corruption: How widespread people believe corruption is within their government and businesses.

GDP, life expectancy, social support, and a low level of corruption are all great, but are they the defining elements of happiness? Why does the report not consider income, education, housing, crime rates, divorce rates, or access to healthcare and other essential services? Finland is a wealthy nation with solid democratic institutions, and living there is undoubtedly desirable if you don't mind the cold, dark, and lack of sightseeing attractions. But why are the people happy there?

In contrast, the longest-running study on happiness in the United States has identified close relationships as the primary driver of a happy life. The Harvard Study on Happiness began in 1938 and followed two groups of men for over 80 years. The study suggests that strong social connections, such as those with family, friends, and communities, are crucial for overall well-being. People with strong relationships are more likely to be happier, healthier, and live longer than those who are more isolated. The study also identified other factors contributing to happiness and health, including maintaining a healthy lifestyle, managing stress, engaging in lifelong learning, and having a sense of purpose in life.

Bhutan famously introduced the concept of Gross National Happiness (GNH) as an alternative to GDP in 1970 to prioritize the happiness and well-being of the Bhutanese people over material growth. Again, the criteria contributing to happiness are different. Next to sustainable and equitable socio-economic development for the citizens and good governance by the government, Bhutan places emphasis on environmental conservation and the preservation of its culture, including language, customs, and traditions.

Bhutan is not included in the World Happiness Report, and it would be interesting to see how they would score vis-a-vis Finland. According to a 2015 GNH survey conducted by the Centre for Bhutan Studies & GNH Research, 91.2 percent of Bhutanese citizens were considered "happy," with 8.4 percent being "deeply happy," 32.6 percent "extensively happy," and 48.7 percent "narrowly happy." Only 8.8 percent of the population was considered "unhappy."

Despite all this happiness, I doubt Bhutan would measure highly in the World Happiness Report because of the criteria set by the United Nations. Bhutan only ranks #109 of all countries in GDP per capita (2017) and #25 on the Corruption Perception Index (2022). Their life expectancy at birth of 72 years is slightly less than the global average of 72.8. Despite their focus on happiness for the past 50 years, their self-reported happiness would be discounted based on these metrics of development.

The misconception of all these studies is that they assume objective criteria exist for happiness. The physical world has no concept of sadness or happiness; hence, external factors can never guarantee a specific outcome. Strong relationships or financial stability will likely contribute to your sense of fulfillment, but it is still up to you if it ultimately does. It is a deeply subjective affair driven by how you process events and whether this leads to an increase or decrease in certain hormones, which make you feel joy, sadness, anger, or other emotions. Happiness is a direct result of how you evaluate the world around you. The universal law applicable here is:

Happiness is your perceived reality against your expectations.

The same rain shower will make the farmer happy and the sunbather sad. The same objective event in the physical world will increase the joy-inducing hormones in one person's brain and lower them in another. The difference is in perceptions, expectations, hopes, and desires. Your expectations are clearly subjective, but, as we saw, your perception of reality also. Your experience is a director's cut of what your brain thinks is important and has a bias toward the negative.

We sometimes observe small children overreact to benign events. The scoop of ice cream that drops to the floor can cause a flood of tears in a child while an adult rarely reacts this way. The difference is not in expectations. Both would have looked forward to tasting the delicious ice cream and are disappointed by the anticlimactic event. The difference is in how they perceive reality. The grown-up is more relaxed because they know that ice cream is a commodity available everywhere at a small price. A child does not have this perspective. It is focused on the one ice cream that now is no longer.

Naturally, most of us desire a safe, comfortable, wealthy, and pleasurable existence, so objective criteria supporting a high standard of living will contribute to a happy life, but they don't define it. The Harvard study puts close relationships at the center of their findings. Would the same be true if they had studied Finnish men for 80 years, who culturally are less outgoing and contact-seeking than Americans tend to be? Maybe Finns are more focused on a secure and organized life and are very satisfied with what they have. And in Bhutan, there seems to be a broadly shared expectation to preserve Bhutanese culture, which is why they include this aspect in the definition of happiness specific to their country.

Happiness does not depend on objective conditions of wealth or community. Instead, it depends on the correlation between objective conditions and subjective expectations. If you want a pair of shoes and get one, you are happy. If you want a house on Lake Como in Lombardy, Italy, and only get one on Lake Iseo, 70km to the east, your life is practically over.

Happiness is, therefore, something a healthy person can influence. Your health and wealth are impacted by external forces outside your control, but happiness is determined by the interplay of nerves, neurons, synapses, and biochemical substances such as serotonin, dopamine, and oxytocin. If one of these processes didn't work, you could win the lottery and feel nothing. And indeed, for people diagnosed with major depressive or anxiety disorder, the priority is to restore the neurochemical pathways that allow them to be happy in the first place.

The neurochemistry of your brain is, how else could it be, homeostatic. As we saw with addiction, sensations of pleasure and displeasure get evened out by homeostatic regulators. Consequently, there is no higher level of serotonin for a rich life than for a poor one. When you place the last bushel of straw on the mud hut you built for your family, your serotonin rises to a certain level as a reward. When the contractors finish building your new house on the lake, serotonin increases just the same. Both individuals feel equally happy. The brain doesn't care that the lake house is much more comfortable than the mud hut. On the contrary, if the house owner got Lake Iseo but hoped for Lake Como, her serotonin might be lower.

The key, again, is balance. It is not about stimulating and maximizing your neurotransmitters and hormones all the time. Homeostasis will downregulate you automatically, if you like it or not. The happiness you feel about the mud hut or lake house will fade quickly. We will talk about this "hedonic adaptation" in more detail. Too much happy stimulus, like with addiction, will adjust your neutral set point. The second Ferrari doesn't stimulate your brain chemistry as much as the first. But losing your Ferraris will feel worse than if you never had them in the first place because your neutral set point now includes them. A life of desire, want, regret, aspiration, greed, and other sentiments of longing, leads to permanently low levels of serotonin, dopamine, and oxytocin, resulting in depression and anxiety.

This principle of inner happiness is long established. Buddhism already highlights the importance of eliminating craving and external attachments, the root causes of suffering. As Siddhartha Gautama, who later became the Buddha, said 2,500 years ago, "All that we are is the result of what we have thought." By recognizing that the mind is the master of our experiences, we can shape our reality and cultivate inner peace. The key lies in taming the mind through mindfulness, understanding the nature of impermanence, and acknowledging that seeking happiness in the material world is futile.

Happiness does not depend on what you have or who you are. It mainly relies on your thoughts. It is a state of calm in which everything is alright the way it is. There are no regrets, no worries, and no nagging thoughts that prevent you from enjoying life as it happens at this very moment.

Frame

The imagined order we live in reinforces the opposite. Happiness today is almost entirely about what you have and who you are. Our Western societies are built on capitalism, an economic system of private ownership and the pursuit of profit, and meritocracy, a social system that rewards individuals based on their abilities, talents, and achievements. Both systems have strong merits but inadvertently promote the notion that wealth and success are the primary measures of personal worth, leading to feelings of inadequacy or failure for those who do not achieve these external markers.

This wasn't the intention. The United States Declaration of Independence famously includes "Life, Liberty, and the pursuit of Happiness" as the inalienable rights endowed to all human beings. Thomas Jefferson, the primary author of the document, was strongly influenced by Enlightenment philosopher John Locke who argued for the natural rights of individuals to "life, liberty, and property." Scholars and historians believe that Jefferson's inclusion of the "pursuit of Happiness" suggests a broader interpretation of well-being and fulfillment, which extends beyond material possessions. It is seen as an expression of individualism, self-determination, and personal freedom.

Hedonism

The pursuit of happiness for its own sake is called hedonism. This philosophy encourages the pursuit of pleasure and the avoidance of pain as the guiding principles in life. Sensual indulgence, leisure and relaxation, personal interests, and material possessions all promise a life free of adversity and suffering.

When we started dating, my wife and I spent a winter in Florida. The weather was unseasonably cold, and we opted for the two things America excels at: eating and shopping. One of our favorite pastimes became roaming the aisles of drugstores to find the silliest over-the-counter medications. We laughed at stool softeners, marveled at odd-shaped snoring aids, and tried various detox cleanses (which we later regretted). There seems to be a remedy for every ailment you can think of in America. Watching TV commercials there teaches you that you don't have to tolerate discomfort. There is always some pill you can take. Instead of addressing the underlying cause of obesity and other preventable conditions, pharmaceutical ads suggest that you can simply just ease the symptoms.

Focusing solely on short-term pleasure naturally hinders personal growth and the development of resilience. As discussed, facing adversity and overcoming challenges leads to improvement, learning, and a more profound sense of fulfillment. A life devoid of stress limits one's ability to develop the resilience necessary for dealing with life's inevitable difficulties.

Herein lies the fake promise of hedonism. No matter what the marketing agencies will have you believe, life isn't always pleasurable. Reality is messy and far removed from the beautiful scenarios companies paint for you. If you seek a hedonistic life, you will ultimately be disappointed. It is better to lower your expectations and reframe your reality, not to get upset about all the things that can and will go wrong.

Society, political parties, and companies constantly overpromise on things they cannot deliver. As a result, you overestimate the happiness you will gain from future events or rewards, such as a promotion, a new car, or a vacation. This can lead to disappointment when the actual experience fails to meet your inflated expectations.

One particularly fake aspect of hedonism is consumerism. Our economies are fueled by growth, which, in turn, requires a high level of consumption. The constant bombardment of marketing messages promotes the idea that purchasing and owning the latest products will bring you joy and fulfillment. Whatever problem you might have — real or invented by someone — there is some good or service that can solve it and give you the happiness you deserve.

Not lasting happiness, of course, as consumerism needs you to spend continuously. Goods must be constantly replaced and upgraded to keep up with the latest trends and features. Fashion, for example, used to cycle in two main seasons per year: Spring/Summer and Fall/Winter. So-called "fast fashion" now introduces new collections as frequently as every few weeks. Some brands turn over as many as 12 to 24 "micro seasons" per year, leading to tremendous waste.

My best friend and I used to prank each other with useless kitchen utensils as Birthday present. Single-use kitchen gadgets like banana slicers, melon ballers, or egg separators provide little value compared to more versatile tools like knives and spoons. But they address imaginary problems that you didn't know you had before. How else would I create perfectly round melon balls? Think of all the variations of knives they came up with: butter, steak, fish, bread, cake, and so on. And nobody understands their use anymore. If you order a fish fillet at a restaurant, they swap out your regular knife for a fish knife, which was designed to fillet the fish in the first place. The most absurd item in our exchange was an electric garlic roaster, a device specifically designed to roast full garlic bulbs and shaped like a giant head of garlic.

We don't know where to put all this stuff anymore. According to the Self-Storage Association, the rentable self-storage space in the United States has grown almost eightfold over the past 40 years. In 1984, around 27 million square meters of self-storage space were available for rent, which grew to 214 million square meters in 2021. During the same period, average house sizes increased by almost 50 percent, from 154 square meters in 1984 to 210 in 2021.

Consumers keep spending more every year. According to the World Bank database, household consumption per capita doubled globally in the last 50 years in constant currency while debt levels have risen constantly. The median ratio of household debt (mortgage and consumer loans) to GDP has increased from 36 percent in 1996 to 60 percent in 2016 for advanced economies in a sample of 80 countries.

People worldwide are spending more and taking out higher loans to buy more things but end up storing them in their larger houses and rented self-storage spaces. As The Rolling Stones put it, we can't get no satisfaction. In a 1978 landmark study, psychologists Brickman, Coates, and Janoff-Bulman investigated the happiness levels of lottery winners and people with spinal cord injuries. The researchers found that lottery winners experienced an initial boost in happiness after winning, but their happiness levels returned to a baseline level over time. Similarly, people with spinal cord injuries initially reported lower happiness levels, but their happiness gradually increased and approached the levels of the control group. This study provided early evidence for the idea of hedonic adaptation. Also known as the hedonic treadmill, this psychological phenomenon describes the human tendency to return to a relatively stable baseline level of happiness in spite of positive or negative life events.

Conformity

Books, songs, and movies have been created around the notion that you should never give up on your dreams. Indeed, the need to self-actualize and be our unique, authentic selves is part of Maslov's pyramid of human needs. But who is defining those dreams? Is it you who deeply understands your life's potential and seeks to fulfill it step by step? Or has the image of your unique self been created as part of your social conditioning? Is your self trying to live up to standards set for you in advance?

Chances are you are conforming to a narrowly defined path of what your life should look like. The type of home you desire, the perfect garden for your children, the trendy breed of dog, the clothing you wear, the drinks you prefer, the restaurants you love, the shows you enjoy, the social events you host with your friends, the festivities you care about like Christmas, Easter, Mother's Day, Valentine's Day, Halloween and the rituals they come with, are all predetermined by society. While there's nothing wrong with conforming to these norms, it's important to remember that certain festive occasions, such as Valentine's Day and Black Friday, are merely commercialized events to encourage consumerism. Online retailers picked up on this trend and created "Cyber Monday," which extended into a whole Cyber

Week in the 2010s. In China, "Singles' Day" is the pinnacle of consumerism. It was started in the 1990s on 11 November (11/11) at Nanjing University by students to celebrate their single status. For some reason, it became the most significant retail day on the planet. In 2021, Alibaba and JD.com, two e-retailers in China, turned over US$ 139 billion on Singles' Day. That's US$ 1.6 million on average for every second of that day.

Women and, increasingly, men exert tremendous effort to preserve a youthful aesthetic and conform to societal beauty norms. They undergo various medical procedures to keep appearing young without gaining any functional benefits. Next to minimally invasive interventions, like Botox and derma fillers, one of the growing areas of self-optimization is plastic surgery. According to the International Society of Aesthetic Plastic Surgery, the number of (officially recorded) cosmetic surgeries nearly doubled worldwide in the last ten years, from 6.7 million in 2010 to 12.8 million in 2021. Liposuction, breast augmentations, and Brazilian butt lifts, a procedure that removes fatty tissue from the stomach and injects it into one's behind, are the most popular.

Getting some aspect of your face or body surgically changed seems commonplace nowadays. Celebrities and influencers enhance their exteriors, making it desirable for fans to follow suit. The webpage of the American Society of Plastic Surgeons sums up the latest trends for 2023:

If you've scrolled social media lately, you may have noticed several influencers looking slimmer, leading people to speculate about whether they've reversed their Brazilian butt lifts in favor of smaller hips and buttocks. In past years, many celebrities took a 'bigger is better' approach to plastic surgery, with large breasts and buttocks setting the desired aesthetic, but that seems to be changing in 2023.

I am shocked at this actual quote for two reasons. Firstly, these are serious and risky surgeries. After increasing the size of one's behind, the new 2023 trend seems to demand slimmer posteriors. But these major inventions impact your skin, muscles, posture, nervous system, and more. A 2018 study published in JAMA Dermatology estimated that the overall complication rate for cosmetic surgeries was around 1 percent, ranging between 0.7 and 1.3 percent for different procedures. So, for the 12.8 million (recorded) surgeries in 2021, 128,000 people would have experienced complications that partially would have been serious or even life-threatening.

Secondly, it seems celebrities and so-called influencers have authority over how people will medically alter their bodies. Ironically, people who want to express their individuality end up following arbitrary trends set by completely irrelevant people they do not even know. We are back to putting the bones of our ancestors into our swords because we believe it will make a better weapon.

By impersonating a random person who can sing or act well, I suppose people think they will harness some of their powers.

All this makes you unhappy. By trying to be like the famous person you idolize, you are setting yourself up for failure. By trying to conform to society's dictate that wrinkles, grey or thinning hair are signs of weakness, you are putting yourself and your health at risk, partially with grotesque results. Even celebrities whose capital is their exterior appearance sometimes end up looking disfigured and fake. Despite their financial means and access to experts in the field, they lose themselves to the idea that everything and anything can be changed.

It is impossible to conform to everything society defines as desirable. Bucket lists, the "hundred things to do before you die," the ever-changing fashion trends, and the beauty and youth norms are impossible to adhere to. You might want to convince yourself that, at a basic level, there is a blueprint for the good life and some general agreement on what matters most. But there are only different approaches and perspectives on the big questions in life, and what works for one will not necessarily apply to others.

Approval

The motivation for conformity is to seek approval from your peers. In our evolutionary history, we have always lived in groups or tribes. Humans have evolved as social animals, relying on cooperation, communication, and social bonds for survival and reproduction. Getting banned from your tribe would likely have been a death sentence. So, genetically we have a strong desire for tribal recognition. Oxytocin is often called the "bonding hormone" because it is crucial in social bonding, trust, and attachment. It is released during activities such as hugging and is involved in forming and maintaining social bonds, including the recognition of familiar individuals or group members.

Today, our tribes are often virtual and organized around interest groups, social circles, and other communities we form in daily life. People continue to seek acceptance and recognition within these modern tribes to fulfill their inherent need for social connections and belonging. Social media platforms, for instance, have become a primary means through which individuals connect with others who share similar interests, beliefs, or backgrounds. These virtual tribes can provide a sense of identity, validation, and camaraderie, much like traditional tribes or communities.

Social media interactions, such as receiving "likes" or positive comments, trigger your reward system and release positive neurotransmitters like oxytocin, endorphin, and dopamine. As interactions tend to be shallower and more transactional, the increase in dopamine dominates. This dopamine response can be addictive and may not necessarily promote deep, meaningful connections or foster genuine trust and attachment between individuals.

A study published in Behavioral Brain Research in 2020 investigated the relationship between social media use and dopamine release in the striatum, a brain region involved in the reward system. The results indicated that heavy social media users showed increased dopamine release in response to social media-related cues, similar to the response observed in individuals with substance use disorders.

The slippery slope of social media is maximizing dopamine secretion. Like trained dolphins, people quickly learn which tricks to perform to get their dopamine treats. Photos and posts documenting adherence to the commonly established symbols of the good life gain the most approval. Showcasing one's beauty is a fundamental source of approval, even though often heavily curated by selecting favorable settings and using digital enhancement tools. People create virtual personas of themselves that are far removed from reality. This includes documenting how they enjoy life and what kind of access they have to great foods, company, or locations.

Beyond social media, we are strongly driven by a need for peer approval in our daily lives. Your clothing styles, tattoos, holiday destinations, and activities are often narrowly defined by the groups you seek approval from. Approval triggers a dopamine reward, and the more you can get, the more you will reinforce these rewarding behaviors. Digital platforms are like refined sugars in the world of carbohydrates. They give you easy and immediate access to the neurotransmitters that make you feel good. You pay for the experience with your data and attention to advertisement, which is why platforms do everything to keep you captive for as long as possible.

I care more about oxytocin from deep, personal relationships than the transactional dopamine release from shallow approval-seeking actions. Digital tools are fantastic and expand the scope and reach of our relationships. Still, you need to mentally keep some distance and learn to differentiate when you are consuming the complex carbs of a meaningful relationship or the raw, refined sugar of quick, transactional "likes."

FOMO

Fear of Missing Out (FOMO) captures the notion of people being unable to commit to one thing and wanting to keep all options open. It refers to the anxiety that arises from the perception that others are experiencing more fulfilling or rewarding experiences, events, or opportunities. This fear can lead people to be indecisive and constantly seek new options to avoid the feeling that they might miss out on something better.

The grass is always greener on the other side. Even when we get what we originally wanted, we question whether this was the best choice after all. Because of hedonic adaptation, happiness from the new thing fades quickly, and new desires bubble up. Long-term relationships are the perfect example. Being married systematically raises life satisfaction levels compared to their unmarried counterparts. A study titled "The Longitudinal Effects of Marriage on Happiness" by the National Bureau of Economic Research confirmed this by looking at thousands of individuals over several years. Also, the World Happiness Report consistently finds that married people report higher happiness levels than single, divorced, separated, or widowed. This does not imply that the relationship between marriage and happiness is causal. Happier individuals may be more likely to get married. The average also obscures the individual quality of a marriage which can be poor or even abusive for one or both members of the partnership.

Indeed, many marriages get divorced. In the United States, there are about seven marriages and over three divorces per 1,000 people annually. Researchers estimate that 41 percent of first marriages end in divorce. For people getting married for the second time, about 60 percent separate again, and almost three-quarters of third marriages end in divorce. You would think that people get better at marriage on their second and third try, but the opposite seems true. The more often people get married, the higher the probability of them splitting up again.

The reason is a statistical one. Divorce rates increase with the number of divorces because the proportion of people who are "bad at marriage" or "prone to separation" increases in that subsample. There are many good or bad reasons for dissolving a marriage, and one of them is FOMO. People often get married early in life, physically at their prime, full of hope and expectations, but with little track record against fulfilling them. As time passes, the physical state naturally declines, expectations are not always fulfilled, and new tempting options pop up everywhere. You start asking yourself, "Have I made the best decision? My life is short; should I settle for this person for the rest of my life?" The same questions arise on other topics, like your job, the house you live in, the car you drive, the holiday home you bought, and more.

Only you can judge if your choice needs reversing. But living in constant doubt will make you unhappy. The constantly nagging thought that there might be a more attractive option prevents you from enjoying what you have. When I am at a restaurant, I sometimes catch myself obsessing over whether I chose the best dish. When the waiter brings the food and others have something that looks better, it is all I can think about. I don't appreciate the lovely meal I have in front of me.

The word "decide" comes from the Latin word "decidere," which means "to cut off." In the context of a decision, it implies cutting off other options. This does not mean you should settle for less but commit to the option you did choose. Whenever you are unhappy with your spouse or other life decisions, reflect on what is driving this feeling. Is it the person or the fact that you might be bored and seeking novelty? Is it because someone has a new (younger) spouse and seems happier? It might be FOMO.

More importantly, it is impossible to make the "best" choice. In every alternative, there are always aspects that seem better than what you have. But your evaluation of these aspects will change over time. What is better now will not necessarily be better ten years from now, and what you consider most important today might only rank second or third in the future. How would you know anyway? When you compare two alternatives, you are oblivious to the millions of unknown options that might all be better than the two you are considering. You can only statically evaluate what is in front of you but never their potential, development, and future optionality. You also cannot forecast your own personal growth and evolving views and values.

Recognize that whatever you choose can only be the best option of the choices you are aware of in the moment. There will always be a better spouse, job, country, sport, or friend out there somewhere. People who claim they have found "the one" are deluding themselves — in a helpful way that will positively impact their happiness.

The question is, do you want to spend your life searching for that incrementally better option and risk never finding it? Even if you do find it, will you then settle or start obsessing about the next-best option? The opportunity cost of FOMO is likely higher than the investment into committing to your decisions and making them work.

Reframe

When you grow up and reach middle age, you realize that many promises of the imagined order are empty. You achieve all the conventional milestones of a good life but still feel like you are missing something. Money and power helped you to advance, but they didn't solve your quest for happiness. If you could finally have enough money and retire, you would spend more time with your family and travel the world. If only you got this promotion, your frustrations and annoyances at work would end. If only you got a bigger house, your spouse would stop seeing you as a failure. If only.

The grass is greener on the other side until you start watering the side you're on. Your happiness is your reality against your expectations. Start by reframing your expectations and then your reality. Happiness is an individual skill that can be learned. It isn't about material possessions, other people's expectations, or avoiding suffering. It is about freeing yourself from your worries about life. It is accepting how things are to achieve a sense of calm, free of regret, filled with compassion and love. To calm your mind, you need the following.

- **Composure** — Compose yourself to prime your emotional state
- **Acceptance** — Accept the world and your fate as it presents itself
- **Love** — Love who and what you have right now
- **Motivation** — Live your deeper sense of purpose.

Composure

On January 15, 2009, US Airways Flight 1549 experienced a bird strike shortly after takeoff from New York's LaGuardia Airport, causing both engines to fail. Faced with a life-threatening situation, Captain Sullenberger remained calm as he assessed the options and decided to attempt an emergency water landing on the Hudson River. As a result, all 155 passengers and crew members survived the incident. Flight attendant Doreen Welsh later recounted in an interview with CBS News how Captain Sullenberger's calmness helped keep the crew focused and in control during the emergency landing. She said, "He was extremely calm the whole time, and that just set the tone for all of us." Passenger Dave Sanderson described Sullenberger's demeanor during an interview with ABC News: "He was so calm when he talked to us. He said, 'brace for impact,' and when he said it, I knew we were going down, but I knew we would be okay. I just knew that in my heart because of how he said it."

Captain Sullenberger's ability to maintain his composure during a high-pressure situation played a crucial role in the successful outcome of the emergency landing. His body composure and communication reassured those on board and allowed him to execute the difficult maneuver with precision.

There are countless examples of leaders making a difference by radiating calm and control in times of immense pressure. One of the things credited to John F. Kennedy during the Cuban Missile Crisis in 1962 was his composure during one of the hottest moments of geopolitical tension. His body language and confident tone resonated with the American people and the international community, instilling a sense of reassurance. The press widely recognized President Kennedy's composure, and it played a crucial role in projecting the image of a steadfast leader capable of navigating the world through a difficult situation.

Composure, in terms of physical aspects, refers to how an individual carries themselves with poise, steadiness, and self-assurance, particularly during challenging or stressful situations. A composed person maintains a calm and neutral facial expression, avoiding frowning or other signs of emotional distress. They speak clearly and steadily without raising their voices or displaying signs of agitation. When walking or moving, a composed individual exhibits a deliberate and steady pace, demonstrating control and confidence in their movements. Their hand gestures are controlled and do not convey nervousness, such as fidgeting or rapid movements. Composed individuals also keep their shoulders relaxed and slightly back, maintain an upright posture, and stand with their feet shoulder-width apart, distributing their weight evenly. Their eye movements are steady and purposeful, avoiding darting glances or excessive blinking. These physical attributes, when combined, create an overall impression of composure that can positively impact one's emotional state and influence the perceptions of others.

It sounds like trickery, but how you compose yourself influences how you feel. When discussing happiness, we think of the mental state as something metaphysical. But as we saw, your emotions result from physical and biochemical processes. It is the release of neurotransmitters that gives you joy. Without the chemical compound, you feel nothing. Whether due to dysfunction, illness, or hedonic adaption, your enjoyment suffers if you cannot stimulate the right neural pathways. Your physical constitution influences the secretion of these hormones just as much as external stimuli or internal deliberation. We will discuss the essential mindsets you need to adopt to avoid negative and promote positive emotions. But before you start there, you must ensure your physiology supports you.

Many experiments have shown that if your body is calm, you will feel that way. Conversely, if your body is tense and dominated by the sympathetic nervous system, you will feel that way, too. Your starting point is to be healthy. I believe there is a sequential necessity for the order of Health, Happiness, and Wealth. Everything starts with health. Not to say, you cannot experience happiness without full health — quite the opposite. My entire framework is built on reframing your limiting beliefs, and you can be calm and free from regret even with a terminal illness.

Wealth, on the other hand, is a multiplier. Beyond a nominal amount that secures a dignified existence, it is not the prerequisite for health or happiness. I see it as a range expander. It provides access, optionality, and resources. But it is neutral. Tanks yield tremendous power, but it makes a difference if Ukraine or Russia use them to attack or defend. The benefits of wealth depend on the intent you use it with. As a multiplier, being wealthy can amplify a miserable life just as much as a happy one. When you are happy on a solid foundation of health, wealth unfolds its full potential. Hence, the sequence of Health, Happiness, and Wealth.

There is a strong link between your physical and mental states. Some medications that are used as muscle relaxants seem also to have antidepressant benefits. Tizanidine (Zanaflex) is primarily used to treat muscle spasms associated with multiple sclerosis and spinal cord injuries. A 2016 study reported that tizanidine helped raise serotonin in animal models. Cyclobenzaprine (Flexeril), another muscle relaxant, is structurally similar to tricyclic antidepressants. While not typically used for depression, cyclobenzaprine may have some secondary antidepressant effects.

The connection between muscle tension and mood is clinically well-established. Chronic muscle tension can contribute to stress and anxiety. Relaxation techniques, such as deep breathing exercises, progressive muscle relaxation, and mindfulness meditation, can help mitigate muscle tension and improve mood. Individuals can reduce stress and anxiety by learning to relax tense muscles and improve their overall mental state consciously. Similar effects have been ascribed to massage therapy.

Studies have found that adopting "power poses," expansive and open postures, can lead to increased feelings of power and higher risk tolerance, while "low-power poses," contractive and closed postures, lead to the opposite effect. A 2012 article, "Increase or decrease depression: How body postures influence your energy level," highlights how body posture can affect energy levels and mood. The authors found that adopting an upright, open posture increased energy and improved mood. A randomized controlled trial showed in 2015 that adopting an upright posture during a stress-inducing task led to lower self-reported stress, better mood, and higher self-esteem compared to slumped postures. This suggests that maintaining an upright posture may positively impact mood and stress levels.

If you want to set yourself up for success, play the part. They say, "Dress for the job you want, not the job you have." It seems to work the same way with happiness. Compose yourself as if you were happy and calm, and your mind will follow. The signaling pathways of emotion seem to work both ways. A positive mood expresses itself in positive body language, while an optimistic body constitution leads to more positive thoughts. We saw a similar effect with the benefits of well-dosed stressors. The physiological effects of a sauna bath mimic the symptoms of exercise (increased sweat, heart rate, etc.), which lead to similar benefits. Mimicking the symptoms of happiness, it seems, helps generate happiness.

Acceptance

Imagine the history of the universe condensed into one calendar year. The Big Bang occurs on January 1st. On February 25th, our galaxy, the Milky Way, forms. Much later, on September 2nd, our planet Earth forms from a gas cloud surrounding the sun, which came to be just two days earlier. Time goes by, and dinosaurs appear on Earth around December 13th. Just 12 days later, on Christmas Day, they become extinct. The first anatomically modern humans (Homo sapiens) emerge on the last day of the year at 11:52 PM, eight minutes before midnight. All of recorded human history (starting around 5,000 years ago) begins December 31st, 11:59 PM, and 47 seconds. So, everything from the Sumerian script onwards happened in the last 13 seconds of the year.

It's humbling to recognize that our individual lives and the entirety of human history comprise a tiny fraction of the cosmic scale. The age and size of the universe are awe-inspiring. Whether you like it or not, everything you want, have, and do is insignificant in the grand scheme. Remember Rule Number 6.

We are imperfect biological machines whose primary purpose is to pass on genetic information. An evolutionary coincidence gave us the brain capacity to imagine and criticize things, so we developed knowledge and technology to enhance our brief lives. But while our cognitive abilities advanced, our biology remained the same. We tripled our life expectancy but added decades of suffering from chronic diseases to many peoples' existence. We increased our standard of living but are putting our entire habitat at risk in the process.

Most of the narratives that hold our societies together are made up. We must collaborate to survive and, therefore, are obsessed with what other people think of us. Realizing our brief lives, we adhere to impossible standards to minimize shame and disappointment. We try to enjoy life but are at the mercy of a paranoid brain that filters and edits our sensory inputs based on primitive heuristics of risk aversion and pattern recognition. We interact with the physical world, but everything we think or remember is a derivative of this solitary and unconscious process. The bottom line: life is tough, and then you die.

The good news is that you alone determine how this makes you feel. Whether you lead a happy or a miserable life depends on your mindset. It is irrational to get upset about things that lie outside your control, and it's unproductive to waste energy on them. Philosophers throughout history have recognized this, and the most pronounced school of acceptance is stoicism. But the underlying notion has been a recurring theme for millennia. Here are ten thinkers spanning more than 2,500 years who have maintained the same thought throughout:

- Laozi (Lao Tzu): 6th century BCE — The founder of Taoism, who encouraged living in harmony with the Tao, or the natural order of the universe, by practicing non-action and accepting the impermanence of life.

- Buddha: c.563-480 BCE — The founder of Buddhism taught that suffering arises from our attachment to transient things and that we can achieve enlightenment through mindfulness.

- Zeno of Citium: c.334-262 BCE — The founder of Stoicism, Zeno, emphasized that true happiness comes from focusing on our own actions and virtues rather than external factors.

- Epictetus: c.50-135 CE — The Stoic philosopher who taught that we can achieve tranquility by focusing on what is within our control — our thoughts, judgments, and actions.

- Seneca the Younger: c.4 BCE-65 CE — A Roman Stoic who argued that our reactions to an event are the sources of our suffering, not the event itself.

- Marcus Aurelius: 121-180 CE — A Stoic philosopher-emperor who believed that inner strength and self-mastery are key to a contented life, regardless of external circumstances.

- William James: 1842-1910 — The American psychologist who suggested that we can actively shape our emotional states by choosing how to interpret and react to events.

- Viktor Frankl: 1905-1997 — The Austrian psychiatrist and Holocaust survivor who proposed that individuals can find meaning and purpose in life by choosing their attitudes and reactions, even in the face of extreme adversity.

- Jon Kabat-Zinn: born 1944 — The founder of Mindfulness-Based Stress Reduction, who teaches that mindfulness practice can help individuals develop an accepting and non-judgmental attitude toward their thoughts and experiences, leading to greater peace of mind.

- Ryan Holiday: born 1987 — A contemporary author and philosopher who popularized Stoic philosophy in modern times, emphasizing the importance of focusing on what is within our control and letting go of what is not.

We have some level of control over our thoughts, judgments, and actions. Everything else is partially or entirely outside our control. The key to a content life is learning to differentiate between these and focusing on improving our inner selves. Where things are only partially in your control, focus on what you can contribute, and don't judge others or the overall outcome. Focus on your contribution and ask yourself whether you did your best. Like Captain Sullenberger, we should cultivate resilience and self-discipline to remain calm in adversity.

It seems obvious, yet very few think that way. Acceptance is the last thing to cross our minds. Incidentally, it is the last of the five stages of grief: denial, anger, bargaining, depression, and finally, acceptance.

We get upset about trivial things, blame others for our misfortunes, and pretend everyone will live forever. To convince ourselves, we apply anti-wrinkle creams or have doctors fill our skin and lips to create the illusion of youth. If this is us grieving our inevitable deaths, we are stuck in the first stage of grief: denial. We call it "anti-aging," but none of the products in this category do anything to decelerate or even reverse aging. The imagined order is in denial. Larger breasts, buttocks, muscles, fuller hair and lips, longer eyelashes, and nails are all illusions to feeling good about us, attracting a mate, or simply avoiding being reminded of our pending demise. To give our fear of death closure, we need to accept it.

Love

Accept, appreciate, celebrate, and even love it! Friedrich Nietzsche, the 19th-century German philosopher, developed the concept of "Amor fati," or the love of one's fate. Amor fati is the attitude of embracing everything that happens in life, including suffering and loss, without resentment or regret. Nietzsche believed that by fully accepting and loving one's fate, one could rise above hardships and embrace life with enthusiasm and joy. He argued that life's inherent suffering should not be seen as an obstacle but as an opportunity for personal growth and self-affirmation. Embracing discomfort, pain, suffering, and loss serves a deeper purpose. It reminds us of what we care about most — what we love. It calibrates our inner compass and briefly switches off the autopilot to help us see and appreciate what is good in our lives.

"You don't know what you've got 'til it's gone," but don't let it get this far. The second half of your life is full of reminders of what you will lose. Physically, the balance point of homeostasis has shifted, and you need to expend more energy to lessen the entropy building up in your cells. Mentally, you still see yourself as the 25-year-old with everything ahead of you. And socially, you are at the center of an intricate network of relationships with your family, friends, work associates, social circles, and communities. Ironically, at the peak of your influence, everything starts unraveling again into nothingness. Just when you think you are indispensable, everything goes downhill. My wife says, "The cemetery is full of irreplaceables." Or so they thought. Everything will end. For everyone you know, there will be the last time you speak to them. For every activity you enjoy, there will be the last time you do it. There will be a last breath and a final heartbeat.

Remind yourself in every encounter you enjoy that this might be the last time. Stoics call it "negative visualization." Take my dog, Lisa. She is the kindest and most reassuring companion I have. When we got her from the shelter, she was about two years old and completely black in her face. Now, going on ten, she is full of white and gray hair, has gained weight, and is much less mobile and energetic. I travel often and usually don't see her four or five days a week. One day, my wife or our housekeeper will call me to say Lisa is dead. If I am lucky, I will be there for her like I was for my last dog Luka who died in my arms at age 14.

I remind myself that today might be the last time I see Lisa. What is the consequence? Do I cancel my trip or start crying? No, I go over to her and show her some love. Give her some attention, play with her, or let her otherwise know that she is an integral part of our family pack. She appreciates the attention, and we are both happy. I probably wouldn't have undertaken the extra effort if it hadn't been for the negative visualization. I cannot prevent that she dies in my absence, but at least our last touchpoint was a happy one for both of us. If it happens, I have no regrets.

You have to learn to say goodbye to everything you love. Your parents, spouse, children, pets, important titles, power and influence, and finally, your life. I recommend you become good at it. The more love you give, the less you have to regret.

Philosopher and author Alain de Botton wrote, "Love is a skill, not just an emotion – and to get good at it, we have to practice. Love is ultimately the art of recognition, attention, and empathy." Sometimes it is not easy to express or even recognize the opportunity for love. Our attention is highly sought after by media and marketing, and we are constantly distracted. We forget to appreciate the ones we care about, all the good things we already have, and the fact that we are alive right now. As part of your daily routine, I suggest adopting the following practices.

Mindfulness

Try being present in the moment without judgment. The past is history, and the future might never happen. The only reality you have is this moment right now. It is where life happens. Everything else is imagined: a curated memory of the past or hopes and fears about what lies ahead.

Observe your thoughts, feelings, and experiences as they arise without getting caught up in them or labeling them as good or bad. Mindfulness is a mental state of calmly acknowledging and accepting one's thoughts, feelings, and bodily sensations without judgment. Rooted in Buddhist meditation practices, mindfulness has been incorporated into various modern applications, such as stress reduction, mental health therapy, and personal development. By being more mindful, you can develop a heightened sense of self-awareness, emotional regulation, and mental clarity, ultimately fostering a more balanced and fulfilling life.

Gratefulness

As you become more mindful, start noticing and appreciating the positive aspects of your life, even in challenging situations. Cultivating gratitude can help you maintain a positive outlook and shift your attention away from negative thoughts or emotions.

Because of hedonic adaptation, we take the things and people we have for granted. Those were the things and people you once desired and thought would fulfill you completely.

Don't compare yourself to others. It is the primary source of unhappiness. Someone will always be more prosperous, better looking, and more successful than you. The truth is that no one has an easy life. You just don't see the underlying baggage of problems, obligations, discontent, and other realities that would make you think twice about switching places with that person. Just don't get into it. Don't compare yourself ever. Just be happy and appreciate everything you have. This doesn't mean you shouldn't strive for a better life and value nice things. By all means, go as far as you can if it fulfills you. Just don't make your happiness contingent on something or someone you must have. Once you have it, you will likely lose interest anyway, so be happy with what you have and treat everything else as a bonus.

Open-mindedness

While practicing mindfulness and gratefulness, remain open to new ideas, perspectives, and experiences. Not everything will be positive or make you happy. There will be situations that simply suck. But even those challenging encounters never are 100 percent negative. Most situations and people are a mix of positive and negative elements and can be viewed from several angles. Your ability to reframe the situation and see the good in a person or circumstance will help you lift your spirits and maybe even drive a better outcome.

Loving yourself, what you have right now, and the people around you will make you happier. Love is a multifaceted emotion. Expressing it positively impacts your external relationships and stimulates your brain chemistry, leading to improved psychological and physical health. Implicitly, you are undergoing a cognitive reappraisal, meaning that expressing love encourages you to focus on the positive aspects of your life. It shifts attention away from negative experiences and emotions, lowering stress and fear.

Motivation

With proper composure, deep acceptance of life as it is, and love for who and what you have, you will significantly increase your chances of being satisfied with the moment. You will minimize regret and achieve a state of calm. You will seed kind deeds and moments of joy that others will reciprocate. You will release tension in your body and help achieve mental, physiological, and cellular homeostasis.

But happiness is not just about the moment or the sum of moments. It is not merely a surplus of happy versus unhappy or a positive net balance throughout your life. At any moment, you want to be able to step back, see your life in its entirety and value it as meaningful and worthwhile, especially in challenging moments.

Every individual inherently seeks meaning in their life. A sense of purpose drives our actions and is a cornerstone of our emotional well-being. Without a mission and a clear sense of purpose, we risk feeling lost and unfulfilled, which may lead to dissatisfaction or an existential crisis. Defining our purpose in life helps to ground us. It provides direction that guides our thoughts, decisions, and actions. It enables us to navigate the complexities of life and find meaning even in the face of adversity.

Purpose is often misunderstood and confused with passion or other motivational drivers. Purpose refers to an overarching reason that drives our actions. It is our quest, the noble cause we are pursuing. Your purpose in life is outward-facing and not egoistic, while passion can be. Our passions are plentiful and represent strong emotional investments in specific interests or activities. A passion is something that gives you much joy. A purpose can be fueled by passion, but purpose is a broader, ulterior, more encompassing concept. Having a purpose as your underlying motivational driver makes you feel connected to something larger than yourself.

The question is how to motivate yourself if everything is inherently meaningless. Why should we care about anything, let alone pursue altruistic goals? The practical answer is that it is a proven way to increase the neurotransmitters that drive life satisfaction and happiness. Many studies have confirmed this, like the Harvard Study on Happiness I mentioned. Since we ultimately need to re-engineer the biochemical system in our brain to be happy, we shouldn't leave out this proven lever.

Ethically, it is also the right thing to do. It might not serve any actual purpose on the cosmic scale, but it will nevertheless improve other peoples' lives and the overall human condition. I admit there is a cognitive dissonance to resolve here. On the one hand, we know that our existence has no deeper purpose. On the other hand, we need motivation to connect to something that transcends us. One of my mentors once told me, "Despite all technology, human desire has broadly stayed the same over time. All we ever want is to love and be loved. We want our lives to have meaning and contribute to something larger than ourselves. And we want the hope that tomorrow will somehow be better than today."

Whether you act practically or ethically, you need to delude yourself that what you pursue truly matters. Remember, it's all imagined, so imagine something that works for you and convince yourself of it. By choosing to believe in a purpose, we can overcome feelings of insignificance and find the motivation to engage with life. There is no alternative. Without self-delusion, no purpose, and without purpose, no motivation. Without motivation, no happiness. Without happiness, mental entropy and death.

In the 2014 study, "Purpose in Life as a Predictor of Mortality Across Adulthood," researchers Hill and Turiano found that individuals with a stronger sense of purpose had a significantly reduced mortality risk. They analyzed the standardized measures of purpose in life from questionnaires of more than 6,000 participants in the Midlife in the United States study. After controlling for several factors, including age, sex, race, education, and emotional well-being, they found that for every one-point increase in the purpose in life score, the risk of mortality was reduced by 15 percent.

The secret to happiness is being **CALM** by leading a life of Composure, Acceptance, Love, and Motivation. If happiness is simply the equation of your reality against your expectations, then composure sets the scene. It helps improve your reality and ensures the best physical conditions for experiencing the positive neurochemistry your brain has to offer.

Acceptance, love, and a deeper motivation all help avoid unreasonable and toxic expectations that pull you down. They lower pointless frustration over things outside your control and lessen your desire for shallow sources of joy like material possessions, imagined standards, and other worldly idols. They help you focus your energy outwardly and increase your community's Gross National Happiness, a currency that benefits more than one person at a time.

It is not the man who has too little, but the man who craves more that is poor. What does it matter how much a man has laid up in his safe or in his warehouse, how large are his flocks, and how fat his dividends, if he covets his neighbor's property and reckons, not his past gains, but his hopes of gains to come? Do you ask what is the proper limit to wealth? It is, first, to have what is necessary and, second, to have what is enough.

—Seneca, Letters from a Stoic

WEALTH

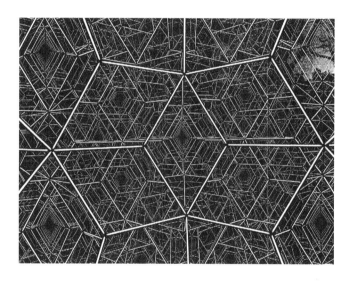

Seek wealth, not money or status. Wealth is having assets that earn while you sleep. Money is how we transfer time and wealth. Status is your place in the social hierarchy.

— Naval Ravikant

MacKenzie Tuttle grew up in San Francisco, California. Her parents, a financial planner and a homemaker, were not considered wealthy but enabled a comfortable life for MacKenzie, who attended a private boarding school in Connecticut and later graduated from Princeton University with a degree in English in 1992. She met her husband as a research associate at the hedge fund D.E. Shaw in New York City. Their desks were side by side, and after a few months of working together, they started dating. She later said that he had a contagious laugh. Just three months later, they got married. When the couple divorced 25 years later in January 2019, as part of the settlement, MacKenzie received company shares valued at US$ 35.6 billion.

MacKenzie Bezos, or MacKenzie Scott as she called herself after the divorce, became the third-wealthiest woman and the 22nd-richest person on the planet. She had helped her husband, Jeff, build Amazon.com from the ground up and received a quarter of the couple's Amazon shares as a divorce settlement amounting to a 4 percent stake in the company. During the Covid-19 pandemic, Amazon's stock price continued to rise, so by September 2020, her net worth was estimated at US$ 62 billion, making her the world's richest woman, according to Forbes.

What did she do with all this wealth? Did she try to conquer space and build rockets like her ex-husband? Did she create a foundation tightly controlled by herself to eradicate diseases and fight climate change like Bill and Melinda Gates? Or did she start a company trying to increase human lifespan like Google founders Larry Page and Sergey Brin?

MacKenzie Scott pledged to give most of it away. In July 2020, she announced she had donated US$ 1.7 billion to 116 non-profit organizations, focusing on various causes such as racial equality, LGBTQ+ rights, climate change, public health, and education. In December 2020, she revealed that she had given away an additional US$ 4.2 billion to 384 organizations, including food banks, emergency relief funds, and support services for vulnerable communities. By June 2021, she had donated another US$ 2.7 billion to 286 organizations with diverse causes, including higher education, arts and culture, and social justice. By December 2022, less than four years after her divorce, Scott had given away a total of US$ 14 billion to over 1,600 charitable organizations. That's roughly US$ 10 million every day for four years straight.

In the film "Brewster's Millions," the main character has to spend US$ 30 million in 30 days in order to inherit a much larger fortune later. The premise of the movie is that it is hard to burn through that much money. MacKenzie made it look easy. The New York Times noted that "Ms. Scott has turned traditional philanthropy on its head... by disbursing her money quickly and without much hoopla, Ms. Scott has pushed the focus away from the giver, and onto the nonprofits, she is trying to help."

What would you do with this kind of wealth? Not that you would likely end up in a similar situation. According to the Forbes ranking, there are only 2,640 billionaires as of 2023. Of these, 186 have a fortune of over 10 billion, and only six people currently net more than US$ 100 billion — that we know of. These are Bernat Arnaut, Elon Musk, Jeff Bezos, Larry Elison, Warren Buffet, and Bill Gates.

Even in affluent countries, people own about one million times less on average. According to the Federal Reserve, the median household net worth in the United States was around US$ 121,700 in 2019. In the Euro area, the corresponding value was around €104,100 or US$ 124,000 at the time, according to Eurostat. With a net worth of more than US$ 125k, you can consider yourself in the top half of the wealthiest countries in the world.

Does that seem wealthy? At which point would you consider yourself rich? If you landed in the top ten percent of your country? In the top one percent? No universally accepted definition of wealth exists, so let's imagine one together.

Wealth has two attributes; it is a means to an end and, as such, relative to that end. On its own, wealth does nothing. It is neutral until you use it for something. To unfold value, you need to be able to access and exchange it for money or something else. Take the example of Stefan Thomas, a German programmer living in San Francisco. He had invested in cryptocurrency early and accumulated 7,002 bitcoin. In 2021, this amounted to US$ 220 million. However, he couldn't access any of it because he forgot the password to his digital wallet. The IronKey hardware wallet allows ten attempts to enter the correct password before permanently encrypting its contents. He had used up eight attempts without success and then gave up. In an interview with The New York Times, Stefan eventually exercised acceptance and said he was "at peace" with the situation. Without the password, his fortune was worth the price of a used hard drive.

Access is necessary but also sufficient for wealth to be meaningful. You don't need to spend any of it. Wealth primarily increases optionality. The more wealth you have access to, the more options you have to wear different clothes, try various foods, visit other countries, live in other countries, work in different jobs, create enterprises, not work at all, or give it away like MacKenzie Scott. When you exercise one of these options, you trade option value for financial value. As a result, your wealth diminishes slightly. With less wealth, your set of remaining choices narrows. Without wealth, you might not be able to afford a good education or live in your preferred location. You will likely be more limited in the kind of experiences you can have. As a general rule, one can say: More wealth, more options. As long as you choose wisely, of course. Flaunting your wealth publicly or acquiring many high-maintenance possessions will limit you in other ways.

Secondly, wealth is a relative measure. Its significance can only be assessed compared to the cost of the options you consider worthwhile. If your dream is to enable human colonization of Mars, your "number" will be different than for someone who just wants to live a healthy, safe, and accommodating life. If you want to leave your children a substantial inheritance, your required wealth will be higher than if you are comfortable with "dying with zero."

If you remember, happiness also is a relative measure of your perceived reality against your expectations. We explored how you can reframe your expectations and, to a certain degree, how to improve your perception of reality. Wealth feeds into this equation as it objectively impacts your reality. Or, more precisely: wealth gives you more options to boost or reset your reality. Wealth can increase your degree of control to be slightly less at the mercy of external factors. I say "slightly" because the fundamental factors influencing our lives cannot, so far, be changed by any amount of wealth, like your biology or the laws of nature. But wealth allows you to upgrade your comfort level and alter your direction of travel.

Wealth, therefore, can be seen as an enabler of happiness despite the adage that "Money can't buy happiness." Both statements are true. Money, on its own, is neutral. However, if it helps you shape a reality that fulfills your expectations, you have a good chance of being happy. And your expectations can actually be quantified.

Their financial manifestation is your burn rate. You require more or fewer resources depending on what and how much you want. Suppose your goal is to enjoy strong personal relationships, good health, and an engaging life of personal growth and learning. Your targeted burn rate will be different than if you desire a garage full of luxury cars, a private jet, and several estates to alternate between.

Whichever version excites you, this chapter is just about the resulting number and the mechanics of getting there. Whether you define your burn rate by what genuinely makes you happy or things that just lead to hedonic adaptation makes no difference to me. To you, however, it might. Living on the hedonic treadmill will perpetually increase your burn rate, so you might have a lot of money but never reach the kind of freedom wealth can provide. Wealth becomes a moving target. Not because it is illusive or unattainable. Because you are sabotaging yourself by chasing things that cannot satisfy you.

Let's focus on the number — your unconstrained burn rate. Many individuals desire more than their current means allow. To determine the total cost of your (reasonable and unreasonable) expectations and obligations annually, you must calculate your unconstrained annual burn rate. Your quality of wealth is determined by your ability to cover that spending rate multiple times over. You will enjoy a sense of independence if you can sustain your expected lifestyle for several years without having to rely on generating additional income. This means you can afford periods without employment due to illness or choice.

When your net worth exceeds the sum of your remaining expenses for the rest of your life, you have achieved absolute independence. This represents freedom. You can choose to work because you want to, not because you must. You will perform better without the pressure or fear of losing your job. You will also be more willing to take risks and do the right thing as you are not dependent on your employment income. Nevertheless, unforeseeable events may still change the situation.

Let's break it down practically. Assume your unconstrained burn rate is €250k net per year. Your monthly cost of living in comfort for you and your family amounts to €10k a month, and you would like to budget €30k a year for extraordinary purchases, €50k for travel, and €50k for anything unforeseen. When your net worth (excluding your primary residence) reaches €1 million, you can sustain your burn rate for four years. This is a good cushion but doesn't make you truly independent. If you plan to retire at 65 and hope to live to 85 or longer, you will have to cover at least 20 additional years if you don't have a substantial pension plan. In this example, we assume that inflation is compensated by your assets' internal rate of return (IRR).

At ten million euros, things look differently. You would be able to cover 40 years of your targeted burn rate. If you are 47 like me, this amount would make you independent.

This is "the number" that rich folk sometimes talk about. It is calculated as your unconstrained burn rate multiplied by your expected remaining lifetime in years. In a well-known 2010 study by Daniel Kahneman and Angus Deaton, the annual burn rate found to maximize happiness was about US$ 75,000 (in 2010 US dollars). Based on data from over 450,000 US residents, they established that further increases in income did not significantly impact people's emotional well-being. It is plausible that people can satisfy most of their needs with this amount and, therefore, broadly feel satisfied. But current household income is a constrained metric and only represents people's current reality.

It's common that "the number" tends to increase as you approach it. If US$ 75,000 annually is sufficient for happiness and you had 40 more years to live, a net worth of US$ 3 million could cover you for the rest of your life. However, if you were to win that sum in the lottery today, it's unlikely that you would be satisfied. Most people tend to adjust their expectations upward after such a windfall. They tend to increase their spending limit and thus lose the optionality and freedom that their wealth represents.

People increase their burn rates willingly or unwittingly. For one, by hedonic adaptation. Things you previously considered luxury or discretionary have become part of your baseline. Inexpensive wine you once enjoyed is now "undrinkable," and a certain level of comfort in travel and lodging has become hard to back away from. Your taste has become more refined, and the level of service and quality you expect has increased. This locks you into higher spending rates for most goods and services. Just the fact that you can afford better choices will push up expenses. It did for me, I can assure you.

Some purchases can lock you into much higher burn rates just by the nature of the asset. Houses, cars, watches, and even art need to be maintained, stored, insured, protected, and so on. Some people dream of owning a yacht, as it is universally seen as a symbol of affluence. The superyachts of oligarchs and tech billionaires have positioned these large vessels as something desirable. But, as a rule of thumb, you can expect 10 percent of the purchase price in annual maintenance costs for the crew, insurance, repairs, docking fees, and fuel expenses. To put this in perspective, if you bought a yacht for US$ 10 million, you must set aside a million annually to operate it. Just moving the boat a couple of hundred nautical miles from port to port can cost you thousands. If you can afford it, and this is your passion, enjoy it. Just recognize that it increases dependence.

While happiness is your perceived reality against your expectations, **wealth is your net worth against the unconstrained burn rate of your remaining life**. It's the same concept, really. While happiness makes you calm and at peace, wealth offers increasing degrees of freedom. From expanding optionality to complete independence, wealth is an enabler, multiplier, and enhancer. You don't need it to lead a fulfilling life full of health and happiness, but it certainly makes things easier if you understand how to generate and maintain it.

Frame

Societal conditioning makes you believe that acquiring more money, possessions, or status will inherently make you happy. On the contrary, the pursuit of wealth itself can become a source of misery if you let your personal relationships or physical and mental health suffer. Building wealth demands sacrifice in the form of time or resources you need to divert from other priorities. It, therefore, needs to be seen in balance with your health and happiness.

Envy

Wealth is essentially about independence. However, for most, it is primarily about status and recognition by others. In a capitalist and meritocratic society, displaying your wealth signals your accomplishments and worth as a person, which in return rewards you with a status score. If you tick the designated boxes of power and success, others will treat you with respect and admiration.

Status is inherently defined by a ranking order and social hierarchy. It involves determining who is number one, number two, and so on, and the privileges that come with each position. This frequently occurs in nature. Dogs, for instance, have a strong urge to establish their place in the pack. We tried to take status out of the equation for our two dogs by having one dog "report" to my wife and the other to me. While we are the boss and number one for both, each dog has an equal second-in-command position, just each with a different boss. This arrangement has been successful as they do not fight over food, territory, or toys and tend to ignore each other. Why bother if you are not competing for status? It's all imagined, even for dogs.

Focusing on status can be detrimental as it involves competition and is ultimately a zero-sum game. To attain the desired position, you must displace the current occupant or prevent others from taking it. Wealth, on the other hand, is a positive-sum game and can grow for everyone. Pursuing status always pits you against others and constantly reminds you of those ahead. But you can never win the game, as someone will always be above you, regardless of your role and position. This can lead to envy, causing feelings of inferiority, jealousy, and bitterness.

Many people strive for wealth and fame to elevate their social standing. In a study titled "The Correlation of Wealth Across Generations," Kerwin Kofi Charles and Erik Hurst analyzed data from the Panel Study of Income Dynamics between 1968 and 1999 to examine consumption behavior in relation to wealth. Their findings revealed that when a person's neighbors experienced a 10 percent increase in income, the individual's consumption of visible goods, such as cars or home improvements, increased by 2.4 percent. This trend is known as the "Keeping up with the Joneses" phenomenon. Economist Thorstein Veblen coined "conspicuous consumption" to describe purchasing and showcasing luxury goods or engaging in expensive activities to signal social status. This behavior prioritizes the display of wealth over the actual benefits of having money. It can create an unhealthy fixation on attaining the "best" as defined by others, ultimately resulting in overspending.

Myopia

Even when building wealth for productive reasons, many suffer from myopia. Also known as short-sightedness, myopia is an eye condition in which a person can see nearby objects clearly but has difficulty seeing ones far away. This, conceptually, is how they approach making money. They manage the short-term but do not know how to compound wealth to sustain 40-60 years of remaining runway. They exchange their time for money linearly and constantly erase any earning surplus by increasing their spending.

Understanding exponential growth and compounding is challenging because our brains are naturally wired to think in linear terms. In daily life, we generally encounter situations where change occurs in a linear or proportional manner, making it easier to comprehend and predict. Our intuitive understanding of constant change or increments in linear growth contrasts with the less intuitive nature of exponential growth, which involves multiplying a quantity by a fixed factor over time. Cognitive biases like the "anchoring effect" cause us to underestimate future growth as we base our expectations on initial linear patterns.

Imagine you are a competent and successful personal trainer. From the outset, the wealth you can create is capped by your available time. Whichever rate you charge, there is a limit to the number of clients you can serve every day. Your income does not scale. Also, you might get ill or want to take a holiday occasionally. You can start a franchise and benefit from other trainers working under your brand for a commission. However, any progression remains linear, albeit on a higher level.

Furthermore, people spend what they earn. Eager to climb the social ladder and satisfy imaginary needs that consumerism has defined for them, they take any increase in their income as a windfall to enjoy immediately. Few think long-term and start investing early. The nature of exponential growth has one powerful component: time. Even modest investments can lead to substantial amounts over longer periods. The sacrifice to regularly put aside a couple of hundred euros at the beginning of your career can cover years, maybe even decades, of your burn rate later in life.

As an aside: your house is not an asset you can consume unless you are willing to downsize and monetize the difference in value. When tallying up your net worth, do not include your primary residence if you own it. You need to live somewhere, whether you own or rent, so your home is an expense. The financial benefit of owning the house you live in is monetizing a potential value increase if you intend to sell it later. However, you also incur the opportunity cost of tying up capital you cannot invest elsewhere.

Greed

Once you reach middle age and start generating a meaningful surplus of cash, your burn rate usually starts increasing. In physics, Boyle's Law states that, at a constant temperature, the pressure of a gas is inversely proportional to its volume. In simpler terms, when a gas can expand into an available space, it will spread out uniformly, filling the entire volume. This is precisely what happens with your spending. But why?

We cannot get enough; the more we have, the more we want. Instead of aiming to reach the saturation point of independence, we continue adjusting our burn rates upward into the void of "available space." Doing so increases the number of obligations and amount of debt. This prevents us from reaching absolute wealth, freedom, and peace of mind, even if we earn a top income. A 2019 study conducted at the University of Queensland confirmed this. The researchers analyzed large-scale global survey data covering 150,000 participants from 78 countries. They found that it typically is the upper class who yearn for even more wealth and status. They labeled this phenomenon "have more, want more."

Hedonic adaptation, the piling up of additional obligations, and the dopamine-induced feedback loop rewarding status and fame all lead to the need for more money. The balance between greed and fear tips toward the former, and you keep gathering stuff. You miss the point of consuming them and drawing down on your wealth. You continue sacrificing time and energy to build something you won't be able to enjoy later.

Reframe

Instead of offering any investment advice, I will provide you with mental models that assist you in selecting the tactics that work best for you. You must determine your risk appetite, priorities, and time horizon for any concrete investment opportunity. There isn't an instruction manual for becoming wealthy. Ultimately, it comes down to mindset. Wealth is about how you show up every day. If you lose everything, which can happen, you need to start over. So, don't get too attached to any of it. Beyond a nominal amount that meets most of your needs, everything else merely provides additional options and is, therefore, optional. Don't allow money to restrict you; it's supposed to make you free, not hold you back.

Avoid comparing yourself to others. We are social creatures, and other people are a source of joy and happiness. However, let each person be themselves, and don't try to imitate their lives. Admire them for who they are and what they have achieved and try to learn from them. But comparing yourself to others only leads to unhappiness and makes you squander your wealth on vanities.

The crucial mindsets to becoming wealthy are.

- **Force** — Be willing to take action; you need to want it.
- **Reserve** — Stay humble and clean; your most valuable asset is your reputation.
- **Equity** — Seek leverage and compounding growth, don't settle for linearity.
- **Evolution** — Cultivate a growth mindset, get better every day.

Force

According to Isaac Newton's first law of motion, objects at rest will remain at rest, and objects in motion will continue moving at the same speed and direction unless a force is applied. In chemistry, activation energy is required for molecules to react with one another. Movement is essential for molecules to break apart and create new ones, and temperature plays a key role in increasing movement within a chemical system.

We all know the person who pontificates all day about how things ought to be. They have all the answers and feel confident to judge everything and everyone. They theorize but don't change anything in the real world. They don't apply force to reality and therefore remain in a state of inertia. You cannot conjure up wealth by pontification and theorizing. You need to do something. You need to act.

The force you apply needs to be directed towards something. In physics, force is a vector quantity, which means it has both magnitude and direction. A force acting on an object will cause the object to accelerate in the direction of the force. Equally, you need to act with intent. If you are not fully committed to getting rich, it will not happen. If you think being rich is evil or that you do not deserve it, you will sabotage yourself. You must want it and exhibit the ambition to get there. I never doubted that I would become wealthy. I am not afraid to lose my job or set myself tough targets, even if I am not sure how I will reach them exactly. Setting the bar high will force me out of my comfort zone and make me learn and adapt to a higher level of performance. Even if I don't make it all the way, I will get further than if I had set out with a more modest ambition or remained inactive.

Once clear about your direction, apply force. Prioritize impact and focus on positive changes in the real world. Make yourself heard and seen. Take a risk. Invest the money you don't need at the moment. Make choices. And don't worry about conforming to the standards of the imagined order. They say, "Conformity keeps you your job; non-conformity gets you promoted."

Smooth talkers can get very far. They usually stay in consulting or venture into other professional services like legal, accounting, or financial services. But they eventually get found out if they don't manage to accomplish anything beyond being intellectual. Keep a distance from them. They don't have skin in the game. They are full of unsolicited advice and thoughtful questions but assume no accountability for an outcome.

Think of the warm, satisfying feeling of actually having done something. Have you ever mowed the lawn and paused to admire your work? It's cutting the grass, not brain surgery. But still, you did it and created a result in the physical world that is a testimony to your efforts.

Remember, it's all imagined. Not everything you undertake will be successful. But you are an actor on the stage of your life. You play the main part while everyone else is a supporting character. Your thoughts, feelings, memories, and dreams are all in your head alone. Only you know the script of your play, and you control the narrative.

In everything that happens, people obsess about "the reason." They look at financial tables, human behavior, stock market movements, and geopolitical events and try to rationalize what they see into simple narratives of cause and effect. People inherently fear the world's erratic, chaotic, and random nature. The daily movement of a stock price is just white noise. It results from millions of individual decisions, but people long for "the reason" it developed the way it did. Give people what they want, a plausible rationalization. On top of being a maker and shaper, you will seem wise and competent.

Reserve

But don't deceive anyone. When applying force, make it a force for good. While striving for success, maintain a sense of humility and reserve. When exercising power or influence, ensure that it is used for the betterment of others and just causes. Integrity, honor, and reliability are fragile qualities, much like sandcastles – they require significant effort to build but can easily be destroyed with a single misstep.

Your reputation is critical when collaborating with others. Losing money can be a temporary setback, but losing your reputation can have long-lasting consequences. Avoid engaging in illegal activities and pay close attention to seemingly insignificant indiscretions. Hold yourself to the highest ethical standards. Be careful when expensing travel and other costs to your company and maintain a strict separation between your professional and personal lives. Refrain from using company resources for personal gain and avoid accepting extravagant invitations from advisors or suppliers, even if your company policy permits it. Always be honest and transparent in your dealings, and never engage in tax evasion or other fraudulent activities, regardless of the amount involved.

All of this sounds obvious, but as you accumulate wealth, you must be increasingly mindful of minor transgressions that might tarnish your reputation. Wealth leads to envy and increased scrutiny by others. Once in the public eye, people may dig into your past and search for any missteps, even those long forgotten. To protect your reputation, it is crucial to avoid giving anyone a reason to doubt your integrity.

And remember Rule Number 6: Don't take yourself so g—damn seriously! Exercise reserve. Embrace humility, inner distance, and non-attachment. Avoid comparing yourself to others or adjusting your lifestyle based on status. Keep your ego in check and recognize that your success may not solely be the result of your intelligence or hard work — luck also plays a role. Enjoy life to the fullest but prioritize what makes you happy. Avoid vanities that lock you into higher burn rates without providing any emotional benefit.

I call this the "runaway" lifestyle. People make the mistake of treating every additional dollar as an opportunity to reward themselves. Myopia. Instead, exercise delayed gratification and trade that money for equity that will work for you in the long run. Treat everything beyond what you genuinely enjoy as leverage to invest. And prepare yourself mentally for the possibility of losing it all and periodically practice living with less. Seneca advised, "A wise man never reflects so much upon poverty as when he abides amid riches."

Remember that wealth can undermine your character and ability to enjoy life. Guard yourself against the pitfalls of hubris and the belief that you have "been there, done that." This false sense of confidence can be dangerous. When people lose curiosity, they risk stagnation and make poor decisions based on overconfidence. That is when people start speculating. They predict the outcomes of fundamentally arbitrary games. Never assume you know the future, no matter how much success you have enjoyed until now. Don't become arrogant and overconfident. Approach each decision with reserve.

Ultimately, wealth is your net worth against your remaining burn rates. It is easier to reduce your expenses than increase your income. Keep the mental reserve capacity to downscale if necessary. It will make you appreciate what you have and minimize hedonic adaptation. It will also make you a better, more grounded person.

Equity

Force and reserve are essential qualities to succeed in any job you are qualified for. However, it takes time to generate wealth if you rely on cash compensation only. You can get there in some highly paid executive positions, but those are rare and often turnover quickly. For everyone else, it takes decades to become wealthy.

The problem lies in the bifurcated distribution of the two currencies that matter most: time and money. When you are young, you typically have plenty of time ahead of you but little money. Your starting salary is low because you don't have seniority. Your need for wealth is high because all major expenses lie ahead. You might even begin with significant debt from your student loan. Indeed, money is a priority at that point, and you are willing to sacrifice your time to earn it. However, the older and more financially secure you become, the more you value time over money.

From Kahneman, we learned that the most significant increases in life satisfaction derive from moving your wealth from zero to a high five-figure amount. Everything beyond that creates additional options with diminishing returns. You can only eat one steak at a time. At the beginning of your professional career, you want to start a family, have a home of your own, and live a life full of rich experiences while you are young and fit, so you prioritize money. This relation flips over time. Your remaining time becomes more precious as you age, and your need for additional money decreases. You have already built a foundation of wealth, and if you avoid the runaway lifestyle and have some equity, you might get close to your saturation point. Many people maximize their wealth at the point of retirement, often with limited remaining time or health to enjoy it. What is the point of dying rich? According to a German proverb, "The last shirt has no pockets," meaning you cannot take any of it with you. Don't miss the point to start consuming your assets.

The salary-based remuneration system is back-loaded for a reason. Society wants to keep you on the hook until the very end. If people reached financial freedom earlier, many would drop out of the workforce — at least for some time. It is a dependency trap that works exceptionally well for those who live runaway lifestyles. They hope their increasing salaries will someday set them free, but they never get there. According to a 2022 survey, 42 percent of Americans saved less than US$ 10,000 for retirement. The life they hope for in their "golden years" will likely be met by the harsh reality of continued hard work.

We must find a way to pull the moment of financial independence forward. Not necessarily to stop working. There is nothing wrong with work if you have a deep affection for your profession. I will never just lie in a hammock all day. I will try to improve myself, generate impact, and have fun as long as I can. But I want to do so independently, not because I am sitting in the golden cage of my obligations, clinging to my job, prioritizing my work over everything else, because I have to.

To pull the moment of freedom forward, you must set aside some of your income early on and invest in equity. Working for money is constrained by you and your time. Your money needs to work for you on its own. This creates leverage. Limit your expenses to set aside resources for investments. No matter how modest these returns might seem initially, reinvesting your gains will significantly short-cut the time required to build wealth. The concept behind this is, of course, compounding.

Albert Einstein is attributed to saying, "Compound interest is the eighth wonder of the world. He who understands it earns it; he who doesn't pays it." It is indeed a challenging concept to grasp for our linear brains.

A simple example of compounding growth is the paper folding challenge. Imagine you had a large piece of paper that you could fold as many times as you like. In reality, you can only fold paper about seven times before you run out of surface area. If you fold a standard sheet of paper (0.1 millimeters thick) in half, its thickness doubles. With each subsequent fold, the thickness continues to double. After ten folds, the paper would be 10.2 centimeters thick ($0.1 \text{ mm} \times 2^{10}$). If you could fold the sheet 50 times, it would reach an astounding thickness of approximately 112.6 million kilometers ($0.1 \text{ mm} \times 2^{50}$), almost the distance between the Earth and the Sun.

To achieve substantial growth through equity, you need to harness the power of compounding. For instance, you need a compounding annual growth rate (CAGR) of 7.2 percent to double your wealth every ten years. To triple it, you require a CAGR of 11.6 percent. You can figure out your own CAGR by taking three variables: a = starting capital, b = target wealth, and t = time in years to get there. Then apply the formula: $\sqrt[t]{b/a} - 1$ or (b/a)^(1/t)-1 if that is easier on your calculator.

You need a CAGR of just under 15 percent to double your money every five years. Private equity investments historically have yielded an average net internal rate of return (IRR) of around 15 percent. In this context, IRR and CAGR are basically the same. Investing into stock market index funds has yielded an average of about 10 percent annually in the long run. The Standard & Poor's 500 (S&P 500) is an index of the leading publicly traded companies in the US. The average annualized return since adopting 500 stocks into the index in 1957 through the end of 2022 is 10.2 percent. The MSCI World Index is a broad global equity index representing large and mid-cap equity performance across 23 developed markets and yielded an average annual return of 10.8 percent between December 1978 and March 2023. A 10 percent return will double your money every 7.3 years.

Note that investing is distinct from trading. When trading, you try to predict the markets based on some differential insight or knowledge you might have. While investments can yield significant gains short-term, they usually are about the fundamental long-term value of the assets. Expect invested money to be tied up for at least five to ten years. When investing in public markets, they say, "Time in the market is more important than timing the market."

These principles of equity apply to all kinds of investments, also non-financial. The way you build your judgment through experience and your relationships through trust follow the same compounding growth curves as building your wealth through equity. While returns are modest initially, over time, they grow exponentially and reach surprising amounts. But you need to give it time (hence start early) and need to roll-over your proceeds (thus don't let your lifestyle run away).

There is one shortcut you can apply, albeit carefully. Leverage. Force or activation energy is a necessary condition for creating wealth. But just like in a chemical reaction, there are catalysts that can speed up a reaction significantly. Typically, catalysts are not consumed by the reaction. They can be removed and used again.

Common leverage typically comes in the form of capital and labor.

It generally makes financial sense if you can borrow money cheaply to invest at a higher return. If your cost of debt is lower than your expected IRR, you will still gain value. However, ensure you can service the cost of debt and safeguard yourself against sudden increases in interest. You don't want to end up in a crunch. If interest rates increase substantially, homeowners with floating mortgage rates may be forced to sell their houses at unfavorable times.

When investing in an asset that generates cash, taking on debt makes particular sense. If you buy an apartment, you can rent it out and use these proceeds to service the debt. The asset basically pays for your debt during the holding period. Again, make sure not to overextend yourself and be able to cover a potential dry period without rental income, just in case. The idea is to become independent, not create more worries and obligations.

Your time is another resource you should think about leveraging. Assess everything you are doing and try to identify non-value-adding activities like maintenance work, admin activities, and other time-consuming chores. It might make more sense to outsource these things. If you can use the freed-up time more productively to earn money, mainly by acquiring and managing equity, then paying someone else to do your chores might be sensible. If you can have your groceries delivered to your house for a small fee, you free up hours of driving and in-store shopping. Embrace technology and digital tools wherever they can save you time, even if you don't use the time you gained for anything in particular. Time is our most valuable resource; every minute you free up gives you options. You decide whether to spend it on health, happiness, or wealth.

Evolution

Remember the Vikings from the second chapter? Without realizing it, they added carbon to the iron they were smelting to create much harder steel. In chemistry, minor variations in the makeup of a material can lead to substantially different properties. Over 5,000 years ago, people discovered that adding about ten percent tin to copper made bronze, a metal alloy much stronger than copper or tin. This was deemed such a significant development that the entire age became known as the Bronze Age.

Biological evolution can work similarly. Changing a single gene of an organism can lead to vastly different characteristics impacting its chances of survival. There is no bias or judgment involved. The concept of "survival of the fittest" is a misnomer. Gene variations are random, and those that get replicated most will prevail for whatever reason. Fitness is irrelevant. It should be called "survival of the most adapted to reproduction."

In evolution, slight variations can lead to unpredictable outcomes. Feedback mechanisms ensure that specific variations are favored. In biology, these mechanisms are reproduction and death. In forging metal alloys, these are trial and error as to the specific properties of the material. In the volatile macroeconomic background of investing, these are curiosity and agility to learn and adapt as you go.

In the three years preceding this book, we went from a global pandemic to a war in Europe with several phases of unprecedented economic developments. From lockdowns that put sectors like travel, leisure, arts, and entertainment out of business, we went to a phase of hypergrowth and stockouts in which the limited availability of critical components like microchips halted entire assembly lines for months. Global supply chains simply broke apart due to social distancing measures and lockdowns.

What nobody anticipated was how long it would take to restart them. With orders for safety stock and pent-up demand piling up in 2021, delivery times went through the roof. Used car prices, for example, shot up as waiting times for new vehicles went from weeks to months. Together with the Russian attack on Ukraine in 2022, this triggered several waves of inflation that impacted raw material prices, logistics costs, energy, and, finally, salaries. Natural gas prices increased by nearly 400 percent when Russia cut supply from its pipelines to Europe. Companies wrestled with liquidity, inventory, worker absenteeism, and passthrough of inflation while still struggling with defaulting suppliers and the unavailability of critical components. Public company valuations took a nosedive when central banks started raising interest rates to curtail household inflation. Companies went out of business, and many lost their investments.

I worked with several companies during these turbulent times. Management teams rose to the challenge and took bold and sometimes tough decisions to safeguard their enterprises. The learning curve had to be steep for all of them, including me. In the short period of ten quarters, we had to let go of several paradigms and truisms of conducting business. Less productive plants with coal-fired boilers in the US suddenly were more competitive than modern facilities burning natural gas in Europe. Commodity parts like simple microprocessors suddenly had to be shipped by air to prevent halting entire plants. And order books went from oversubscribed to virtually empty within months end of 2022 with no visibility on when this would normalize. Not to mention how we all had to learn to recruit and collaborate remotely.

Our environment changed abruptly several times, and those who could not or would not adapt quickly suffered badly. Companies had to evolve, and investors had to anticipate and react to tectonic shifts in underlying drivers. The post-pandemic phase, so far, has been extreme, but it could get even worse if a Chinese-American conflict erupts. The uncomfortable truth is that nothing is safe. People will tell you that gold or government bonds or real estate or something else is the investment that will prevail in any crisis. None of this is true. In today's world, virtually any market can collapse or be severely disrupted. Just think of the latest development in generative AI that suddenly puts creative work like writing, composing, or painting into the realm of automation, something that would have been considered science fiction five years ago.

For many, the current pace of change is overwhelming. People who seek simple answers and are susceptible to conspiracy theories find it hard to accept how nonlinear and chaotic the world really is. Most of our lives have been characterized by perceived stability. This is, of course, nonsense. During my lifetime, the Cold War ended with the collapse of the Soviet Union, and we moved from an analog to a digital to a connected World. We have undergone massive change, but our post-hoc rationalizing brain makes up a linear and logical storyline based on cause and effect.

You can be lucky and pick the right sector at the right time. But if you are not a gambler, you must continuously evolve your understanding of the world and its drivers. You need a growth mindset to recognize your gaps and improvement opportunities. A growth mindset is a belief that one's abilities, talents, and intelligence can be developed and improved through dedication, hard work, and perseverance. Individuals with a growth mindset see challenges as opportunities for growth, embrace learning, take risks, and overcome setbacks. On the other hand, a fixed mindset is the belief that one's abilities, talents, and intelligence are static and cannot be changed. People with a fixed mindset often avoid challenges, fear failure, and may give up easily when faced with obstacles. They believe their success depends on innate abilities rather than effort and growth.

A fitting example of a growth mindset is aviation. Every time an airplane crashes, a detailed investigation is conducted by agencies like the National Transportation Safety Board in the US. Investigation teams are formed with the support of technical advisors from the aircraft and engine manufacturers. The teams collect evidence from the crash site, including aircraft parts and any available flight recorders ("black boxes"). They also gather data on weather conditions, air traffic control records, aircraft maintenance history, crew training, and much more to determine the sequence of events and identify the factors that led to the accident. Their report will typically lead to changes in regulations, aircraft design, and operational procedures to prevent similar accidents in the future. As a result, flying has become very safe, with a hundred times fewer fatalities per billion kilometers traveled than driving.

Hospitals operate very differently. Until recently, the traditional hierarchy in healthcare often discouraged questioning senior doctors. Fatal mistakes in procedures were sometimes viewed as inevitable. This could lead to under-reporting of errors, lack of learning from mistakes, and missed opportunities to prevent future harm. A 2012 report by the US Department of Health and Human Services found that hospitals reported only about 14 percent of the harmful medical errors and near misses that Medicare beneficiaries experienced during hospital stays. Moreover, a landmark report by the Institute of

Medicine in 1999 estimated that between 44,000 and 98,000 people in the US die each year due to preventable medical errors in hospitals, underscoring the magnitude of the problem.

In recent years, efforts have been made to shift this culture towards a more open, learning-oriented approach. One of the principles of a growth mindset is a non-punitive response to errors, which encourages healthcare workers to report and learn from mistakes without fear of punishment. These efforts have been associated with reductions in specific healthcare-associated harm, such as central line-associated bloodstream infections, which decreased by 50 percent in US intensive care units between 2008 and 2014.

An open mindset of learning and continuous improvement is the basis for improvement in all areas of life. Without learning and refining how to interact with and influence others, you will not be effective in building your career. Without learning healthy habits, you will not sustain your body's homeostasis over your lifetime. And without learning to appreciate what you have, you will never be satisfied with your existence. Learning isn't something you can buy or shortcut. Learning takes time and is cumulative — every new insight builds on your existing knowledge and exponentially grows the connections you can make to other domains. Evolution works the same way. Gene variation happens on top of all the adaptation that has already taken place.

What is the implication for wealth? In a volatile environment, past success does not predict future success. Stay curious and open to new input and ideas. All notions of "beating the market" or anticipating the winners are fallacies. Accept that everything you do is an increasingly refined process of trial and error. It started when you put your hand on the hotplate as a child and received the sensory feedback not to do that again. While building your wealth, it will come in the form of massive blunders that cost you a lot of money. Don't judge yourself by the outcome, neither the good nor the bad. When things go well, don't credit yourself too much for the success. When things are under pressure, don't beat yourself up over it. Just keep whatever works and stop doing whatever doesn't.

Lastly, recognize that evolution and adaption are a fundamental part of life. They are not just about advancement but are needed to preserve the status quo. A fixed mindset, by definition, will lead to deterioration. Only by applying the principles that sustained life on this planet for more than 4 billion years will you maintain your current level. There is a fitting concept called the Red Queen Effect, after the Lewis Carroll character from Alice's Adventures in Wonderland. The Red Queen tells Alice, "Now, here, you see, it takes all the running you can do to keep in the same place."

In summary, your primary objective when building wealth is to set you **FREE** by acting with Force, exercising Reserve, focusing on Equity, and embracing Evolution.

In the language of chemistry, you need activation energy (force) in a controlled environment (reserve) with a catalyst (equity) to find new alloys (evolution). Wealth is about providing options, and you are wealthy when your net worth exceeds the sum of your expected burn rates. To get there, you have to spend less than what you make, have to work to earn more money, and have to invest the money you don't spend. What destroys and misdirects wealth is comparing yourself to others, adjusting your burn rate upward, and not understanding when you have enough.

Do not save what is left after spending, but spend what is left after saving.

—Warren Buffett

STRONG, CALM,
& FREE

The best time to plant a tree was 20 years ago. The second-best time is now.

— Chinese Proverb

In 1913, Arthur E. Andersen founded a company in Chicago that became one of the "Big Five" accounting firms globally. By 2001, the firm provided auditing, tax advising, consulting, and other professional services to large corporations and had grown to 28,000 employees worldwide, making close to US$ 10 billion in revenue. The firm stood for integrity and accountability, and its founder was famous for his quote, "Think straight, talk straight," which became encapsulated in the company's values statement:

> We believe in integrity, respect, and always speaking as one firm. We believe in maintaining a passion for excellence in people, service, and innovation. And we believe in demonstrating a commitment to personal growth through training and development. In fact, these values are minimum standards for anyone within our organization. Each has roots in the thinking of Arthur Andersen himself. And each guides us toward a brighter future ahead.

The future was less bright for Arthur Andersen once they became involved in the Enron scandal in the early 2000s. Enron was one of the largest energy companies in the world and had been falsifying its financial reports to make the company appear more profitable than it was. Arthur Andersen, Enron's auditor, was found guilty of illegally destroying documents related to the Enron audit amid the Securities and Exchange Commission investigation. Their professed value of integrity did not align with their actions. The firm was supposed to conduct accurate and independent audits, but in the case of Enron, it failed to uphold these standards. The fallout was disastrous: Arthur Andersen lost its license to audit public companies, effectively ending its existence, and Enron filed for bankruptcy.

The demise of Arthur Andersen is an example of what can go wrong when beliefs and behaviors do not align. Proclaiming a value like integrity is meaningless if it isn't embodied in your daily actions and decisions. Similarly, you can hold strong convictions on how to get healthy, happy, and wealthy, but they are ineffectual if you don't put them to practice every day.

Virtues

Values and beliefs need to be reflected by virtues — how one leads their life. Virtues embody values and are a tangible manifestation of your convictions. If you value honesty, your corresponding virtue is to be truthful. Only by telling the truth, even when difficult, does your value become evident. If you treasure responsibility, be dependable. If you uphold compassion, develop the virtue of kindness, acting in ways that are considerate and helpful to others. If you honor wisdom, be prudent, making thoughtful decisions considering the long-term consequences.

While beliefs and values are abstract and internal, virtues are concrete and observable in a person's actions and behavior. They require consistent effort and are what we communicate to the world through our actions.

To become more human, we must actively practice the virtues I outlined for health, happiness, and wealth. Many of these habits require discipline and postponing rewards. Nature doesn't prioritize healthy and active 90-year-olds, nor does it prevent them. But our bodies are only programmed to ensure our survival long enough to reproduce. To enhance the potential of our lives, we must understand and reprogram these algorithms to our benefit.

Modern life revolves around satisfying our short-term desires and addressing our momentary discomfort. Constant prioritization of fun and pleasure leads to self-defeating choices and behaviors. We have access to an abundance of energy-dense foods but, at the same time, hardly need to engage in physical activity anymore. Our pursuit of happiness is so intimately linked to material possessions and consumption that the resulting over-stimulation of our reward systems robs us of the ability to experience any of it.

Our modern lifestyle is one of the greatest achieve-ments of humanity. Never before have so many people enjoyed access to food, shelter, safety, healthcare, education, leisure, culture, self-fulfillment, and every other conceivable possibility. But there is a price to pay if we overindulge. Consequently, most of the traditional virtues of philosophy and religion teach us to exercise restraint, live in moderation, and forgo instant gratification. It is a struggle deeply rooted in our civilization and many societal norms have been imagined to justify poor choices and alleviate cognitive dissonance.

Deep inside, we know that changing course does not come easy. If it were, thousands of self-help gurus would be out of a job. We don't want to put in the effort, exercise restraint, delay gratification, or be disciplined. We seek out quick-fix solutions instead of putting in the necessary work. We want the pill, the short-cut, the simple and short intervention that magically solves our problems. We believe that drinking apple cider for breakfast will allow us to somehow eat whatever we want without consequences. We get convinced that a cheap set of plastic and rubber cables will effortlessly help us achieve a Chris Hemsworth-like physique. The current fad at the time of writing is Ozempic (Semaglutid), which is touted as a magic weight loss drug. Nobody discusses that any weight lost while using the substance is quickly regained once discontinued. There is no free lunch. But we've become conditioned to assume that there must be an easier way. This fixation on quick fixes is well-captured in the 1998 movie "There's Something About Mary."

Hitchhiker: You heard of this thing, the 8-Minute Abs?

Ted: Yeah, sure, 8-Minute Abs. Yeah, the exercise video.

Hitchhiker: Yeah, this is going to blow that right out of the water. Listen to this: 7… Minute… Abs.

Ted: Right. Yes. OK, all right. I see where you're going.

Hitchhiker: Think about it. You walk into a video store, you see 8-Minute Abs sitting there, there's 7-Minute Abs right beside it. Which one are you gonna pick, man? (…)

Ted: That's right. That's — that's good. That's good. Unless, of course, somebody comes up with 6-Minute Abs. Then you're in trouble, huh?

Hitchhiker: No! No, no, not 6! I said 7. Nobody's coming up with 6. Who works out in 6 minutes? You won't even get your heart going, not even a mouse on a wheel.

We want a great body but are only willing to invest minutes, if at all. Because there is no short-term reward. You go to the gym and start working out, but your near-term cost (soreness) outweighs any immediate gains. Even after a week of training, your body will still look more or less the same. There are a lot of upfront costs before you start reaping the benefits. With bad habits, this sequence is reversed. You eat the pizza and instantly feel good. When you finally have become obese from repeating this behavior over and over, you don't connect how bad you feel to the original event. In his book on habits, James Clear attributes this to the immediacy of feedback: "The cost of your good habits is in the present; the cost of your bad habits is in the future."

Our "present bias" prevents us from seeing the full picture. I have experienced this when people complain that electric vehicles (EVs) cost too much. They don't. Their initial purchase price might still be higher than comparable combustion engine vehicles. But the higher energy efficiency of electric motors alone more than makes up for this. In a combustion engine, most of the energy you pay for gets wasted as heat. Also, EVs have far fewer movable parts and, therefore, less maintenance cost. They recuperate energy when braking, and electricity is cheaper than gas in most places. Looking at "total cost of ownership," EVs are clearly more affordable. But people fixate on the upfront purchase price.

Linked to "present bias" is our propensity for over-weighting risk. Daniel Kahneman calls this "loss aversion." He discovered that we tend to only risk US$ 100 for every US$ 250 we hope to gain, a loss aversion coefficient of 1:2.5. In other words, not only are we hesitant to incur a perceived cost without any visible short-term gain. The gain has to be at least two and a half times larger to make the investment worth our while. To overcome this, we must push past our "inner pig-dog" — a term coined in German to describe the resistance, laziness, and procrastination we feel when trying to complete a task or overcome a challenge. To decide in our favor, we need to perceive the benefit to be 2.5 times higher than any potential loss, such as giving up a donut or glass of wine.

Again, it isn't the individual sausage that gives you cancer, nor the single workout that lowers your blood pressure. The compounding effect of small behaviors on your cellular health, state of mind, or bank account changes the outcome over the decades. You need to sustain these behaviors to have an impact. Moreover, your habits must evolve over time as your body, expectations, and burn rate change. It is the strangest thing that people form habits in early adulthood and expect never to change or adapt to an aging system with different calorie, nutrition, and recovery requirements. Hormone secretion, muscle and brain function, metabolism, and most of your homeostatic regulators change decade by decade, so you must adapt accordingly. Despite our unique thinking abilities, we humans are poor at incorporating time and evolution into decision-making.

To tackle your biases and adopt better habits, embrace living the virtues I suggest. If you want to succeed in an ever-changing environment, try to make these virtues part of your identity. Don't just define a to-do list or follow a set of guidelines. Try convincing yourself that **you are a healthy, happy, and wealthy person, so act as that person would.** It is the ultimate reframe and probably my most important piece of advice.

Once you embrace these virtues as part of your identity, making better choices won't be a negotiation with yourself anymore. You remove the mental accounting of cost versus benefit, near-term versus long-term. Reframe yourself as the person you want to be. Doing one workout doesn't make you fit, but it is evidence against your identity as a fit and healthy person. People do it all the time. When someone tells you, "I am a vegetarian," they assume the identity of someone who does not eat meat. There is no inner struggle, temptation, trade-off, or decision to be made. They don't weigh the cost of forgoing a juicy steak against the long-term benefits of potentially having a lower cancer risk, reducing animal suffering and their ecological footprint. They are a vegetarian and are acting consistent with this identity.

Embrace the identity of a healthy, happy, and independent person. This person would live by the virtues that make up the acronyms STRONG, CALM, and FREE. Virtues are characterized by consistency. One-off interventions don't move the needle. The more consistent you are, the sooner you will experience the benefits. Keep in mind that our brains economize to only notice deltas. You will notice an initial improvement, but the feeling of accomplishment disappears when you plateau at an optimal state. To make matters worse, your optimal state is age-dependent and will likely deteriorate over time. Track and remind yourself constantly of where you are against that optimal state.

Even when you don't feel the immediate effect of an intervention, think of it this way: **In everything you do, you are either speeding up or slowing down the clock.** Every action slightly changes the speed of your aging process. When choosing an indulgence, you might not feel different today, but your remaining time just got reduced by a small amount. If you've seen the 2011 movie "In Time" starring Justin Timberlake, you can picture what I mean. It features a future society in which people stop physically aging at 25 but have a display on their forearms tracking their remaining lifetime. The countdown is constantly running down, but people can extend their lives by buying more time. Think of your virtues in a similar way. Getting good sleep, exercising regularly, or being satisfied with things, buys you more time. High-quality time. Shortcutting your recovery, stress, or constantly comparing yourself to others speeds up the countdown. You don't immediately feel the effect of it, but your cells keep track. You can still get hit by a bus, develop cancer, or prematurely die of some other cause. But who wouldn't want to extend the clock and give themselves the best possible chance of living longer and stronger?

Health Tactics

After exploring strategy, we finally get to some tactics. They haven't been the focus of this book because tactics are highly dependent on the individual's starting point, context, and ambition. Particularly for happiness and wealth, my concrete challenges and choices will mean nothing to your situation. If you apply the strategies (virtues) I outlined, you will be well-equipped to derive your own conclusions and actions.

For health, however, I chose to share some examples as we all have a similarly built physical body as the starting point. Remember that my genetic dispositions, environmental conditioning, and concrete targets will likely differ from yours. My appetite for risk, propensity for utilizing technology, and the lifestyle I prefer determine many of my choices. Don't blindly copy any of these tactics; see them merely as options to evaluate against your objectives and preferences.

Stress

Applying well-dosed stress to my various energy systems is something I do every day without exception. Here are some of the tools and methods I employ.

Apple Watch for accountability and consistency

While more of a governance tool than a stressor, the Apple Watch is deeply connected to my various activities. I used to be a fan of Garmin because of how long the battery lasted. The Apple Watch typically doesn't run for an entire 24-hour cycle on a single charge and therefore is hard to use for sleep tracking. But at some point, I decided to buy a second Apple Watch and now alternate between the two. They synchronize perfectly through the Apple ecosystem. With the much larger battery of the Apple Watch Ultra and other means of sleep tracking (Oura ring, in my case), one watch has now become sufficient to track all your activities.

Apple encourages you to complete daily activity goals by closing three rings. You set targets for activity calories, exercise minutes, and standing time, each represented by a ring, that you need to close daily. Personally, I aim to burn at least 800 kcal above my base metabolic rate, exercise for at least 30 minutes, and stand for at least one minute per hour at least 12 times. I have successfully closed all three rings for 1,686 consecutive days without fail, even when facing challenges like Covid, a slipped disk, or long flights. I have gone to great lengths to meet my goals, waking up very early to work out, hiking up and down airport terminals, or walking on a treadmill when I was too ill to exercise. I even walked up and down the stairs at home to reach my movement target after a trip. Although I am still waiting for a call from Tim Cook to acknowledge my achievement, the habit of closing my rings has become ingrained in me. After building a streak of several hundred days, I became committed to maintaining my progress and staying on track. Sharing my data with two friends, one of whom is equally obsessed and slightly ahead of me, has also helped me stay motivated. Despite its seemingly trivial nature, gamification has proven to be an effective tool for forming my habits and driving motivation.

Standing desk and walking pad

The nature of my job is sedentary. Rather than sit all day, I incorporate different methods to keep me moving. The standing-hour metric of the Apple Watch helps with this. If you haven't moved for a while, the watch will alert you at 50 minutes past the hour to get up. I also use a standing desk at home for video conferencing and computer work. This can get quite tiring on a long workday, so I added a balance board on the floor to shift my weight from leg to leg when I fatigue.

The feature many ask me about on video calls is my walking pad. It is a flat, foldable treadmill that lets you walk in place in front of your computer screen. In my experience, a speed of 4 kilometers per hour is ideal to remain focused and not bounce around too much on screen. I don't advise using the pad for every call, as people can get irritated by the continuous movement. But when I use it, I easily accumulate ten kilometers and more.

Obviously, I use every opportunity for additional movement, like taking the stairs and walking to places rather than taking a car.

Mobility and stretching

I've experimented with various types of stretching but haven't found one that stuck. Unfortunately, it's one of the things I tend to neglect. Recently, I began incorporating a brief stretching routine before my runs, especially since I was diagnosed with a Haglund deformity located at the back of my heel. This condition puts my Achilles tendon at a higher risk of inflammation or tearing if I don't stretch properly. Despite my efforts, I'm not very flexible. My posterior chain, which includes my hamstrings, hip flexors, and upper and lower back, remains rigid.

Last year I discovered an app called Pliability which utilizes long, passive poses to mobilize various muscle groups. The stretches are mostly static; you hold them for several minutes to soften fascia and connective tissue. There is an ongoing debate on the merits of static versus dynamic stretching or range of motion exercises. The Pliability approach makes me feel better temporarily but doesn't seem to improve my mobility noticeably. My posterior chain and glutes, quads, and calves remain tight. This is an area I will need to further refine.

Cardio training

It has been nearly four years since I started running. It used to be my least favorite activity, and I had convinced myself that long-distance running was not for me. I don't know what I was thinking. Running is fantastic. It hardly needs any equipment and can be done in most places. I admit I am a "comfort runner" and hit the treadmill when it is dark, cold, or wet outside. But when conditions are acceptable, nothing is more satisfying than a long run.

My regime revolves around two half-marathon races I perform annually, one in April and the other in October. I usually start training for each of these 12 to 16 weeks prior. This involves intervals, tempo, and endurance runs to train my aerobic and anaerobic systems. Half-marathons are the perfect distance to train both speed and endurance. Training runs in the weeks leading up to a race are usually around an hour, with the longest at 90-100 minutes. Committing more time, for instance, to run a full marathon, is difficult for me next to my job. I also worry about the increased injury risk and load on joints and connective tissue. Many who get hooked on running start adjusting their targets upward and want to run a marathon, then an ultra-marathon, then some form of iron man. I am not sure how beneficial this is for the body. It feels more driven by ego. Just like with the runaway lifestyle, I try to avoid the tendency to keep adjusting upward. I am happy with the half-marathon distance.

Many gadgets and devices promise to help with running performance. Though all you need is a pair of shoes, companies have developed various products to address needs you didn't know you had. The gadget I use most is a Stryd sensor. It attaches to your shoelaces and accurately measures your running stats, including power. As with biking, you can train by pace, heart rate, or power; the latter is a good indicator of the zone you are in as it considers incline, friction, wind, and other factors. You can also use heart rate but measuring it on your wrist is not very accurate. Heart rate lags in how it responds to exertion and is influenced by other factors, such as the food you eat or the music you listen to. Power in watts is a clean metric and only measures your current output. Stryd calculates Functional Threshold Power (FTP), representing the power you can sustain for a full hour. The tool provides other statistics, but FTP best predicts my running performance. To run a half-marathon in 1:45 hours, I must output an average of 320 watts, achievable at my current FTP of 330. Without ever having run the distance, I know I could run a marathon in 3:46 hours

(+/- 4 minutes), which is my predicted race time based on FTP.

I typically do three to four cardio sessions a week. One will be high-intensity interval training (HIIT) that I do on a Peloton or run all-out intervals of varying lengths. One will be a tempo run, during which I try to continuously increase my speed and finish at the fastest pace I can sustain. These typically last 45 minutes and expand my reserve capacity as I try to squeeze out more power when my legs and lungs are getting exhausted. The last type will be a long zone-2 exercise, mostly a 90-minute run at a moderate pace.

Resistance training

Two to three times a week, I hit the gym for resistance training. Regimes vary depending on how tired various muscle groups are, which equipment, and how much time I have available. I have a gym set up at home, but I spend at least three nights a week traveling, so I need to adapt to the circumstances constantly and tend to plan each week individually. In London, I have been working with a brilliant personal trainer for the past seven years who taught me all the principles of strength training I apply. We usually work out in a small hotel gym that sometimes gets crowded. If a bench or mat is taken, Stuart knows dozens of variations to each exercise, and we never miss a beat. I have learned barbell, dumbbell, resistance band, or bodyweight variations for most muscle groups that I can apply when working out alone. During the Corona pandemic, we continued meeting up via video chat. He would join me remotely for most sets with a kettlebell in his kitchen, his kids sometimes peeking into the picture.

Regarding apps (I tried them all), I can't follow a particular program for practical reasons. I like Centr by Chris Hemsworth, but I just don't have enough consistency in my daily life to do the required workouts in the recommended order. I mostly use Fitbod, a flexible app with a few learning algorithms to suggest weights, sets, and reps depending on my previous activities. I can set up various gyms, like a home, professional, and hotel gym, and enter the available equipment. Fitbod will always devise a workout based on the muscle groups I want to train. It's straightforward and intuitive to use. To check the quality of a hotel gym, there is a helpful site called hotelgyms.com. For most hotels, they provide a rating of the facilities and equipment.

I focus on heavy compound lifting in my training and loosely follow the 5x5 approach. A typical workout takes an hour and is structured as follows.

- I start with a few mobilizing movements like "cat-cow" or "the world's greatest stretch," notably to loosen the spine, shoulders, hips, and glutes.

- Then, I try to activate all muscle groups that I am going to train with simple bodyweight or resistance band exercises, like "band pull-aparts" or "frog pumps." The idea is to warm them up through their range of motion without straining them too much at this stage.

- Next, I do a round of heavy compound exercises like pull-ups, bench presses, barbell squats, and deadlifts. Typically, I have time for two or three of them, usually at five sets of five repetitions with at least one-minute breaks in between. I try to go as heavy as safely possible. Because of poor form on deadlifting, I go lighter on those and try to fit in more reps.

- For every major muscle group I stressed with compound exercises, I try to do another set of dumbbell or kettlebell exercises, like a single-leg "Romanian deadlift" for hamstrings after barbell deadlifting or a dumbbell incline press for the chest after bench pressing.

- I finish with a few dumbbell exercises targeting smaller muscles like the deltoids, triceps, or lower back.

- Before heading to the shower, I often think I should do another round of stretching, but I usually don't which I regret the next day.

Toxins

Here are some of my tactics to limit my exposure to toxins.

Air and water quality

I periodically check the air and water quality in our home. For air quality, there are measuring devices you can use at home (Awair) or carry with you (Atmotube) to alert you to any dangerous particles in the air you breathe. I have large Philipps air filters in my living and workspace that constantly monitor the amount and size of particles in the air and adjust the fan speed of the filter accordingly.

For water, I take a sample once every few years and get it tested by a lab. We have a Grohe water filter that we use for drinking water. It can also carbonate your water if you prefer. Apart from testing the water we drink, I also take a warm water sample every five years and have it tested for salmonella in case the boiler is not sufficiently killing off bacteria.

No drugs apart from coffee

I stopped smoking more than 20 years ago and stopped drinking any alcohol close to four years ago now. When I stopped drinking, I didn't intend to quit altogether. I did a dry January, then February, and when the lockdowns started in the Corona pandemic, I didn't feel like starting again. So, I just kept going, and after some time, I realized I didn't miss anything. It is awkward in the beginning. You will be surprised how many occasions there are to drink. People treat you like a recovering alcoholic. But it is much easier this way for me. I decided that part of my identity was being a "non-drinker."

You needn't be that strict with yourself. Research shows that alcohol does nothing good for you, and there is no safe amount to drink. However, having a few glasses per week carries such a small risk that it probably doesn't make a difference in your lifetime. If we lived for 500 years, you might see these differences in risk play out. With our current lifespans, the occasional glass of wine will not harm you. However, this changes considerably for more than one or two glasses per week. Drinking daily, having more than one glass in a sitting, or being female significantly increases your risk.

I have smoked marijuana, but very infrequently in the last two decades. The last joint I smoked was very uncomfortable due to the smoke. Since I am generally happy and energized, I don't take mood-altering substances. I also avoid pain medication as much as possible. My only vice is coffee. I probably have four to eight cups a day, which is on the high side. However, I never have coffee after 4 PM to not affect my sleep. The idea of having an espresso after dinner seems absurd to me.

Sensible food choices

I avoid ultra-processed foods and any form of pro-cessed meat. I don't buy frozen meals or ready-made sauces and avoid fast food. Besides being lower quality without nutrients, they also don't taste good. I often eat out while traveling during the week, so we home-cook most of our weekend meals from natural ingredients.

I eat unprocessed meat but try to buy organic as much as possible. If there is high-quality air-dried ham like Jamón Iberico, I will have it, but this may happen once a month. Like with alcohol, my sense is that infre-quent consumption carries a negligible cancer risk that is too small to measure or matter. The difference is that alcohol also lowers your sleep quality, which hasn't been established for Jamón.

One of the areas I struggle with is sugar. I have a bit of a sweet tooth and enjoy ice cream and everything va-nilla. I don't miss it if it isn't available, but if sweets sit in front of me, I will likely have them. At home, at least, I have been substituting sugar with Allulose, a monosac-charide similar to fructose in its chemical structure but with vastly different effects on your body. It has a tenth of the calories of regular sugar and does not impact your blood sugar or insulin levels. It tastes the best of all the sugar alternatives and is a great substitute.

Recovery

I take recovery very seriously and track sleep quality, resting heart rate, and heart rate variability. The Oura ring captures these metrics well and provides a daily readiness score that includes recovery, sleep, heart rate, body temperature, and respiratory rate. The Fitbod app indicates how fresh or tired my muscle groups are depending on prior load, while Stryd measures my running stress scores and warns me if I am ramping up too quickly. Recovery prevents my stressors from overloading my body and inflicting chronic stress. Recovery also allows my body to repair and adapt, essentially strengthening various systems.

Post workouts

After workouts, I try to have some protein, hydrate, and get adequate sleep the same night. On days with heavy lifting, my deep sleep phases typically extend by half an hour. There seems to be a real need to repair tissue and reduce inflammation after resistance training.

Against soreness, I use a Theragun to massage thighs, glutes, or calves. I have a large massage gun and a small travel version that is incredibly powerful for its size. I also have inflatable leg cuffs that apply pressure to different parts of your legs and thereby improve circulation. However, given how large the device is and how short the effect lasts, I am not a fan. I prefer a therapeutic massage I try to have once a month, not the superficial feel-good variety, but something deep into the tissue.

Weekend routine

On weekends I regularly use the dry sauna. I set it to 93 degrees Celsius and usually do two rounds of 15 minutes. Before entering, I place a few menthol crystals on a copper bowl resting on the hot stones. This opens my sinuses and bronchi very effectively. I have a device that grinds sea salt to a fine powder and blows it into the air. This is also supposed to open your lungs and bind pollen and other particles to the salt. However, the machine makes a lot of noise and requires regular cleaning. Menthol crystals do the trick for me.

Located next to the sauna, I have a cold plunger that cools down water to a specified temperature and disinfects it. I keep the water at 12 degrees and take a dip right after exiting the sauna for 5 to 10 minutes. Two rounds of hot and cold exposure improve my sleep quality and lower my resting heart rate.

Sleep

Ever since reading Matthew Walker's book on "Why we sleep," I have protected and prioritized my slumber. By avoiding alcohol and limiting coffee, I have removed two of the most disruptive substances regarding sleep quality. But I also try to be consistent with my sleep times. I go to bed around 11 PM and get up around 6:30 AM. Even though I sleep in many environments that are not always perfectly quiet, dark, and cool, I generally have no difficulty falling asleep. I might wake up once or twice for a bathroom visit but then fall back asleep again within minutes. When I set an alarm for an earlier time, I somehow manage to wake up a few minutes before the alarm. I don't understand how that works. But then, I also don't understand how our dogs know exactly when it is their feeding time.

As a consequence of these tactics, I avoid late-night activities. Unless necessary, I stay away from late dinners or parties. If socially acceptable, I excuse myself and leave. In some countries, this is a challenge. In Spain, food is served very late, and restaurants sometimes don't open before 9 PM. However, I would rather go to bed without dinner or just an appetizer than with a full stomach and a bad night of sleep.

The biggest challenge is traveling between time zones. I try to stay in my time zone for shorter trips, not to reset my circadian rhythm. However, flights from the US East Cost to Europe are particularly exhausting. They can be as short as seven hours, realistically leaving you with four hours of sleep. You arrive in the morning and have an entire day of work ahead of you. Those days, I know I am not at my best.

Meditation

As mentioned, I have tried many different meditation approaches. Nothing has stuck so far. Popular apps like Headspace or Calm felt more like chores than stimulating my parasympathetic nervous system. Playing the piano, walking the dogs, hiking in nature, or my weekend routine mentioned above all induce the effect I want. These activities reset my emotional balance and offer a welcome pause from the constant news and message stream.

Overhaul

Recovery helps to maintain homeostasis, but overhaul protocols go one step further. They try to reset the balance point to a more youthful state by cleaning out or reversing some aging-related deterioration.

Fasting

I have already outlined my fasting practice. Rather than intermittent fasting, which mainly addresses insulin resistance, I opt for prolonged water-only fasts of 72-hour durations every two to three months. Fasting is challenging to study scientifically in humans. It doesn't offer many financial benefits for companies, so we don't have sufficient evidence for the ideal or minimal effective dose to maximize the geroprotective effects of abstaining from food. We know that it significantly increases autophagy, a beneficial cell protocol we cannot enjoy if we constantly provide exogenous energy. Autophagy seems to be the only available cleanup program for reducing cellular and mitochondrial debris, and we can most effectively stimulate it through multi-day fasting.

Hyperbaric oxygen

A more experimental device I bought is a hyperbaric oxygen chamber. In combination with an oxygen concentrator, it provides pure oxygen that you breathe in a pressurized environment of 1.4 atmospheres absolute (ATA). In my case, you lay in a cylindrical tube made of fabric for 90 minutes and can use an iPad to watch movies or work. Parts of this book were written lying in the tube.

The basic principle is that increasing the amount of oxygen delivered to tissues can stimulate cellular healing, reduce inflammation, and mitigate some aging effects. When you measure blood oxygen saturation at sea level, it typically is already close to 100 percent. However, this metric represents the amount of oxygen-carrying hemoglobin (red blood cells) in the blood relative to hemoglobin not carrying oxygen. The pressure in the chamber dissolves oxygen molecules into all your body fluids, including your blood plasma, central nervous system fluids, and the lymphatic system. Hence, oxygen reaches all tissue, not just the areas that hemoglobin can get to easily.

Some research has suggested that hyperbaric oxygen therapy may be able to slow or even reverse the shortening of telomeres, thereby extending the lifespan of cells. Some studies suggest it contributes to reducing senescent cells. The evidence is inconclusive, but I enjoy the treatment and always feel refreshed and energized when I exit the chamber. Hyperbaric oxygen therapy is typically used for non-healing wounds and tissue damage by radiation, similar to age-related degradation of our cells in senescent or mutated cells. The treatment is without side effects, so the benefit-risk relation seems positive.

Preventative supplements

Apart from nutritional supplements (see below), I take preventative supplements intended to slow down or delay the hallmarks of aging.

NAD+

NAD+ (Nicotinamide adenine dinucleotide) is a crucial coenzyme in hundreds of metabolic processes. It plays a role in cell energy production, repairing DNA damage, and regulating cell aging. However, NAD+ levels tend to decrease as we age.

Supplements aim to raise levels of NAD+ by administering one of its precursors, mainly Nicotinamide Riboside (NR) or Nicotinamide Mononucleotide (NMN). NR and NMN have shown promise in preclinical studies, mostly in rodents. They can be converted into NAD+ in cells through different steps of the same biochemical pathway. However, a key point is bioavailability: how much of the ingested precursor reaches the bloodstream and the cells where it can be converted into NAD+. A randomized, double-blind, placebo-controlled study from 2017 demonstrated that daily supplementation of NR and the antioxidant Pterostilbene (a form of Resveratrol) led to 40 percent higher NAD+ levels in humans versus baseline after 30 days. I take 250 milligrams of NR with 50 milligrams of Pterostilbene or Resveratrol daily.

Metformin

Metformin is a prescription drug primarily used to treat type-II diabetes. It works by decreasing the amount of glucose your liver produces and your stomach and intestines absorb. It also increases your body's response to insulin.

Many aging-related conditions are brought on by metabolic syndrome and insulin resistance. Prematurely lowering glucose is thought to delay or even prevent some of the worst killers like diabetes, heart disease, cancer, or dementia. A large-scale trial called TAME (Targeting Aging with Metformin) has recently launched with 3,000 participants to test whether those taking metformin experience delayed development or progression of age-related chronic diseases.

It will be six years until we get the study results. I see no downside to taking it today and lowering my glucose as much as possible. I take 1 gram of metformin daily and don't experience any side effects. There is some evidence that taking metformin increases blood lactate levels which could potentially decrease athletic performance. As I don't compete professionally, this does not bother me.

Rosuvastatin

Statins are an established way of lowering blood cholesterol. I have genetically elevated lipid levels at the higher end of the normal range or slightly above. Doctors have given me confusing advice, from not doing anything on the one end to medical intervention on the other. Some have advised taking over-the-counter supplements like red rice extract, though those have not impacted my test results.

I check my blood lipid scores at least once a month with an at-home test kit from Mission which measures LDL, HDL, and Triglycerides in a finger prick test. When a screening identified a plaque at a junction in my carotid artery (also genetically caused by how the artery branches off), I decided to take a 30-year risk perspective and prevent any further build-up of plaque and calcifications. I take a very low dose of 5 milligrams of Rosuvastatin which has significantly lowered my cholesterol metrics.

Rapamycin

Rapamycin, or sirolimus, is a compound with potent immunosuppressive properties. It was initially discovered in the soil of Easter Island in the Pacific Ocean. In medicine, rapamycin is primarily used to prevent organ transplant rejection due to its ability to inhibit the immune response. It achieves this by binding to a protein inside cells to form a complex, which then blocks another protein called mTOR. The mTOR pathway plays a crucial role in cell growth, proliferation, and survival. In recent years, rapamycin's inhibition of the mTOR pathway has attracted significant interest in aging research due to its potential to slow aging and extend lifespan, at least as observed in several animal models.

I currently don't take rapamycin as the protocol remains unclear. Taking the wrong dose can inhibit your immune system and frequently leads to bacterial infections. Bio-hackers experiment with intermittent doses taken once every week or every two weeks. It seems to be a promising substance that will attract further research, but I will wait until there is more clarity on how to administer it without any meaningful side effects.

I take several other preventative supplements, like quercetin to eliminate senescent cells or curcumin for its anti-inflammatory properties. These are primarily natural substances that are safe to take but don't have strong scientific evidence backing their efficacy in humans. Neither the minimal effective dose nor the bioavailability of oral supplementation is established. I won't go into detail on these, but I take them as a no-regret move.

Nutrition

In what I eat, I follow my own advice of plentiful protein, complex carbs, and favorable fats. My go-to breakfast is porridge that I prepare in a Thermomix, a device that weighs, cuts, cooks, stirs, and more. I add oat or apple fiber powder and allulose or a banana to sweeten the meal. When done, I mix in whey protein powder and add a ton of blueberries. I love blueberries. My wife jokes that we need to hire a full-time blueberry supply chain manager for the amounts I consume.

We make a large salad bowl for lunch and add eggs or lentils for protein. I have a device called PlantCube, which looks like a fridge in which I grow my salad. You insert pods with seeds, and the machine automates hydration, fertilization, and optimal light exposure. The salad tastes fantastic and is as fresh as it gets. Unfortunately, the company was taken over by Miele, who discontinued the product. Not many people are willing to spend ridiculous amounts on a commodity like salad, it seems. I bought as many seed pods as possible and hope to use my salad-growing fridge for a while longer.

For dinner, I prefer meat or fish with some steamed vegetables smothered with olive oil. I love oven-roast chicken, rib-eye steak, and salmon. I reflect a lot on whether I should eat meat because the industrial production of it is truly disgusting. The environmental footprint and how we treat living beings with feelings and emotions are revolting. I have gone vegetarian or switched to game meat for some time as a consequence. It remains a difficult tradeoff. Animal protein is superior to anything plant-based. While you can sustain a healthy diet just by eating plant-based foods, it requires much more thought, preparation, and supplementation.

I avoid plant-based meat substitutes from soy, lentils, or other protein sources. Besides the fact that the vast majority of them taste awful and nowhere like meat, it is ultra-processed food. There are so many additives and chemicals to imitate meat's texture, color, and taste that I doubt these are healthy alternatives. When I buy meat, I buy organic, free-range, grass-fed, or any other form indicating that the animal suffered less than in highly industrialized production facilities. In Germany, most supermarkets classify meat from 1 to 4, with 4 representing the highest level of animal welfare, if one can call it that. I find it a vital step in the right direction, but I would like restaurants to also adhere to this system. Transparency regarding the origin and production conditions of meat should be mandatory everywhere.

I discovered meat called "Txogitxu." It is a Basque term that translates roughly to "old cow." The beef is sourced from older cows, sometimes aged 12 to 18 years and, thus, far older than the typical beef cow at slaughter. It is known for its deep flavor and marbling and is hard to get in Germany. I managed to order some through an online service at an eye-watering price. I put the steaks on my kitchen counter to warm up to room temperature and went to fire up the barbecue. When I returned, the steaks had disappeared. When I looked at my dogs, they avoided any eye contact.

I only drink filtered tap water and black coffee. Occasionally, I'll have some tea and, very rarely, alcohol-free beer. But I generally adhere to the principle of not drinking my calories. I also stay away from Coke Zero and other artificial drinks. There is likely a low risk of consuming these, but I don't need the excessive flavoring. My underlying approach is to take food as naturally as it is. Food doesn't need sauces, seasoning, or other condiments if you have fresh, natural ingredients. Why do people buy a steak and then cover it with a sauce?

Good quality meat tastes excellent on its own. You can enhance its natural flavor with some salt or add butter to accentuate the umami. For me, real food is the best choice.

I supplement a few vitamins and minerals. For instance, I take a combination of Vitamin D3 and K2 daily. D3 enhances calcium absorption in the body, while K2 ensures the calcium is directed to bones and teeth, where it's needed most. These vitamins work synergistically to support strong bone health, promote cardiovascular wellness by preventing arterial calcification, and aid in immune system function.

I also take magnesium and, before races, potassium to prevent muscle cramping. Magnesium helps with muscle relaxation and also promotes good sleep quality. A known effect of statins is that they lower co-enzyme Q10 (CoQ10) levels, which can lead to muscle aches. As I take Rosuvastatin, I also supplement CoQ10 to compensate for this deficiency.

Governance

I identify with the "quantified self" movement and love to understand how the body responds to certain stimuli and environmental changes. I am not a body hacker who would typically experiment with different substances and regimes to achieve desired outcomes much faster. I am skeptical of quick fixes and shortcuts. They usually come at some hidden cost.

The data I collect is intended to show me the longer-term developments of my vital stats that are not easily captured by point-in-time measurements. For example, measuring weight or body fat can yield very different results based on hydration, bowel movements, and current diet. On a prolonged fast, I can lose 3 kilograms, mostly from reducing water after depleting glycogen stores. I have been tracking my weight since 2011 and can see seasonal patterns throughout the year and the influence of certain lifestyle choices, like quitting alcohol.

As mentioned, I capture all my activities and heart-related data in the Apple Health app. It doesn't provide much insight but connects easily to other apps that offer analytics functionality. So far, apps can do little more than correlate metrics or compare data to cohorts similar to you in terms of age and gender. Life is multi-dimensional, and for advanced analytics algorithms to derive actionable insights, you must capture as many metrics as possible. Tools like Gyroscope try to be that encompassing data hub but still only playback the data in a more accessible way rather than providing real insights. Some apps are more useful on particular topics. I mentioned that I wear a Continous Glucose Monitor (CGM), and a tool called Veri compares my glucose to my activity, sleep, and nutritional data, which has been very interesting for me.

To capture the data that matters most to me, I built a simple spreadsheet in Google Sheets that sits in the cloud. Every two weeks, I capture average weight and body fat over the period, average resting heart rate, and average heart rate variability. Notice that these are all averages I pull out of Apple Health because I try to eliminate data outliers. I have a small device called Bello that gives me a separate reading of my visceral fat by performing scans of my biceps, thighs, and above my belly button. I measure blood oxygen saturation, take a blood pressure reading with a cuff, and count my blood lipids with the Mission home test kit I mentioned. I also regularly get a reading of my blood uric acid and perform a 6-lead ECG with a small device from Kardia. Every few months, I conduct a fecal occult blood test, an early indicator of colon cancer.

I am a sucker for healthcare gadgets and have tried pretty much every device out there (yes, also the Whoop band), but these are the ones that stuck. For people with a lower affinity for technology, I recommend, at a minimum, wearing an Oura ring. It is tiny for the data it delivers, allowing you to wear your super-expensive analog watch or no watch if you prefer. It only weighs 4 to 6 grams, depending on your ring size, is waterproof, stays charged for 4-5 days, and measures heart rate and other metrics very accurately off the capillaries of your finger.

Phanta rhei

Scientific research and my thinking will continue to evolve. The Ancient Greek phrase "phanta rhei" means "everything flows" and is attributed to the philosopher Heraclitus of Ephesus, who lived around 500 BCE. More than 2,500 years later, we experience the ever-changing nature of life with full force and must continuously adapt. As insights evolve, I will continuously challenge and adapt my habits and tactics. But in writing this book, I intended to offer something more constant to stand the test of time. The virtues and strategies I outlined are either a direct consequence of millions of years of evolution or are based on thousands of years of human thinking. They provide direction and guidance in a world of volatility and short-term trends.

Remember that most of our convictions and conventions are imagined. You can reframe yourself as the best version of who you aspire to be and reframe all the limiting beliefs that prevent you from becoming that person. As the world evolves, "phanta rhei" also applies to you. You are not the same person you were 20 years ago, and you certainly won't be 20 years from now. You will evolve if you want to or not, and the question is whether you will take agency over that process. The reward is a deeply fulfilling life full of optionality. What could be more meaningful than the ultimate prizes of health, happiness, and wealth? What stops you from achieving them are your thoughts and beliefs.

I recently heard the adventurer and pioneer Bertrand Piccard speak at a conference. He became known as the first person to circumnavigate the Earth in a balloon and later in a solar-powered aircraft. He said many discoveries could have happened much earlier if people had just opened their minds to them. Humans have observed birds for thousands of years that provide the blueprint for how an airplane works. In the 15th Century, Leonardo da Vinci sketched several flying machines, none of which got built. George Cayley, considered the "father of aviation," finally created the first full-sized glider to carry a human and briefly flew in England in 1853. It was built of wood covered with fabric, materials available to us for eons. It is peculiar that no one had ever attempted to make a plane earlier. Building a glider or hot-air balloon could have technically been achieved as far back as the Ancient Egyptians if they had opened their mind to the idea that humans could fly.

Our ancestors had been staring at Mount Everest for millions of years. Only in 1953 did Edmund Hillary and Tenzing Norgay successfully attempt to climb it. Then, only seven years later, people reached the Mariana Trench, the lowest point on Earth. Just nine years after that, we landed on the Moon. Once we open our minds to the possibility of something, there is no stopping human ingenuity. Reframing our reality is a shift in perspective that lets us see previously hidden things. Reframing unlocks new possibilities.

It is ultimately your choice. You can take the Blue Pill and return to your life of comfort and instant gratification. You can continue to chase some "tomorrow life" of pleasure and bliss and numb the fear that you are wasting your life with alcohol and consumption. The years tick by, your body gets worn down by decades of bad food, insufficient sleep, and half-hearted exercise, and you spend the end of your days fighting chronic diseases, worried about what kind of legacy you leave behind.

This book offers you the Red Pill. It is a less comfortable choice in the short term. It requires discipline, adherence to virtues, and frightening thoughts about death, loss, and insignificance. But it will expand your set of options and provide you will the resilience and mental tranquility that will make you an agent and lover of your fate. Depending on where you are in life, you have a couple of decades left before you switch off forever. Make it count, be your best, and take humanity one step further.

What lies before us and what lies behind us are small matters compared to what lies within us. And when we bring what is within us out into the world, miracles happen.

— Ralph Waldo Emerson

Printed in Great Britain
by Amazon

33920117R00225